Alpha City

Alpha City

How the Super-Rich
Captured London

Rowland Atkinson

VERSO
London • New York

First published by Verso 2020
This paperback edition published by Verso 2021
© Rowland Atkinson 2020, 2021

1 3 5 7 9 10 8 6 4 2

Verso
UK: 6 Meard Street, London W1F 0EG
US: 20 Jay Street, Suite 1010, Brooklyn, NY 11201
versobooks.com

Verso is the imprint of New Left Books

ISBN-13: 978-1-78873-798-2
ISBN-13: 978-1-78873-799-9 (UK EBK)
ISBN-13: 978-1-78873-800-2 (US EBK)

British Library Cataloguing in Publication Data
A catalogue record for this book is available from the British Library

Library of Congress Cataloging-in-Publication Data
A catalog record for this book is available from the Library of Congress

Typeset in Sabon by MJ & N Gavan, Truro, Cornwall
Printed and bound by CPI Group (UK) Ltd, Croydon CR0 4YY

Contents

Acknowledgements   vii

Introduction   1

1. Capital's City   9

2. The Archipelago of Power   33

3. Accommodating Wealth   61

4. Crime, Capital   83

5. Cars, Jets and Luxury Yachts   109

6. My Own Private Stronghold   139

7. Life Below   165

8. Too Much   201

Afterword   229
Bibliography   247
Notes   251
Index   255

Acknowledgements

This book represents the culmination of my interest in and research on London over the last quarter of a century, work that has included studies of the city's middle classes, gentrification, gated communities and, latterly, its wealthiest residents. Some of this work has been conducted by myself, much of it with colleagues and friends. A good portion of the research presented here was supported by two public grants from the Economic and Social Research Council for work on the research projects *The Very Affluent Worker* and *Alpha Territoriality in London and Hong Kong*, whose teams included my long-term co-lead Roger Burrows alongside the excellent support of researchers David Rhodes, Hang Kei Ho and Luna Glucksberg, as well as Richard Webber, Tim Butler, Caroline Knowles and Mike Savage. I am particularly grateful to Richard Webber, who acted as a reliable pathfinder, statistically and literally, on forays into the alpha territory – a term he coined to describe urban elite areas and which was the inspiration for the title of this book. I have also been helped in framing and appreciating the spaces that appear in this book through a photographic project with Alan Silvester, whose work is also featured here.

I am deeply grateful for the conversations with and general support of all those who have spurred and challenged my work, in particular Andrew Baker, Andrew Bebbington, Sarah Blandy, Talja Blokland, Sam Burgum, Stephen Graham, Katie Higgins, Keith Jacobs, Loretta Lees, Rex McKenzie, Simon

Acknowledgements

Marvin, Tim May, Anna Minton, Emma Morales, Simon Parker, Dennis Rodgers, Phil Stanworth, Malcom Tait and Paul Watt, and especially to Emma Brown for her support throughout. The invisible, invaluable and patient efforts of my editor at Verso, Leo Hollis, are gratefully acknowledged.

Introduction

During the refurbishment of a London home a sink was thrown out. An unremarkable event were it not for the fact that the house, in the plushest of districts, had been installed with a feature that offended the sensibilities of the new owner: a floor-to-ceiling solid Italian granite unit costing around £30,000. The size of the unit meant that it could only be smashed out, yet out it had to go. Lots of money, too much money, enormous waste – even the new and perfectly functional destroyed in the name of some subtle change in the markers of good taste. Such stories abound in a city in which growing numbers of the world's super-rich seek a home, whether they intend to live in it or not.

As money circulates through the city both the old and the new are destroyed through the making and remaking of places and, of course, the making of even more money. This spin cycle of capital operates under hyper-active economic conditions in which massive gains are mainlined to a select few. The result is a wealthy elite who have come to achieve staggering purchasing power, with the acquisition of multiple homes, sports teams, newspapers, media companies, industries and votes. But to really understand such power we need to be able to place it: London, the alpha city, is in many ways the pre-eminent site of the rich.

London competes on the world circuit to be the natural habitat of the rich thanks to its good homes, culture, history, society, financial heart, and its cluster of corporate command centres. The city's more or less unrivalled position has come about through its single-minded pursuit of the rich, creating seamless, open borders for capital while ignoring its working population and its poor. In adopting this strategy, the colours of those in power are pinned firmly to the mast of a ship propelled by the variable winds of global capital. The city is like a vessel buoyed by cheap and flexible labour, all the while throwing its provisions for those in need overboard. Participation in the alpha city's undoubtedly vibrant social life is increasingly predicated on the ability to pay. The psychology, economy, politics and deeper operating system of the city are run more and more for money, its reason for being in many ways forgotten and its vision of the future indifferent to the plight of many of its residents.

Change in cities is rarely as dramatic as it has been in London over the past twenty years. A veritable crescendo of activity, reaching a climax of capital investment: a move from cool, to Cool Britannia, to an Olympic peak achievement, to the hip, and then to a city associated more than anything else with the rich – each shift echoing and integrating the dividends of the global economy. The London of the 1990s still resounded to slam-door trains, noxious diesel buses and a sustained economic reverse. The East of the city remained an index of enduring poverty while the West accommodated long-standing wealth and a series of comfortable suburbs beyond it. Today the East has been claimed by a creative class as gentrification has transformed many of its neighbourhoods. From a low-rise city with a comfortable skyline, hundreds of new towers have emerged, including the largest in Europe, with many more still to come. A city economy that was once the site of a gentlemanly capitalism now embraces the mantra of cash at all costs, without heed to the social consequences. Perhaps most visibly, the presence of an internationally sourced super-rich cadre is now evident to everyone.

The pursuit of money, and of those with lots of it, infiltrates and reshapes the spaces and culture of the city, physically changing old streets and creating entire new districts, lifting house prices, attracting waves of international capital and the temporary gains generated by asset sales. It seems that if a pound sign can be placed on anything, it can be put up for sale. One of the key challenges of governing a city economy running hot on international capital and an influx of the world's super-rich is how to ride and tame this flailing force. But as capital flowed into London at every new opportunity, the only question asked was how to create the right conditions to let the city's economy accelerate still further.

These massive changes and apparent improvements helped to mask their flipside – disinvestment in local neighbourhoods, demolished estates, evictions, rising homelessness and, alongside these changes, the apparent loss of an ethos of care as support for those in need was systematically withdrawn. As the money flows of finance and property seeped into numerous districts, providing many with windfalls, city governors were reassured that all of this stuff was a simple and self-evident good. Yet viewed today, the rise of an alpha city seems to have been based on a Faustian pact, a contract taken out on the zero-contracted, with the price for success being the exclusion of the poor souls of the city while capital and the rich ride on.

London is a vast, almost unknowable automaton, a complex city machine incorporating new and old elites, modern-day merchants, immense homes and corporate megastructures. Taken as a whole, this city, alongside a handful of others globally, is a key node in a global economy founded upon endless cycles of extraction and growth. The beneficiaries are small in number and rewarded in an abundance beyond everyday comprehension. What this also means is that those doing well out of the system are less concerned about its more pernicious outcomes. Today we know that the system's economic priorities yield winners and losers in a rigged game designed to channel ever larger dividends to those already winning.

To understand the condition the city finds itself in, we must understand the traditional alliances of state, capital and City. To be sure, the positions, networks and interests of each overlap in complex ways. Yet the power of money also lies in its subtle ability to co-opt and align those whose work is in some way connected to servicing capital or the rich themselves. This of course includes the bankers and other servants of wealth, but it also includes politicians, local councillors, planners, developers, builders, real estate agents, luxury fashion retailers, department store workers, chauffeurs, restaurateurs, art, wine and antique dealers, auctioneers, bank clerks, servants, car dealers, tailors, delivery folk and indeed anyone whose livelihood is connected to the wealthy. Wealth becomes a city industry in its own right.

To understand this confluence of interests we must look beyond what is happening to house prices one month, or observations about where the city is going another. To get at the substance beneath the froth of such commentary we need to examine the deeper structures of the economy, the nature of the political system with its conflicting interests, alliances and divisions, the standing stock of housing, and the influence of money and the moneyed on the city. It doesn't matter too much whether prices for mansions are tumbling or rising because the rich have already occupied them (unless you happen to be an estate agent or a government relying on tax revenues from such sales), nor does it matter when price falls simply generate new opportunities for cash-rich international buyers to snap up assets at bargain prices – the same people are in power, and the same logic of capital is in operation. We need a longer-term and macroscopic view of such matters, one capable of tracking the processes, institutional life and socio-economic forces that are making and remaking the city in the interests of the wealthy.

4

Members of the city's power bloc – a complex amalgam of networks, institutions and elites whose perspectives are shaped by a common interest – now seek to move away from a sense of patrician obligation and stewardship. Whether this be moving to residences behind gates and high walls, holidays on yachts or inaccessible beaches, investments in schemes to avoid or evade tax, or in exclusive hotels – the general sense is of a grand escape, the ever further secession of the successful and of the cash they command. Understanding what has happened to the city as money has reshaped it requires work, but the dividend is an insight into how to devise and plan for a city better based on principles of fairness, inclusion and social justice.

To understand London is also to comprehend the workings of our society, economy and polity, of which it is both product and creator. But to really know the city we must become analysts skilled in divining the complex social and economic forces that ultimately shape its material fabric. A city is not a natural occurrence. To be sure it evolves, but it does so according to the designs of its politicians, builders and planners, the competing interests of the powerful, the existing laws and regulations, and the accommodation of the regressive results of these forces by the powerless. In the past, the state and ruling class came to have an interest in maintaining, preserving and securing the amenity of the city. Projects were undertaken in the form of recreational parks, hygiene works, new infrastructure, public housing and transport networks, as a means of preventing dissent, disease and disharmony among the working classes, but also for the middle and upper classes who collectively benefited. Today's elite appear to show little interest in such social contracts or obligations. London is a city apparently the poorer for the wealth condensing there.

This book offers an impression of London at this moment, as a city facing the paradoxes of a post-crash decade, defined by an increasing meanness in terms of social support, alongside the simultaneous rise of the super-rich and their capture of the city. This disconnection of fates has been arbitrated by its less wealthy elites, through their efforts in the political and corporate domains. We must remember how the commitment to public cuts was forged in a class politics born of a machine hardwired to protect the position of the corporate, political and capitalist elites. But perhaps what is new today is that even those managing this system sense that its limits may have been reached, that its injustices and excesses have become too much, or perhaps too obvious. The decision in July 2019 to deny planning permission for the proposed 'Tulip' viewing platform in the City – funded by a Brazilian billionaire and designed by a super-rich architect with an 'educational' agenda – was a sign perhaps that such white elephant projects will at least be challenged when they lack any genuine social benefit.

Social need has been put into the shade by the easy wins of free-floating global capital and the billions of laundered cash flowing through real estate and finance. That shade has been amply provided by the many tower blocks built for wealthy investors. The needs of the city's poor, most of them in working households, appear to be further eclipsed and side-lined by the statistics highlighting service sector growth, the contribution of finance to the economy, and the rocketing redevelopment of the city – the stuff that has to be kept going because it is good for us all! This impression of good health is a story enthusiastically narrated by those among the political class favoured by capital and the wealthy.

Many may feel that this book's central argument is overplayed and unjustified. In what possible sense could this cascade of wealth into the city have a contaminating effect on its life? What kind of naïve, envious position is being privileged in an account that questions the contribution of the rich? What would we do without these great wealth creators if they all upped and went somewhere else? The time-honoured claim made for established wealth and corporate life in general is that their activities and investments have the effect of 'lifting all boats'. But this core proposition, indeed this ruling set of ideas, today appears increasingly unsustainable and is everywhere being challenged.

According to Oxfam's annual survey, in 2018 the number of billionaires who owned as much as the poorest half of humanity stood at twenty-six – enough to fill little more than a third of the seats on a new London Routemaster bus. Yet the system that produces such evident excesses has its massed ranks of defenders. While the world rushes headlong towards numerous precipices, whether they be political, ecological, economic or social, its fundamental structures continue to create subsidiary winners who become the cheerleaders of capital and capitalism. Today the hollowness of this vision is everywhere being pointed out and denounced. Increasingly, the exclusive and excluding landscape of new and unaffordable homes is generating a simmering rage, a substrate of feeling throughout the city whose consequences we do not yet know.

What does a city run for the rich mean for everyone else? Certainly its effects and costs can be calibrated in social terms: in the shifting, unrecognisable and often alienating urban landscape; in the creeping privatisation of public space; in the subtle messaging and forms of control relayed through the city's media and politics. But what does it say about the influence and power of money, and about capitalism itself, that it can create a city that appears to be both flourishing and floundering at the same time? The heart of this system appears to beat ever faster, running the risk of overload or systemic breakdown. Yet if another crash is around the corner, we know that it will not be footloose capital or the wealthy who will suffer.

The global financial crisis of 2007–8 marked the beginning of a new level of indulgence towards the wealthy, with tax cuts, quantitative easing, asset price inflation and a reduction of interest rates among the measures taken. Since that moment there has been a long boom in property generated by the effects of the crisis, motivating the wealthy to pour money into those cities that appeared safe bets in an unstable world. The alpha city is today more a place for money and the moneyed than it is for living in, and this has had significant consequences. The most important result perhaps lies in our losing sight of what cities are for – as places where people live and thrive, where the city's economy is set up to serve its residents' needs, rather than being a magical playground for the super-rich in the hope that a few others may be enriched as a result.

1

Capital's City

London is a world city, one of a select few that command and control the world economy. In fact, it is not simply one of the world cities, but *the* world city, the paramount member of a group producing and receiving vast fortunes within a global economy run increasingly for finance. Simply put, London is the alpha city.

The alpha city presents itself as the domineering, swaggering and altogether ruder sibling of those cities lower down the global hierarchy. Like a posturing man in a meeting, it jostles to maintain its pre-eminent place, as the one to whom all others should offer respect. A language of entitlement flows from this status. It is found in the effusive adjectives of the brochures describing the city's most select trophy homes and luxury high-rise apartment blocks. There can only be one One Hyde Park, 1 Kensington Road, 77 Mayfair, Clarges Mayfair or Embassy Gardens among the myriad unique residences and palatial homes dotted around the city's West End and beyond. As in the market for rare art or wine, appeals to the unique, to luxury and to marks of good taste are found here in abundance.

This is a city increasingly for money, not for people. It is here that capital, capitalism and the capitalist elite come together. In doing so, these combined forces have torn up the mission statement of the city as a place for all. Now, perhaps more than ever before, it is a playground for the wealthy and a hothouse

One Hyde Park

in which to grow capital under hydroponic conditions, carefully tended by the city's politicians and financial institutions.

The argument of this book is that for all the spectacle and beauty of a city created by expanding personal fortunes, such decorations are distractions from the more vicious and discriminating impacts of wealth on the life of the metropolis. Beyond the facades of the luxury homes, the smoked-glass nightclub entrances and the comfortable private clubs, lies a city in the process of being hollowed out.

This city above all others appears to the wealthy like a beacon in a storm, a luxurious harbour in which to weigh anchor in a restless and troublesome world. London sits at the top of those rankings showing where the world's wealthy, political and social elites reside. These groups of the super-rich are distributed across a constellation of fine residences in select quarters of the city and beyond, in comfortable suburbs and small satellite towns – untroubled by the split fortunes of a city in which vast wealth co-exists with significant hardship and social stress. It is to London that so many of the world's ultra-wealthy come to live, invest or indeed hide. The city's abundant luxury homes and quiet districts offer them safe spaces insulated from the intrusions of unsightly poverty or anything else one might find disagreeable about city living.

Whether measured in terms of its wealth, GDP, cultural offering or liveability, London can confidently lay claim to being *the* alpha city. Its bright lights only cast other cities into the shadows. The dusty cloth of the establishment, old boy's networks and gentlemen's clubs has been re-cut and tailored to suit a new power elite formed out of a mash-up of old and new money, political and corporate power, and new or dynastic wealth. The international rich come to the city in search of prime assets to buy and sell, to take advantage of house prices cheapened by strong foreign currencies, to escape the insecurities or dangers presented by their own governments, or to offload bundles of criminally sourced cash, laundered through London's real estate. Some even come to the city to live.

Compared even to New York or Tokyo, the two other truly 'world' cities, London has the largest number of wealthy people per head of population. It is the epicentre of the world's finance markets. It is also an elite cultural hub, offering enviable open streetscapes, swathes of green space, a reputation for safety and low levels of state intrusion. Within what is referred to as the world urban system, London is the most brilliant celestial body. But, we should remember, even stars die.

'Alpha' denotes both the beginning and the most powerful member of a group. London as an alpha territory is sufficiently large to generate its own gravitational field, a force that pulls in much of the world's wealth and many of its most wealthy individuals. But it is also a kind of social centrifuge that increasingly, to paraphrase Shelley, spits out those damaged or unhoused by its workings – the poor and the unwanted. All of this goes on under a regime of interests operated effectively by the city's elite of politicians, governors and financial institutions. This group defends markets and rising inequality while courting the wealthy at a time of enormous hardship for many.

All of this raises the question of how we might begin to understand the city and what it stands for when the rich sip £8,000 gold-infused cocktails while swathes of public housing are demolished and those on low incomes are evicted from tenancies to the city's hinterlands. Such uneasy comparisons might be defended as simply representing instances of diversity in a city that has always offered massive contrasts. In reality, these and many other examples of exclusion and poverty are connected to the fortunes and positions of the wealthy by deep, subterranean flows of capital, political ideology and social networks. Despite being invisible to the naked eye, these underlying forces drive the stellar gains of the wealthy, seduce and enroll those who come to rely on their spending, and assist the development of programmes that further exclude those on low incomes. In one sense London is shared, but its various prizes and dividends are most definitely not.

London's position as the heartland of capital is revealed in the newspapers every day, whether the reports are about traffic jams of supercars on Regent Street, the hundreds of high-rise riverside apartments reserved for the wealthy, or the exchange of football teams between one oligarch and another or the parties at which politicians, media moguls and artists mix. The stories are familiar, but how should we understand what is going on, who benefits, and the broader impacts of alpha city status?

In this book I want to show that there are significant and damaging consequences that come from the city's increasing devotion to capital. It is critical that we grasp the extent to which massive wealth, produced in a global economy that seems to generate new fortunes each day, has real and grounded impacts on the everyday life of the city. Capitalism delivers incentives for a relatively small group to rework the

Back street boy racers

operations of the city. These tweaks bring further benefits to
the wealthy and their adjuncts while casting adrift those in the
wider community. Whether the result is a new crisis or a resurgent boom, the wealthiest continue to reap massive rewards
while defending the workings of the city as the best there is
to offer.

It is difficult to understate the ability of the wealthy to influence and reshape the world around them, given the power of
money. Yet, in both more subtle and forceful ways, money also
has the capacity to ensnare and colonise the minds and values of
all those who benefit from it – politicians, developers, planners,
corporate lawyers and financiers, but also interior decorators,
club and restaurant owners, real estate agents, hotel owners,
personal service providers and so on. This is what some describe
as the ideological function of money: it gives one the ability to
buy stuff, but its deeper influence lies in its power to conscript
the hearts and minds of many to the domination of markets
and the demands of capital.

Money is a force that shapes our mentalities and the models
we use to understand how the world around us works. When

today's global wealth surveys display images of green shoots and graphs with sharply rising lines, it is easy to forget that the financial crisis of 2008 was considered to present a near existential threat to the capitalist system. Instead, that threat was diverted, towards the vulnerable through public cuts and austerity programmes. The arrogance that so often goes with wealth and power appears as a particular insult to those forced to endure the government-sponsored collapse of public services and spaces.

Many of these issues are delicately interwoven, but a lot of the changes brought to the city by the rich and powerful are quite blatant. As we will see in this book, much of the form and function of London has been modified by large houses, skyscrapers and megaprojects, while the needs of the rich for luxury and personal security have transformed the look and feel of the city as their homes become fortified and their streets secede from the city's public realm. This gathering point of super-affluence, a great wen of wealth, grants visibility and superficial legitimacy to the insanely unjust reward system that the global economy has generated and to the kind of city for the few that this brings with it. As will already be clear, the mark of the alpha city should be considered less a badge of honour and more a source of concern. But let us start to dig a little deeper.

*

The world's 'top' cities have got where they are less as a result of hard work and more because of the accidents of history and locational advantage. Despite the myths pinned to effort, entrepreneurial brilliance, strategic know-how and various other unrivalled qualities, the reality is that many of the features supposedly unique to the world cities are of course also offered by others. Nevertheless, a confluence of historical, cultural and colonial factors have undoubtedly contributed to London's near-alchemical success. These factors include its fortunate position at the midpoint of global longitudinal time zones

(Greenwich Mean Time), and a national history of imperial expansion that generated enormous wealth, bolstered more recently by its dominance of the global finance economy for at least three decades, alongside Tokyo and New York.

London is an enormous honeypot of personal wealth: in 2017 it was estimated that its residents held around $2.7trn.[1] This figure does not include the city's richer hinterlands that have long accommodated wealthy county and 'City' types who wish to live within reach of the fumes of finance in the capital. Today, many of these commuter locations also attract the interest of extremely wealthy international buyers. Small towns like Windsor, Ascot, Virginia Water, Leatherhead, Weybridge, Henley, Marlow and Bray form part of a long-standing island formation, environs whose established wealthy are joined, as in many parts of London, by the newly minted global rich.

There has long been the sense that London and the South East are effectively another country, but recent estimates show them breaking off from the rest of the UK even more emphatically.[2] One mark of this transition is the seemingly improbable fact that the total value of homes in Elmbridge – a small, very affluent town to the west of London with a population of 130,000 – is now greater than that of the city of Glasgow. Likewise it is hard to comprehend that the top ten London boroughs by property wealth are now worth more than North Wales, Northern Ireland and the whole of Scotland put together.[3] This regional rump of wealth, a 'fat ass' of property riches and the presence of the rich themselves,[4] is an attractive prospect for the world's wealthy who have increasingly wanted a piece of it.

London is a rich city however you measure it, and long has it been so. But one of the thornier debates regarding its advantages rests on the degree to which its wealth really contributes to the fortunes of the nation more generally.[5] Much of this wealth comes through the ownership of property, as well as investment portfolios from which incomes can be extracted and wealth further supplemented – the very definition of what might be considered a truly capitalist class. Part of this story of split fortunes – between those who live from the proceeds of their capital and the rest – was revealed in the 2015 *World Wealth Report* which showed that around one in twenty of London's population was a 'high net worth individual' (a dollar millionaire or with around £660,000 in non-property wealth), representing nearly half (44 per cent) of this group nationally (840,000).

Many of London's rich don't consider themselves to be particularly well-off in a city in which the average cost of a terraced home is now just shy of half a million pounds.[6] Yet the city also boasts 431,000 property millionaires, that is, households living in homes worth a million pounds or more (roughly one in twenty people). Some will remember the comment from the model Myleene Klass that two million pounds wouldn't buy a garage (a figure mooted at the time as the basis of an annual property tax), but many might suggest that she either had particularly high standards for car storage, or else was among the many now somewhat detached from the housing needs of the average Londoner.

By 2018 the amassed fortunes of the roughly 18.1 million global super-wealthy topped $70 trillion dollars – a lot of wealth for a tiny fraction of the world's roughly 7 billion population.[7] In 2008, at the outset of the austerity decade, there were only 11 million in this group, highlighting the fact that the public cuts that have hit so many so hard are part of a system that has continued to enrich the wealthy.[8] Indeed, as many now argue, the austerity project can be linked to a political and economic machine devoted to protecting and expanding that wealth. The fortunes of the world's rich are large enough to wipe out the third world debt of $2.4trn twenty-five times,[9] clear the US and UK budget deficits,[10] and perhaps still have enough left over to bid on a few cases of nineteenth-century Bordeaux at Sotheby's.

If there are nearly half a million millionaires in London, then who are the city's real wealth elite? They constitute roughly the top 1 per cent of wealth (rather than income) holders in the city, around 88,000 in a population of 8.8 million. But this measure belies the vast variations of wealth even within this group – the tiniest cluster of the top 0.001 per cent are considerably wealthier than the remainder. Many in London possess wealth that has been generated within the UK, and which may have been transferred across generations. But many of its most monied are what used to be called the nouveau riche; they possess wealth that was not inherited and that, in the case of many of the richest, has been generated as a result of regional and global economic and social instability. This instability has seen changes in national leadership, corporate ownership and the extraction of value through mechanisms that have created new and dramatic clusters of wealth, particularly among those benefiting from the shift to capitalism in the former Soviet Union and from financial and economic liberalisation in Latin America. Alongside these are the resource-based wealthy of the Gulf states as well as the new rich of East Asia and, to a lesser extent, Africa.

The billionaires, despite the inevitable attention they receive, are really only the tip of the iceberg. If we want to understand the wealthy and their impact on the city we need to go much further. To get the full picture of how London works for the rich and for capital we must include not only the other tiers and categories of the super-rich but also, critically, those who court, support, laud and defend them. Real wealth is often defined in the various rich lists in relation to three bands: first, the High Net Worth Individuals (HNWIs) who hold between $1m and $5m in investable wealth, described somewhat cutely by Capgemini as the 'millionaires next door'; then there are those worth between $5m and $30m (known as the mid-tier millionaires); finally there is the rather wide band of those who have $30m or more, known as Ultra High Net Worth

Individuals (UHNWIs). There are around 353,000 HNWIs and 4,944 UHNWIs, the latter forms only 0.05 per cent of London's population (or just 1 in 1,785 people in the city).[11] Of those classified as multi-millionaires, that is those with £6.6m ($10m) or more, there are 12,000 in London.[12] Many of the best-rewarded company directors (median income £3.9m[13]), as well as the wealthiest of politicians (such as Jeremy Hunt, who sold his company Hotcourses for £30m), pale in comparison with these upper echelons of the city's rich.

Roughly 22 per cent of the global super-rich (UHNWIs measured here as those with $50m+) live in Europe. The majority reside in the US (51 per cent) and Asia-Pacific regions.[14] In the UK we can find roughly a hundred billionaires, with their combined wealth of $253bn, of whom around 95 live in London itself according to the *Sunday Times* rich list, more than in any other city in the world. The city's rich are located mostly in the central districts of Mayfair, Belgravia and Knightsbridge (the core of the super-prime property market), the city's northern suburbs and outside it to the west.[15] London has also become increasingly popular over the past decade as a destination for the world's rich: 2018 saw the largest single-year influx of HNWI 'golden passport' seekers (over 114,000) in the past ten years looking to use investment in the UK as a means of accessing citizenship.

The rich are not islands, even when they live on them – wealth is never simply self-made, nor does it make one self-sufficient. They are dependent on a range of bespoke private services, advisers and institutions as well as the publicly planned, designed and managed city around them. They are supported by the property buyers and agents required to source the right home, family offices to manage accounts and personal affairs, the lifestyle managers needed to locate tickets, contacts or access to key events, and numerous financial service providers who offer advice and products. All this can be conceived of as nothing less than a life-support system firmly located in the alpha city and without which the wealthy would soon struggle, like a luxury yacht in the doldrums.

The lifestyle and service needs of the rich create a distinctive geography driven in large part by their seeking maximally advantageous locations for their homes (whether first, second, third or fifth). Choice of location is determined by the proximity of workplaces (if they are so burdened), financial service providers, private schools (such as the French school in Kensington or the American schools to the west of the city) and leisure and cultural infrastructure. Neighbourhood and home life is set alongside the need for additional rooms for visitors, and the use of one or more of the seventy-five 5-star hotels (the most in any single city – New York has fifty-nine, Dubai sixty-one) and the seventy Michelin-starred restaurants in the city. For transport, the twenty-five luxury marque car dealerships are essential; for leisure, the opera houses, theatres and public art galleries (of which two, the Saatchi and Newport Street, have recently been built with private money, while a further four have seen extensions or wings added thanks to the largesse of the rich). There are more than 250 banks in London representing 26 countries, many offer bespoke services for the wealthy, even among many of the larger banks as well as by so-called family offices that run the financial and practical affairs of the richest. London also has four universities ranked in the world's top forty (New York has three) for educating offspring.[16]

Some of the most spectacular changes generated by the rich and their investments can be seen in the city's many new buildings, the product of perhaps the most dramatic construction programme undertaken in the city in the post-war period. The built environment, in the shape of new housing developments and a transformed skyline, expresses in solid forms of steel and glass the flows of capital beneath them, indexing the rising fortunes of the wealthy themselves. The many and massive high-rise constructions in particular reshape the city's ambience, infusing it with the aura of money and signifying the acquisition of the city by capital. This shining new built environment offers a glimpse of the deeper economic and political forces reshaping the city, creating new ranks of beneficiaries and changing the look, feel and function of London for everyone who lives in, works in or visits it.

One way to appreciate the scale of the changes is to focus on the city's new high-rise skyline, a massive alteration to the built fabric of a city that, like its European counterparts, had always been characteristically low-rise. This is still an unfamiliar landscape to many – the average age of London's skyscrapers (buildings taller than 100m) is only fourteen years.[17] Even by 1950 New York could lay claim to 140 such buildings, and Chicago twenty-nine: high-rise buildings signified the technological and economic advances of the US, which itself epitomised the meaning of urban life in the twentieth century. London had to wait another decade before it saw a building that exceeded the height of St Paul's Cathedral (111m) – Pimlico's Millbank Tower, built in 1963 and soon to be converted into a 5-star hotel and luxury apartments by one of the city's billionaires, who was given planning permission, with no requirement for affordable housing, by the then mayor, Boris Johnson. The first London skyscraper to exceed 150 metres was the NatWest Tower, built in 1980 in the City of London, just prior to its 'big bang' deregulation and expansion in 1986. In fact, only thirty-three buildings higher than 100 metres were built in London as a whole between 1960 and 2008, or roughly a skyscraper a year.

It gives some idea of the step change in the city's economy, and its links to real estate, to know that in only the past decade (the alpha years of 2008–18) a further forty-four towers have been completed. The city has arguably been a late developer, but much more is to come, as we will soon see. London's dramatic new skyline divides opinion between those who feel it speaks of a new confidence and see it as a mark of global success, and the many others who argue that the rampant reach skyward has destroyed the character of a once distinctive and beloved city.

*

London's geographical centre does not lie at Buckingham Palace or the Houses of Parliament – symbols of the city's regal and democratic power respectively. Any milestone or sign showing the distance to London terminates at the equestrian statue of the last absolute royal, Charles I, in Trafalgar Square. If we were to seek the city's political heart we might look to Westminster, the traditional home of Parliament and the various ministries clustered along Whitehall, and to 10 Downing Street. We might also want to bring in the city's thirty-two local governments and their role in planning and administering the capital, as well as the relatively new role of the mollusc-like City Hall, designed by a super-wealthy architect, and home of the city's mayors since 2000. These places symbolise the democratic sources of regulation and management of the city, but are they the locus of its power today, or should we look elsewhere to understand what makes the modern capital tick?

In order to understand the ways in which political and democratic institutions are connected to the interests of capital, we might begin our search in the discreet offices of the hedge funds located in former merchant's homes in Mayfair, in the City of London certainly, and perhaps in the Bank of England. Yet, in many ways, a search for the city's economic, social or political power base is doomed to yield empty chairs in spacious rooms – power is a more elusive and deeper capacity than any particular building or institution might suggest. As the city changes and new institutions, wealthy individuals and those binding these sites and key players together emerge, a contemporary search for the centre of the city must recognise the power that emerges from the laws, movements and interests of capital and the few winners it has produced. Here we may be reminded of the claim to the heart of the city made by the

Center Point tower, built in 1966, longstanding emblem of a previous housing crisis and now of the alpha city's resurgence as it is converted into super-luxury flats.

Seeking the heart of a city that runs in ever greater alignment with the interests of wealth and the wealthy, we might look to key buildings such as the Shard, within spitting distance of City Hall and emblematic of the key forces shaping the city. The ninety-five-storey, roughly 1,000-feet high building, a mix of offices, hotels and residences (most of them still empty years after completion), was bankrolled by Qatari sovereign wealth fund monies. Like many others in central London, this was a building constructed by new international wealth searching for a place to grow.

Similar funding bankrolled the Candy Brothers' One Hyde Park development (designed by Richard Rogers) overlooking the Harvey Nichols department store in Knightsbridge. Such buildings exemplify the sway of capital and its imprint on the city today. Very little of this architecture offers a sense of public contribution or new spaces for circulation and social life, unless one counts the sky garden of the Walkie Talkie building, 20 Fenchurch St, where this concession to provide a public space had to be wrested from the developer. The 11th commandment underwriting this cityscape is that if you have, you shall receive much more.

A contender to replace the Charles I statue as the central point of the city today might be the sculpture that stands beside the ultra-prime residences at One Hyde Park. Walking the canopied length of the road to the side of this building one will find the five curious figures of Jacob Epstein's work *The Rush of Green*. Completed in 1959, it seems unlikely that its title was intended to refer to the future sea of cash that would come sloshing into what was then a city arguably in economic and demographic decline. There they stand, a mother, father, child and dog, figures seemingly distended in their attempt to evade the god Pan who chases them. With a little poetic licence we might suggest that they are running away from the antiseptic emptiness of the new apartments at One Hyde Park. Yet the rush of cash and rivers of gold have since flowed like a biblical deluge, making any such escape impossible.

If we continue to walk along nearby Park Lane, we might spot a low-loader truck delivering Porsches to one of the handful of luxury nearby dealerships, their young male staff shuttling them to waiting clients. Sit in nearby Mayfair itself for a while and you will likely see well-groomed women exiting from beauticians in perfect synchrony with the arrival of a powerful chauffeur-driven car. With even fairly modest resources one can access a small part of this world by buying a coffee in some of the most famous hotels in the world: the Dorchester, Claridge's (for the old school), Jumeirah Carlton (for the Arabs) or Bulgari (for the quite simply loaded). Old photographs in the lobby of the Bulgari portray a charming and grounded class of artisan leather-workers and fashionable strollers in charmingly decaying Italian urban centres. Such images appear as the fantasised retreats nostalgically hankered for by the wealthy – quaint, peasant-filled settings that money power has often since destroyed. The reality here, as in the city more widely, is that such luxury is often built upon the destruction of the authentic places and ways of life around it.

Knightsbridge forms the focal point of the global investor's imagination. The overall effect at street level, belying the luxury and calm within, is the sense that the intersection outside Harrods is perhaps less the heart of a former empire than the central conduit along which capital flows into the city – a place with no allegiance to anything but money, untethered from social obligation or affiliation to place. If you come from China, the Middle East or Russia, and lack direct knowledge about where best to live in London, you can come to rest in these environs, safe in the knowledge that the extended larder and dressing rooms of Harrods and Harvey Nichols are but a step away among a vast array of

For sale (Harrods)

personal service providers, restaurants, clubs and comfortable neighbourhoods.

Walk through some of the back streets of Kensington to Chelsea and the growing honeycomb of below-street excavations is indicated by elaborate apparatuses of skips, conveyer belts and impossibly noisy jackhammering, a source of enormous resentment on the part of those who see themselves as London's true residents and guardians, its long-term wealthy. If this area is the heart of the city, it feels more like a device to enable wealthy bodies and their cash to rest, rather than a living, breathing social space.

*

Cities are key components of the global market economy and of the capitalist world system of accumulation. They are centres for the creation, processing and storage of wealth, but they are also places in which value that has been extracted elsewhere is then invested and circulated. This is why the City, as the financial heart of London, has become so important to its apparent success. Cities with significant financial sectors are the key nodes in a world economy that is itself increasingly financialised as more and more aspects of social, economic and political life are dictated to by the finance economy with its proliferation of financial instruments and investments.

The intensity of the flow of capital, both to the City and into London real estate, tells us much about the operation of this system and the state of the world around us. It also says something about the ability of particular urban centres to become major condensers of wealth and points of confluence for the wealthy themselves and their investments. Such cities are sticky places that hold onto these flows through cultural, architectural, historical and social qualities that help them attract business and maintain their economic dominance. Economic theory might suggest that the functions of the City could be fulfilled equally well in a field in Northumberland or on a large rig built in the middle of the Atlantic. In reality, the reason the rich themselves choose to live and invest in particular places like London, New York or Tokyo lies in their need for economic networks as well as the satisfactions to be derived from social connections, the cultural patina of tradition, and the inviting ambience generated by fine streets and residences.

The economy and the city are not run according to some master plan. The city is formed of a highly complex set of interactions within and between politics and commerce and their various captains. The perceived magic of the markets lies in the idea that even without some central system of allocation, the city as a whole works to bring goods and services to companies and consumers with little or no fuss. In reality, such a system is also deeply implicated in political processes that cast these alchemical operations as disembedded from social and civic life, even when it is clear that the markets are closely monitored and managed by governments working in concert with leading economic actors and institutions. The power of markets is ideological as well as economic – their portrayal as open, unfettered and efficient methods of resource allocation remains a deeply held principle among many in the political and commercial worlds. Nevertheless, apparently beneficial market systems have been strongly associated with deepening inequality and the massive enrichment of particular individuals even as they are lauded for creating wealth.

For several decades the allure of the market has inveigled its way into forms of political thinking that have become aligned with the needs of business and finance. This becomes problematic when the background assumptions of pro-market systems become deeply embedded in political and economic life to the detriment of social needs and functions. In short, markets come first and social essentials, like housing, education and health, become secondary issues, instead of being understood as part of a system in which the needs of citizens are paramount. Market principles have become so deeply entrenched that the functionaries of the operating systems underpinning capitalism – government ministers, local authorities, planning departments, chambers of commerce, business leaders and financiers – all begin to sing from the same hymn sheet.

Even after the financial crisis, market-based economic models and ideas continued to dominate discussions, frequently without reference to the ultimate rationale for economic life itself – to address human need. Much of this lopsided thinking can be linked to the way such ideas were connected to the ability of markets to generate enormous windfalls for political honchos, captains of the financial system and dealers in real estate. The danger of these beliefs is that they enabled a massive expansion of wealth among a few while doing little to benefit the city's residents as a whole.

Conspiracies are not required to bring to life a working model of these interests, systems, ideas and networks. We can call the effect of these processes 'city capture'. This notion may help us think through what is happening to many cities globally, where the demands of capital are being met with open arms and minds by local elites keen to attract and benefit from the money of the wealthy. The term plutocracy literally means 'money power', often conceived in terms of government by the wealthy or the sense that government itself is run at the whims and instruction of the rich. In a plutocratic city like London, this makes local politicians, builders, decorators, butlers and estate agents, among many others, the mediators and facilitators of a process in which the rich themselves appear to have significant power.

That power does not reside solely in the overt actions of plutocrats lobbying government and politicians directly; there is an interleaving of interests and assumptions about what is best for the city that runs much deeper. This makes power, as the capacity to exert some kind of force, something more diffuse and complex than the traditional idea of a power elite or establishment tends to convey. The availability of many tens of thousands of the global rich presents itself as a significant business opportunity. Politics becomes the very stuff of this business. Similarly, the social mission statement of the city becomes subtly realigned with, for example, the idea of realising the value of any and all 'underused' assets as the city intensifies investment activity (housing associations selling homes, local authorities selling playing fields, care homes, housing estates and so on).

London's contemporary power bloc consists of many key individuals, but these people are almost incidental to the exercise of power. It is the roles they perform and the resources they hold that bring power to life. There is, however, a sense that the traditional establishment has undergone a change, not so much in terms of its personnel, but in the reconfiguration of its underlying operating system. The old political and economic order is not dead, but its fabric has been rewoven to include the very rich and their agents acting, lobbying and building on their behalf.

The city's power bloc is thus a complex amalgam of forces, money flows and wealth. This is not to suggest some kind of fully integrated, coherent network of individuals and institutions. Wealth is not just about a coterie or an elite, it is also about an idea or a set of values to which many in the city and beyond now subscribe. These values are transmitted through training in neoclassical economics and underwritten by the tenets of financial journalism and the discourse of politicians who are themselves often the beneficiaries of dynastic or new wealth to say nothing of those who aspire to be wealthy themselves. The result is the capture of the city by money and those whose interests are served by it.

City capture is a process that involves not so much conflict and strategic gain as an apparently voluntary acceptance and submission to the ruling logics of capital and its expansion.[18] Making lots of money is understood as a positive sign, and good things come to those who can attract more money and inward investment. This means that those with money can profit from and subsequently dictate how the city and its various resources are to be used. This can be seen in the way planning authorities in the city have come to identify private developers as critical to the remaking of many districts, while presiding over the demolition and loss of desperately needed public housing. This capture of place has been achieved without battle or bloodshed, if not without some degree of localised protest and significant social pain.

The capacity of market logic to colonise the minds of those occupying positions of power is an important aspect of what has been termed cognitive capture – the influence over government of key economic ideas and principles of the importance of markets and the high value to be placed on financial institutions.[19] In the present context this means that political institutions become preoccupied with the idea that finance capital is central to economic vitality and are thus supportive of whatever it needs in order to flourish. These assumptions run

28

so deeply that they often remain unquestioned. The power of Wall Street and the City of London arguably resides not just in their daily business activity but also in their ability to perpetuate deep assumptions about what is good for all.

These influences and processes are periodically exemplified by the comments of key politicians, keen to show they are not antagonistic to the interests of capital and its primary beneficiaries, the rich. Whether it be the 'intensely relaxed' attitude towards the wealthy famously expressed by Peter Mandelson, or the lauding of the rich as 'tax heroes' by the former London mayor, and now prime minister, Boris Johnson, this open and welcoming environment gives those holding fortunes significant power. Yet their influence in reality works its magic in indistinct ways. Billionaires and UHNWIs do not generally make direct demands on political parties, though we are increasingly learning more about the role of the rich and international wealthy in political funding and lobbying. More often politicians, seeking investment in their town or city, simply act in tandem with the needs of capital by second-guessing the agendas of the super-rich, because, in essence, they identify these with their own needs.

Of course, plutocracies do sometimes operate by way of large bribes or expensive and laborious lobbying (the influence on electoral politics of hedge fund managers and rich individuals being but one example), but at the city level these processes become more opaque and complex, even though the results are everywhere in evidence around us. These include proposals for costly projects like the unbuilt Garden Bridge, the undermining of public planning rules by developers seeking to avoid having to build affordable housing, the incorporation of city councillors into the property machine via hospitality and gifts, the drive by developers to build almost exclusively for the world's wealthy and for investors, the evident lack of capacity to police the vast flows of laundered money in the built environment, the demolition of viable and essential public housing and the banishment of tenants beyond the city.

None of these things happened because some billionaire picked up the phone and called the mayor. They happened because it became acceptable and was deemed necessary to think that these processes represented the most efficient and best use of the city in order to ensure its maximal profitability. This is why the story presented here cannot be fully understood simply through the traditional tropes of old boy's networks, private clubs or meetings over liquid lunches in the City.

A number of key changes can be identified that undergird these shifts in the operation of the city. Certainly the city's elite and its networks have, over time, become increasingly efficient at recruiting those whose primary allegiance is to making money, rather than to notions of class or indeed nation. These changes have altered the formation of existing elites while building new and more complex ones. Constellations of interests, including the City and its various institutions, the government and cabinet, underwrite systems of regulation and rules of trade that facilitate rounds of accumulation by the affluent. The game of politics and corporate life has changed significantly during the neoliberal era, with self-serving, short-termist and reckless behaviour increasingly evident.[20] Politicians have arguably changed in their role and position in relation to the (newly) wealthy. They have become what some now describe as a kind of butler class – functionaries who see their role as one of subordination to the wealthy, supporting, guiding and pampering them.

This is the way of urban life in a plutocratic city in which money power is courted and channelled wherever possible by central and local government officials, who are either themselves signatories to the mantra of footloose capital and trickle-down economics or who believe that they have little agency over such forces. Critically, the results impact not only on the lives of the elites; they also have the effect of underwriting arguments made for dislodging the poor or for ignoring middle-income groups who are seen as less valuable to the urban economy. There is a real savagery to these processes, even if it is frequently cloaked in a language of opportunity or described in terms of new horizons of international investment. Meanwhile the policy-making elite are able to live sheltered from the consequences of their own decisions, in leafy districts, comfortable clubs and on exciting leisure circuits, uninterrupted by envious workers or lazy benefit recipients.

Money has real power – it can generate a new skyline, subvert planning principles and rules, buy apparently unpurchaseable club memberships and secure privileged access to policy-makers and governments or to important power networks that are less visible. Money doesn't force its way in; it slides into the scene and is usually welcomed. Money power is the binding and guiding logic of the city, dictating, influencing and shaping the parameters of what is possible. The overall effect has been that London, a city that has long worked for capital through its financial services sector, increasingly also works for the rich.

2

The Archipelago of Power

The alpha city is to the rich what bones are to the human body. It is here that the rich are supported by fine homes, clubs, power networks and a diverse cast of assistants. The close-knit presence and availability of the alpha city's support system means that the rich are clustered in its finest and most luxurious districts. There is something about such places, an almost indefinable aura that attracts the super-rich to the city's fine streets and homes but also to its multiplying social potential. These qualities leaven an almost globally unique mix of heritage, prestige and culture. All of this combines to create a city to live in, but also one to be seen in by the right people at key moments in the social calendar. While the patrician circuits of court and nobility have faded, it remains the case that in order to find a position among the world's global elite one must find a place in the city.

As a destination for international capital investment, London is a place in which fortunes are made. But it is also a place where those with massive personal wealth seek to make and enrich themselves still further, socially and financially. This is a diverse and international group, originating from around the globe and in particular from the new and booming segments of national economies around it. Of course, London has long been a wealthy city that has attracted the world's rich, but where in the past they could be found clustered almost exclusively in the West End, today the geography of super-affluent enclaves extends to the city's North and South and to numerous areas beyond its formal boundaries.

What binds these networks and wealthy quarters together is the dependence of the super-rich on proximity to the social and economic life of the city proper. The key circuits of social life, deal making and political connections have been extended by luxurious and rapid modes of transport that effectively expand the geographical limits of the formal city to take in new suburbs, wealthy towns, and villages with mega-homes. But within all of this the city itself remains critical to the functioning and daily life of the rich and to attracting a global flow of new and visible wealth.

Who are London's rich and where have they come from? Why are they so attracted to this particular city? The core argument underlying the analysis offered here is that London is critical to the creation of a group identity among the rich, even if there are clear divides and sub-networks within their ranks. This group forms a kind of congregation; we can see them in the city out in force, but there is no clear sense of community among them due to their increasingly diverse national, economic and political backgrounds. The city also operates as a kind of theatre in which money is translated into social and cultural displays of good taste sought out by new money (and which old money believes it already knows).

A new nouveau riche, today's super-wealthy arrivals have come to London as one of only a very few possible locations. They come to do business but also to be received within the city's existing power networks and those domains that confer status. This kind of access begins with residence in the city's established luxury districts, its alphahoods, joining its notable clubs, and connecting with others in less formal settings where dusty codes and prejudices can be circumvented in new and often highly dynamic private circuits. If much of London was originally constructed to woo the wealthy from its rural hinterlands, today it plays the same role on a global scale.

A theatre of riches

Much of the city that today we so closely associate with the wealth elite was already well in place over two hundred years ago. At the beginning of the nineteenth century, the West End was already the focus of new residential developments for the wealthy, speculatively built by the owners of landed estates to accommodate aristocrats, merchants enriched by their imperial adventures, and the bourgeois owners of new industries who came to rent properties in these prestigious enclaves. The history of the alpha city begins with this space and its key role in acting as a melting pot that brought together British and international wealth elites. In this sense the city still acts as this point of social confluence and processer of people and capital, a place in which new social alloys and class compounds are forged and mixed over time.

An important outcome of the work of this machine has historically been its production of a sense of common identity, consciousness and solidarity among its elites, generated by shared residence in these immaculate districts. From this has also flowed the sense of new money jostling to be accommodated within the ranks of the long-term national elite. The historic city and its established alphahoods have long been the critical ingredients of a process through which rich and powerful groups have been formed. Proximity allowed networks to be built and lifestyles enjoyed that were advantaged by access to an exciting range of services, institutions and social opportunities. Underlying these social changes and the formation of a more urban and self-conscious elite lay strong economic incentives.

The story of the building of the West End was one of speculation by large landholding estates, creating the kind of fine streets, homes and semi-rural squares necessary to lure the growing numbers of the rich. The West End helped them to be close to each other but also to the key institutions of court, the economic institutions of the City, and the rounds of events that brought access to 'Society'. The city of today, now chasing global cash and new ranks of the rich, continues the patterns of association and class formation generated in this formative period.

The social geography of areas like Mayfair and Knightsbridge was the result of building large and thus expensive homes that only the elite could afford. Such homes required a large entourage of staff, and access to shops and services with supply chains for luxury items and fresh food that were necessarily short. Living at the right address was critical to securing a position in society, and historians have noted that careful geographical placement in the city was key to being considered part of the right crowd. As a result, more often than not, the residences of the wealthy and the nobility were almost never south of the river. During the seventeenth century, the Earls of Bedford (Covent Garden), Leicester (Leicester Square) and Southampton (Bloomsbury) created the new swathes of the early West End, a geography that pushed further west in the eighteenth century as the Earl of Scarborough (Hanover Square), Earl of Oxford (Cavendish Square), Lord Berkeley (Berkeley Square) and the Grosvenor family (Grosvenor Square) created the cornerstones of today's alphahoods.

Aesthetically and physically, the arrival of new money gave rise to new urban districts that spoke of the power of this wealth, embodied by massive mansions and palaces and, later on, hotels and clubs. All appeared on a grand scale, often using international styles, such as French-inspired, gothic and classical architecture.

The West End estates were frequently built with a focal point, a central square, with a mansion associated with the estate owner. This would then be surrounded by the houses of new residents and tenants. A degree of town planning ensured more or less self-sufficient neighbourhood units through the inclusion of churches, markets and public houses. Unlike today, servants and other service staff also lived within the West End, making and supplying the goods and services the various households needed. Though elite areas, they were necessarily diverse because of a reliance on 'help' of various kinds. It has been estimated that even in these super-rich districts only around 10 per cent of the population were 'upper class', while the rest were servants, shopkeepers, publicans and smaller manufacturers.

Some areas of the West End were strongly associated with particular political affiliations: Hanover Square (1717), for example, was apparently built by and for people with Whig and military links, while Cavendish Square (1724) was seen as a Conservative enclave. Despite all the networking and sense of proximity, the West End was never a community in the sense of a connected group of individuals living in a locality. It was in reality a very large yet 'part-time' area, as many large townhouses were only occupied during the 'season' for a few months before the rich returned to their rural residences. These patterns have some resemblance to what we see of the life of these areas today.

Estimates have been made of the size of the elite occupying this area: in terms of the titled elite, there were around 5,500 in London in 1800; by 1900, due to urbanisation and the conferment of new peerages, the number had risen to 21,700. Among the earliest wealthy groups that returned to London were the so-called Nabobs, who made their fortunes in India in the mid eighteenth century as employees of the East India Company, as well as the families that had made their fortunes in the Jamaican sugar trade. One of the great anxieties about the Nabobs was not only their massive wealth but their use of it to demand, and allegedly purchase, seats in Parliament. This threat of money power to city, nation and society was perhaps inevitable and irresistible, but the establishment attempted to hold on by reducing the powers and scale of the East India Company.

New money, always somehow outside and representing a threat to existing elites, has arrived at the gates of the city for hundreds of years, seeking to integrate with its existing corporate, political and cultural worlds. Newly rich individuals and families looked to sit alongside and be absorbed into long-standing estates and aristocratic circles through education, emulating good taste, seeking political favour and using strategic marriage as a means of entering the upper social echelons, helping to access and reproduce new and dynastic wealth. This could not be done from a distance and without proximity to the kinds of connections and institutions that were only to be found in London.

Admittance to the upper circles was also pursued through membership of the city's increasing numbers of private clubs (there were around twenty-five in 1837, and ninety-eight by 1900), many of which were connected to political parties. Most clubs were clustered within St James's and Piccadilly, because these districts were historically adjacent to St James's Palace, which remained the royal court even after Queen Victoria took up residence close by at Buckingham Palace in 1837. While today there are clubs devoted to the arts, media, universities and sports, many are still focused on politics or have strong military connections or aristocratic ties (such as the Carlton, home to the Tory Party, Turf Club, White's and Pratts – where all male staff are called George to avoid confusion). With changes in taste and society over the century, clubs devoted to the arts emerged, such as the Athenaeum, Garrick, Savage, Arts and Savile.

A key route to transformation was the use of honours to transform money capital into political and social standing. By 1890 it was estimated that a quarter of business and commercial families had a peerage. Between 1886 and 1914, two hundred new peers were created,[1] highlighting the way in which money was increasingly being admitted to society in what some saw as a kind of 'bourgeoisification' of the gentry. The role of the then existing city establishment, formed primarily of the landed wealthy, oscillated between gatekeeping access to good taste and 'breeding', on the one hand, and, on the other, slowly admitting new wealth by enrolling it into the ways and codes of the long-standing elite. Up until the late nineteenth century the acquisition of a rural estate was still considered the critical means by which the tastes and power of the landed gentry could be emulated. In fact it is estimated that between 1835 and 1889, 500 new major country homes were built. From the early twentieth century onwards, however, most looked to London's milieu as the key space in which to do business and engage with others of a similar background. Here access could also be gained to the annual round of Society functions, the 'season' that ran from May to September in the city.

London's changing wealth elite

How might we begin to unpick the groups and individuals that make up the rich of today's alpha city? One way into this question is to think of them in terms of three more or less distinct blocs. The first consists of the established rich, whose forebears we met in the preceding section. This group includes those with dynastic wealth and the more modest patrician elite who are anchored in the city's established alphahoods. A second key group is today's equivalent of the nouveaux riche of the late nineteenth and early twentieth centuries. This bloc includes the various industrial, tech, finance, commodities, energy and utility barons. In the third group are the enablers, those who play the role of factotums to capital and the super-wealthy. These are the agents and managers who, in many cases, have become rich themselves, often by growing and deploying other people's money. This group is critical to the story of the alpha city because it is they who have helped to create the kind of environment conducive to attracting the flows of mobile global capital and ensuring the influence of new money on the city more broadly. The enablers include key figures working in banking, the managers or CEOs of large firms, financiers, hedge fund managers, some politicians, and those working in real estate including developers and builders.

London's wealthy are by no means a unified establishment, with fractions among the rich who have differing backgrounds, interests and roles. Wealth overlaps with, and has become integrated into, a number of other key domains in complex ways – including politics, finance, the aristocracy and the media. The sense of a capture of the city by the rich is multifaceted, involving the planning of the enablers to bring capital investment to the city as much as any strategic set of actions by the rich themselves. Across the three groups of the old, the new and the enabling rich, there are thousands of individuals drawn from diverse nationalities, working in various sectors, including those whose fortunes are 'self-made' and those who have inherited wealth.

Most of London's resident rich are also residents elsewhere, which adds some dynamism to their relationship to the city

A Whirling Social Circuit

and to other places that compete for their wealth by offering more or less open regulatory regimes, preferential tax arrangements, rapid transport networks and low taxes on property. The alpha city's super-rich include British aristocratic families and estates, media moguls, apparent geniuses from the world of new media, captains of commerce and industry, Russian oligarchs, individuals linked to organised criminal networks, oil barons and other resource magnates, as well as a slew of others linked to old (steel, diamonds) and newer (rare metals, chemicals, pharmaceuticals) commodities that underpin global capital markets today.

The single common denominator of the wealth elite is, of course, their command of personal wealth that has arisen as a result of accidental, strategic or aggressive control of capital. What tends to bind the group is an interest in enlarging or at least maintaining their financial position, an interest which brings with it political alignments connected to the pursuit of low taxes, economic stability and the privileging of finance and open capital borders. Here we also need to consider the enablers, because they are the skilled engineers and mechanics who maintain the magic machineries of capital, looking to ensure that the needs of the rich are met. They are defenders of the rich because their own wealth depends on them, hence their efforts to capture potentially easy money through the lure of the city's offer.

To some extent we have already encountered London's established rich. In many ways this group is very much of the city; they are embedded in its everyday life and have been here, in some cases, for decades or even hundreds of years. While their more obvious power, as political and law lords and land-holders, has waned, they remain an important part of the story of the development of the alpha city. We have seen how the use of peerages greatly expanded the ranks of the landed wealthy as honours were used to bring members of the bourgeoisie and international plutocrats into the ranks of the city's power brokers and political parties. The city's old money today is formed of the really old money, exemplified by the key estates which still own large areas of central London – Grosvenor (300 acres), Portman (110), Cadogan (93), de Walden (92) and Bedford (20 acres covering Bloomsbury) – and whose collective wealth is estimated at around £22bn. The 'old' rich includes the descendants of the 'new' families that had emerged in the nineteenth and twentieth centuries, such as the Rothschilds or Sebag-Montefiores. Yet very few of the richest families of even the 1970s are anywhere to be seen among the ranks of the city's super-rich today.

The patrician wealthy have a strong attachment to place and its use as a social asset. Of course many in the House of Lords were and still are drawn from this group. Here the traditional image is perhaps the Wodehousian archetype of fusty and eccentric landowners eschewing the material trappings of modern life. The former Duke of Westminster was renowned for not being interested in material things, which is easy to say when you own swathes of Britain. While the sense of patrician responsibility has something going for it in a world of tidal money, we must remember that the accretion of luck, land and rents generated a group whose money power is also entwined with forms of political power and more subtle forms of influence. These connections and interests continue to block action on issues like land reform, transparency of property ownership, more progressive wealth taxes and more concerted challenges to money laundering and offshore investment, because many among the wealthy (in London and beyond) are linked to these systems.

The estates are now businesses that have often been taken out of the hands of their respective families. Many have branched out into land and property investments in other cities and nations. Grosvenor, for example, is today run as a Trust and owns property in more than sixty cities around the world. Now as in the past this group maintains its wealth by drawing payments (rents) for land and leasehold properties, but diversification of their portfolios has also been seen as an important element of survival. As a result, long-standing ownership means that this group is active in planning and shaping the look and feel of many of London's alphahood areas that continue to draw in the world's new rich.

Today the city still sees other sedimentary displays of patronage and older class and power structures, whether it be the Lord Mayor London's annual parade, the fading circuit of the royal court, or proms and debutante balls. The annual 'season' has been in decline since the 1960s, as has its role in underwriting the boundaries of Society membership. But the city's richest long-standing families, and of course royalty itself, continue to play a part in the everyday life of the city. Here, land and social position come together, carefully sustained and managed over generations through long-term estate management and succession planning. In 2017 the new Duke of Westminster, inheriting one of the largest wealth dynasties in the UK and indeed the world, paid almost no inheritance tax as the estate was passed to him in a trust. Even so, times and fortunes change, and in 2018 it was estimated that the royal family of Abu Dhabi were now the second largest landholder in Mayfair, while a string of sovereign wealth funds had snapped up enormous amounts of land and assets in the city. The city's largest residential home after Buckingham Palace was now owned by a Russian oligarch, and a billionaire former owner of a mobile phone empire was building a massive mansion in the heart of Mayfair.

The established rich also include quite large numbers of households that are wealthy if not spectacularly so. Many have lived in London's alphahoods for several generations, sit well within the 1 per cent in terms of wealth, and resent many of the changes brought about by new money. This is a privileged group bordering the upper-middle and upper class, often having bought property in the 1960s and '70s, and for whom the massive tide of wealth arriving in the city represents both a symbolic and real challenge to their quiet enjoyment of the city. For this group the major anxieties are the increasing cost of property, the excessive noise pollution from cars and parties, and the question of why the new wealth elite don't seek to become more integrated in the everyday life of the neighbourhood. A frequent complaint of this patrician elite is that areas which were once relatively diverse and lively urban communities now have the feel of ghost neighbourhoods. This is a group that has been and still is privileged, but which now feels threatened by new money and the sense of an overdevelopment of the city exemplified by its new high-rise and luxury developments.

The 'new' new rich

The alpha city has seen its traditionally wealthy groups joined by those who have grown rich in a time of global financialisation, kleptocratic capitalism and the use of new financial instruments and rent-seeking tech platforms as effective methods for making massive personal fortunes. London has been keen to lure this group and, more particularly, their cash.

Changes in the sources of the wealth among the city's rich offer a barometer of changes in the global economy. Those changes, from the dominance of coal, steel and cotton in the nineteenth century to the role played by finance, tech and media today, can be mapped onto the city's alphahoods and the architecture of new waves of development that show distinctive contemporary displays of taste and untrammelled money power. Over time these displays and the rich themselves appear to have become more privately oriented, whereas many among the wealthy of a hundred or so years ago would signal their standing through social and political contributions.

The idea that a crusty, outmoded and undemocratic elite has

given way to the benefit of 'self-made' (the scare quotes are important!) money belies the many contributory factors such as good fortune, selection processes in major corporate outfits (based on schooling or social networks), the use of leverage from monopoly rentier positions, or indeed criminal acts that help to game or infiltrate the system. The rich often occupy a structural position that must be filled while believing no one else capable of doing what they do. Many of them come from a kind of vampiric cluster whose wealth is primarily generated by their ability to draw massive income from their control over capital, property and intellectual property. This group is unchallenged, untaxed and over here. A small coterie of alpha cities are engaged in a competition to attract them, driven by a number of enabling political and economic groups and key individuals.

How might the social location of London's new money be best described? The traditional class types – working, middle

Dead Space

and upper – feel increasingly quaint and unsuited to making sense of the long tail of riches that now extends celestially upwards. Certainly any sense of class or identity founded on traditional measures of occupation, political affiliation or income will not get us far in understanding the gulf between the social top and bottom, and, critically, the ways in which massive advantage and money power are becoming concentrated among the rich. One way to gain some purchase here is simply to follow the money, looking at the sources and systems that deliver such pronounced benefits to such a small group.

This means tackling two key issues head on: first, the question of power captured in the idea of an elite itself; second, how we understand its influence on the urban settings in which it is located. Clearly there are numerous overlaps here, as money connects with other affiliations, institutions, identities and industry sectors. None of this answers the question of whether an upper or ruling class, or an establishment, still exists, or if it does whether it remains influential. However, what we can see is that in many cases old money has become adjunct and facilitator to the new capitalists. In some respects the landscape of established groups and interests has been circumvented by the way that new money has again bulldozed to one side the closed doors of class.

While the idea of an establishment is not redundant, it has in many ways been refashioned by the presence of a newer, internationalised and cosmopolitan group whose wealth is akin to that wielded by the belle epoque capitalists of the late nineteenth and early twentieth centuries. The wealth of those groups was eroded and straitened over the last century by massive wars and the partial triumph of labour and social democratic governments. But a resurgence of class and capital interests can be observed in the way that London in particular has been managed as part of a strategy to restore and maintain power among the wealthy. This restoration and the growth in numbers of the rich themselves have been enabled by a deregulated land and labour market, cuts to the public sector, fewer border constraints or taxes on capital, as well as an enabling environment for international investors and buyers of property. These regulatory aspects of the city, designed to lure the rich, have been supplemented with what amounts to a kind of recorded welcome message from a series of mayors (such as Boris Johnson's claim that London is to billionaires what the jungles of Sumatra were to orang-utans) and other influencers that is played to anyone with bags of cash looking to invest or live in the city.

The key formations seeking to attract the rich are embodied by central and London government (including the thirty-two London boroughs, many of which either by choice or necessity have welcomed international capital) and the City, which sits at the centre of massive corporate flows (including enormous illicit wealth channels) and has sucked in capital via the post-colonial development of the world of offshore finance. Whether during apparent booms or periods of economic crisis, the power of finance has been assured through the ingestion of the logic of money by government.

One important means by which wealth has been retained by potentially footloose wealthy individuals is known as the non-domicile, or non-dom, tax rule. Where trusts have proved useful as a key vehicle for protecting old money, money from overseas or inherited wealth (the tax code can be inherited) was encouraged on the promise that it would remain largely untaxed. It remains possible to live in Britain and hold enormous wealth overseas, with only a very partial tax applied to income brought to the UK. This can get very complicated very quickly. The non-dom tax rule itself goes back to 1799, when the measure was brought in to help rebuild state resources following a series of wars and enormous losses. At the time many wealthy British citizens were living abroad and the question arose of how to tax their foreign holdings of estates, wealth and business operations without putting them off from returning to the UK. To encourage their return the government proposed that so called non-doms be exempt from paying tax on their assets and foreign income.

The rules changed in 2017 when non-doms were asked to pay income tax on their earnings in the UK, but they could still avoid paying any tax on their foreign assets and income as long as these were not paid back to them in the UK. The point here is that one might choose to retain operations overseas and build up a war chest that could be accessed by, say, retiring to France, Bermuda or wherever. The rules also create a series of inheritance tax, business investment and other tax reliefs that UK citizens cannot access. An added complication is that it is possible to pay a charge (the 'remittance basis charge') on income and gains held overseas.

The latest figures show that there are 52,900 non-doms registered in London (2019 HMRC data). This is a group that, somewhat curiously, reside in the city but don't live there (to reduce their tax burden); they are the Schrodinger's cats of the tax world. For wealthy 'non-doms' the city is defined in law as a kind of incomplete home, despite its clearly being their preferred location to live. London non-doms paid £5.3bn in income tax in 2018 (roughly 80 per cent of the total amount paid by all of the UK's 90,000 non-doms). This sounds like a decent enough contribution until we divide it by the total number of non-doms, which then gives us an average take of £100,000 per head. This may still sound like a lot, but then an average school head teacher earning £55,000 would pay around £16,000 in income tax, while a 'low' paid university vice chancellor earning £170,000 would pay a comparable amount of tax (£70,000), this is also equal to the level of pay that a quarter of a million Londoners earn. Since we know little or nothing about the scale of the non-doms' offshore holdings, it is not possible to estimate how much tax is lost by these arrangements. Many think the UK government's tax inspectors should do much more. It is also worth remembering that this group does not include the numerous wealthy 'onshore' citizens who have used offshore savings and investment funds to evade or reduce their tax bill.

The existence of the non-doms is the source of much heated debate. We know very little about who these people are, with the exception of some well-known individuals – such as Mark Carney, the former Governor of the Bank of England, Roman Abramovich, Lewis Hamilton, Sigrid Rausing, Viscount Rothermere (owner of the *Daily Mail* who inherited the exemption from his father) and Lakshmi Mittal – many of whom are among the richest in London. The list also includes entrepreneurs like James Caan, private equity and finance managers, resource and retail magnates and numerous CEOs of major global corporations including a string of UK banks and pharmaceutical and insurance companies.

The non-doms have become a serious point of contention since many have lived for years in London and clearly benefit from living here. The non-dom issue highlights rules that are a legacy of empire and landed interests that permeate through to the life of the contemporary city. This is another good example of the many ways in which capital finds all manner of schemes by which its demands to escape the rules placed on the little people are enabled by a compliant state.

The general impression is of a rotten colonial legacy that serves the interests of the rich, who are able to run rings around tax collection agencies. The fear often peddled by some commentators is that imposing a greater tax burden on them might drive away important contributors to the UK economy. Yet it seems unlikely that long-term residents of the alpha city would be put off living there by a levelling of the tax playing field.

It is clear that London retains a powerful hold on the imaginations, wallets and lives of the global super-rich. In this sense there is reason to be confident that fair and transparent tax rules might not see a significant exodus of the city's rich because they would not be able to access the host of desirable aspects of living there, even if they do so only for part of the year. An obvious dividend of introducing such measures would be the clear message that tax rules applied fairly to all, with the extra revenue used to address problems like the availability of affordable housing in the city.

The new rich of the alpha city are exemplified by wealthy individuals like Evgeny Lebedev (owner of the *Evening Standard*), Sir Cameron Macintosh (entertainment), Dickson Poon (owner via an investment company of Harvey Nichols), Michael Bloomberg (politics and media), Anthony 'Yachtie' Bamford (heavy plant), Anne-Marie Graff (diamonds), Bernard Lewis (retail), Charlene de Carvalho-Heineken (brewing), Ashok Hinduja (steel), Richard Desmond (media), Bernie Ecclestone (sport), Duncan Bannatyne (leisure) and Christian Candy (real estate). Banking and finance also figure prominently. Perhaps the most interesting thing about the lists of London's wealthiest is the unrecognisability of the bulk of their names – those with enormous wealth are for the most part obscure, anonymous individuals.

Also significant are those who provide opportunistic processing and investment of other people's money, the fund managers such as Crispin Odey, Ken Griffin (who spent nearly £200m on two homes in London), Michael Platt and John Beckwith among many others. Among this group, proximity to the City is important, but so too is the key hedge fund district of Mayfair, which has long been deemed a more comfortable and sociable base for those working in high-end finance. The idea that proximity is no longer important in finance is inaccurate – personal deal making, face-to-face meetings to build trust, and the soft infrastructure of watering holes and restaurants are also crucial elements here.

Over the last twenty years or so the internationalisation of the city's wealthy has become increasing evident; this has included groups like the Russians, Turks, Nigerians and Chinese, alongside the longer-term presence of Americans, Hong Kongers,

Arabs and the French. Many of the new rich live in the wonderful homes and massive mansions that were built on earlier
waves of wealth. They include Lakshmi Mittal, who lives in
what is known as the Taj Mittal on Kensington Palace Gardens,
Roman Abramovich, Leonard Blavatnik, Alisher Usmanov,
China's richest businessman Wang Jianlin, the Sultan of Brunei,
Tamara Ecclestone and John Hunt, who owns the elite estate
agency Foxtons. Next to Regent's Park live the Sultan of Oman,
the Prince of Brunei and members of the Saudi royal family,
in the enormous 'lodges' and terraces created by the Prince
Regent's architect John Nash in the early nineteenth century.

In areas like Highgate and Hampstead many of the mansions built by people who made their fortunes in soap, coal and
brewing have been bought by wealthy Russians, who tend to
live much more privately than did the patrician but ultimately
short-lived wealth dynasties that built the residential landscape
on the ridge. Athlone House, which was originally built by a
financier, became a care home between 1955 and 2003, when
it was sold to the Kuwaiti royal family. It was recently bought
for £65m by the head of the private investment company Alfa,
Mikhail Fridman, who started out as a construction engineer.
Like many homes in the key alphahoods, the property was
purchased from offshore. Adjacent to Athlone is Beechwood
House – one of at least two residences in and around London
belonging to billionaire Alisher Usmanov (metals and mining, a
stake in Arsenal, with another home in Surrey at Sutton Place).
It was previously owned by members of the Saudi and then
Qatari royal families.

Perhaps the key home here is Witanhurst. With its sixty-five
rooms it is the second largest home in England after Buckingham
Palace, yet still apparently not large enough for Andrei Guriev
(fertilisers), who bought the property using a company (Safran
Holdings) registered in the British Virgin Islands, and then
reportedly expanded the building to include underground car
parking and a massive indoor pool and cinema.

London has become a world increasingly made by and for the new rich. Yet few of them are fully or even mostly resident in the city. Today, instead of retreating to a rural pile as their forebears did, they are more likely to be found in other tax-efficient cities, such as Geneva, Dubai or Monaco, or in homelands around the world such as India, the UAE, Pakistan, Nigeria, Lebanon or Israel. While the city's new rich are a hyper-mobile group who circulate between many places critical to their tastes and needs, many of them still see London as the key place to engage with others in the wealth bloc – building alliances, advancing business opportunities, and drawing on its uplifting arrangements and configurations of people, places and experiences that London alchemically brings together.

If the nineteenth-century bourgeoisie initially struggled to join the ranks of society, their co-opting of and co-presence in the city eventually became a means of bypassing the strategies of class closure or rejection on the part of the ruling elites. Similar processes have occurred in more recent decades. In the 1970s, when London was on its knees, money talked louder than social networks, while snobbery regarding who was part of society faded by necessity, as new entrants like the oil-rich Arabs came to take up residence in areas like Knightsbridge and Mayfair.

The Clermont Club, a gambling house set up by the middle-class entrepreneur John Aspinall, was the setting for what some have identified as the kind of no-rules capitalism that pervaded the city in the 1980s, and in which new players could enter and vie for power outside of the establishment rules. The Mayfair 'set' offer an interesting case study of the changing power structures as London shifted away from being an imperial force in the post-war period. Key figures like James Goldsmith, Jim Slater, Tiny Roland and the founder of the SAS, David Stirling, adopted a vision of the UK as a fading imperial power whose gentlemanly capitalism and establishment were being undermined by complacency and adherence to rules.

In this context, shareholder seizures of company control and asset stripping proved an effective means of wresting power and generating remarkable if sometimes short-lived fortunes. The group appeared to be anti-establishment while adopting a kind of retrotopic vision of Britain as a nation that could restore its economic pre-eminence at least for those prepared to risk their own and others' capital. The story bears some relationship to the contemporary impression of new money and anti-establishment elites who, in order to usurp power, have sought to use Brexit as a means to construct a narrative of a country in decline.

Today's alpha rich are not a mono-form power bloc. Identifiable sub-groups are clustered by nationality (the British, of which there are still many; Russians, Hong Kongers, Emiratis and so on), source of wealth (commodities, energy, food and brewing, media), and industry sector (finance, development, industry). Much of this money has emerged in recent decades, rather than being dynastic. Where some proclaim a more porous and meritocratic corporate world rewarding a new generation of go-getters and innovators, others have charted shifts in the scale, intensity and asymmetrical reward systems of the global economy. These changes have had the effect of producing many new entrants to the wealth elite, often with relatively little effort on their part, facilitated by state monopoly positions, tax evasion, offshore finance and, in some cases, dubious or criminal trade.

A portrait of London's wealthiest can be painted in miniature by examining media reports of the owners of apartments at One Hyde Park, the epitome of the city's contemporary wealth elite and the destination of the spoils from many mineral and energy-rich countries.[2] This development, in which apartments are frequently purchased via offshore companies, transformed the fortunes of the Candy Brothers, Nick and Christian, one of whom himself owns an apartment in what has been described as the only ultra-prime development in the city. From a variety of sources we can learn something of what others have described as the 'shadowy' residents of the development. There are eighty apartments in this opulent, semi-fortified block that sits a stone's throw from Harvey Nichols, perhaps two from Harrods.

The wealth of One Hyde Park's residents appears to be based almost solely on new money, made from privatised energy fields, from the monopoly control of telecommunications, real estate, pharmaceuticals, oil, property, gambling, and, allegedly in some cases, from organised criminal involvement. The list of nationalities is long, including Russians and those from Lebanon, Malaysia, Australia, Qatar, Nigeria and Taiwan, among others. Only one UK national has been reported to live there, other than Christian Candy, who bought duplex penthouse D for an estimated $270m.

One Hyde Park represents the top tier, the billionaire metropolis in miniature. Across the city, the estimated number of such masters of the universe is almost a hundred. This is a small number of singularly powerful individuals who have a high impact in social, economic and political terms. Among London's billionaires are Brits like Jim Ratcliffe, James Dyson and Philip Green. In addition, Russians such as Roman Abramovich, Oleg Deripaska and Alisher Usmanov are a significant group, as are those from the Middle East and East Asia. They are courted by politicians but often avoided by journalists, who have become fearful of litigation. Such figures are able to construct a world for themselves, a city whose social order and economic underpinnings are designed to place no obstacles in their way.

Many will point out that the alpha rich are also notable for their demonstrations of largesse. Certainly the use of personal foundations and charitable giving has become significant, but this remains paltry when compared with the scale of personal wealth. It is also the case that the British super-rich are significantly less generous than their US equivalents, though some have managed to make a mark on the apparently public world of the city's galleries and museums. For example, Lord Ashcroft reportedly has the largest collection of Victoria Cross medals in the world, estimated to be worth more than £30 million, and paid the £5m needed to build the Ashcroft wing at the Imperial War Museum, in which they could be housed. He is also Chancellor of Anglia Ruskin University. Anthony Bamford has given millions to the Conservative Party and some tens of thousands to charity.

New and international wealth seeks a place in the city by selective giving in order to build reputation and acceptability. In a recent profile of Len Blavatnik, the *Financial Times* reported that he paid £41m for his mansion in Kensington Palace Gardens in order to assist his entry into the London elite. In the process he reputedly purchased the advice of a lord and a knight. Blavatnik has given around £75m to the School of Government at the University of Oxford, £50m to Tate Modern for the Blavatnik building, and a further £5m to the Victoria and Albert Museum in 2018, which renamed its Exhibition Road entrance after him.

The Sackler family (pharma money) have financed a gallery at the Serpentine, and there is a Sackler Studio at the Globe theatre, a Sackler Hall at the British Museum and even a Sackler Bridge in Kew Gardens. Idan Ofer has given £25m to cheerleaders of the capitalist world order at the London Business School to help fund their Marylebone Town Hall campus, while Lakshmi Mittal gifted £47m to the National Gallery (which was also expanded through Sainsbury family money in 1991) and a wing at Great Ormond Street Hospital. This naming of public spaces and facilities continues the practice of the earlier super-rich who helped create the Tate Gallery, the British Museum and the Courtauld Gallery.

At this point we need to look at the goalkeeper and avoid being distracted by the fancy footwork of the new centre forwards. New money may grab the attention, but it is the deeper structures of the city and its social order that we need to focus on to see how the interests and influence of capital shape the city's daily operation – the factotums, or enablers, of capital and the super-rich. London today is, if nothing else, the physical expression of the kind of steroidal capitalism that emerged from the crisis of a decade ago. In this phase of the city's development, more elusive and complex methods of wealth creation have been supported by an increasingly affluent class of enablers (directors, financiers, hedge fund managers), politicians deeply aligned with an expansive market-orientation, and those working in the real estate sector (developers, builders, elite realtors).

We can and should look to the richest of the rich as points of influence and symbols of inequality, but the story of the city also heavily involves those agents and institutions employed and deployed by the super-rich and the managers at the helm of large corporations. Many bankers play with other people's money and are not necessarily super-rich in the terms we have been describing; there are nearly 700,000 who work in finance and banking in the alpha city. However, it is also true that those who are dependent on and work for capital more broadly have a clear interest in the perpetuation and thriving of sectors and mechanisms that are advantageous to them. The enablers are a well-networked mediating class, consciously aware of their role in facilitating capital flows and capitalists because their business depends on them. This is a group that we shall keep returning to in later chapters.

The reinforcement of money and power by place

To be sure, fortunes are made in London, and the rich come here. But more importantly the city itself – its homes, clubs, galleries, restaurants, streets and shops – allows them to gather, consolidate and reproduce their existing advantages. From the early 2000s it became clear that the city operated effectively as a tax haven, particularly through the non-dom tax rules. But this still leaves the question of why this particular city is so important to the rich. London is in many ways the vital space that binds, enables and supports the creation of a complex elite network whose pre-eminent position is defined by its wealth. Getting inside this almost intangible quality of the city requires spending time in the alphahoods and a closer experience of the kinds of settings in which feelings of weightlessness and a sense of unchecked possibilities can be stimulated.

Seen from above, the geography of the alpha city's rich comprises in essence a golden arc that envelopes Regent's and Hyde parks. These are the alphahoods, the so-called prime and super-prime areas to which real estate agents guide foreign buyers with unlimited money to spend. The alpha city has attained its position in large part because only a very few places can succeed in capturing the attention of the world's super-rich. They are attracted to the city's long cultural centrality, its political powerhouse, its commercial and corporate life, as well as the historical legacy embedded in its fine architecture. London is a city advantaged both by luck and by the strategies to capture the rich advanced by its own elites, as these entwine with and play out through the workings of the global and national capitalist economies.

Few cities can compete with the cumulative weight of the alpha city's history. Economic dominance is expressed not only in the tangible institutions and imposing verticality of the financial heart of the City, but also through the links between it and a massive offshore world of money. London's economic centrality helps to generate a vibrant culture and this cosmopolitanism also draws the rich to it. But the city is also part of a wider metropolitan group of cities linked to London by transport networks, by flows of capital and goods. This network is comprised of New York, Hong Kong, Singapore and Tokyo, supplemented by the massive dominance of the wealthy in other urban centres like Geneva, New York, Paris, Dubai and Moscow, where many of London's rich also have homes.

The alpha city is like a vast exoskeleton, whose uplifting and enclosing qualities support and enlarge the lives of its wealthiest residents. Its class of enablers and its homes, clubs and institutions are the very bones that hold up the body of the rich. The society of rich individuals with their subtle and shifting alliances is integrated into and formed by an urban world suffuse with hotels, villas, palaces, clubs, airports and the more general sense of an atmosphere of privilege and service that brings and binds the world's rich together. We cannot talk about the rich without placing them. Yet while there were close on a hundred clubs at the close of the nineteenth century, today there are only around fifty, highlighting the changing locations and circuits of power and influence. The idea of a single round of connection making and displays of privilege within an identifiable Society or season has given way to a multitude of private networks built around national background, sources of wealth, or residence in particular alphahoods.

Today's super-rich are in many ways drawn to the same districts of the city that their counterparts of the past were – but with the addition of new gated communities, super-gentrified villages, and electronic fortress homes in semi-rural areas in the city's hinterlands. In many cases the very same buildings and palaces created by earlier waves of the wealthy are the homes of today's new rich. This is particularly the case in Mayfair, Knightsbridge, Belgravia and around Regent's Park. Taken as a whole, space and Society collide and entwine in the city to form a non-random geography, one structured around locations that allow access to key infrastructure, social connections, facilities and sights. The city is the firmament within which the slowly shifting constellation of its rich is able to hang. In this sense London enables a kind of collective consciousness among the privileged, who cluster there even if they are not part of an active or close community as such.

Many of the city's more overt physical changes – a rising skyline, symbolic buildings and the visible excesses of fashion and cars at street level – highlight the interweaving of capital, the rich and the city itself. Designers, starchitects, enablers and often members of the super-rich themselves have created new residences that bring these elements emphatically together. One Hyde Park was built through a combination of rich architects used by rich developers deployed by national wealth funds to create residences to be sold to an international super-elite. At Chelsea Barracks (strapline 'A heritage, a destiny, a legacy') a billion pound sale of land to the Qatari wealth fund has led to a development in which the smallest two-bedroom apartment costs no less than £5.2m, while its smart townhouses sell for £37m, each with a private swimming pool. Other notable developments – like One Kensington Gardens, No. 1 Palace Street, Canary Wharf's Pinnacle, and perhaps most emphatically, the Admiralty Arch's conversion to a single residence of twelve bedrooms costing around £150m – highlight configurations of local and international wealth. Such spaces also speak of a wider usurpation of the city's social domain and its public functions by an increasingly private and privatised streetscape that screams money.

Many of the rich have sought to adopt, extend and redevelop the city's homes, districts, clubs and political life. They, or their enablers, have destroyed what they deem passé or redundant in a new wave of creativity involving the demolition of homes and clearance of sites for the construction of massive new residences, skyscrapers or apartments.

The fact that there is nothing new about this confluence of wealth and place does not mean there hasn't been a step change in the relationship of wealth to the city, its economy, its polity and to other sections of the rich and powerful. If one sits atop Highgate Hill to the north, or at the Greenwich observatory in the south, and looks at the city's skyline, a good impression can be gained of the city's economic and political cores, marked by the Houses of Parliament to one side and the towers of the City and Canary Wharf – enormous gatherings orchestrated both by market actors and successive city governments. The towers in these locations now dwarf the monuments and church spires of the older city.

The contribution of London's historic elite to the skyline and to a series of grand projects – such as Kensington's Albertopolis (the line traced between the Natural History and Science Museums, the Victoria and Albert Museum and the Albert Memorial) or George IV's winding Regent Street and Park – have been submerged by a shinier high-rise city built steadily by private capital in hand with city government. These transitions symbolise a larger shift from the active service of past elites to the city and its use as a space of accumulation and self-aggrandisement, a site to be plundered or traded through sharp planning practices, tax avoidance schemes, and the making of as much money as one can whether this be within or outside the rules.

In the streets of Mayfair or Hampstead we begin to see something of the animating effects of money, the things that it brings to life, builds and destroys in the city. Even the older landed estates are caught up in frenzied purchasing activity, with the creation and sale of new iconic and centrepiece developments and the slow reworking of the city's geographies of power. But, as we will see, the comfortable micro worlds of the alphahoods and their mansions also help to enshroud the city's wider social life and its rising poverty.

Accommodating Wealth

London's alphahoods tell us a great deal about the desires and preferences of the rich. They also offer an insight into how the machine of capital is harnessed to the city's property market. While London's fortunes are closely tied to its finance economy, its distinctive market in real estate enables the rich and their wealth to be accommodated. To understand this machine of wealth creation, investment and storage we need a sense of where the money goes and why it goes there. The new rich have often purposely moved into areas already long established by the city's elite. But their impact can be felt across the whole metropolis.

In 2017 London saw the largest number of homes sold for more than £5m (1,400 of them). A decade earlier in 2007, just before the financial crisis kicked in, the most expensive home sold in London was £19m. In 2016 three homes were sold in the city for more than £90m each. In 2018 the record was broken again as Nick Candy sold a flat to himself for £160m in the development he built, One Hyde Park, via an offshore company. In 2019 Ken Griffin bought a pair of London homes for £95m (one a home in St James's bought for £65m and then renovated). To cap all of this off, 2020 began with the sale of the single most expensive home ever sold – £200m for a home in Knightsbridge, with 45 rooms, by a Chinese tycoon. Such transactions can be seen either as a sign of confidence or as a kind of madness in the city's prime property market, known in economics as the theory of the greater fool – recklessly throwing money at trophy homes in the hope that a bigger fool will come along one day to buy it at an even higher price. In most cases purchases are made because these homes are like trophies that signal either winning the game or social standing.

Alpha homes sales index a deeper, seismic shift in the mass of wealth commanded by those at the top of the global hierarchy. Here financial capital has been translated into something tangible, something that can be witnessed in the daily life and look of the city as the global wealth elite have re-made many of the quarters and districts that had long housed its traditional elites, including Belgravia, Mayfair and Knightsbridge. For some time such neighbourhoods had become mixed areas devoted to luxury shopping, offices and embassies occupying substantial homes that even the rich were unable or unwilling to service. Now these areas have seen a resurgence of residential fortunes remarkable in their scale; in cases like Grosvenor Crescent, almost entire streets have been bought and redeveloped for international buyers. Such changes also began to indicate how staggeringly wealthy private individuals were able to out-bid competitors, and perhaps more importantly, the city's existing rich residents.

Between 2016 and 2018 alone a thousand homes were sold for somewhere between £5m and £15m. Over the past decade the sale of homes worth more than £1m can be counted at around 75,000 transactions – coincidentally this rather neatly equals 1 per cent of the total number of sales over this period in London. It is estimated that the UK treasury raised around £24bn over the decade on these sales. It seems naïve to think that political and economic interests are not vested in a property system that yields so much to both private agents and public coffers. The increasing internationalisation of London's wealthy buyers has created the impression of an almost limitless cloud of cash descending on the city. Because of this it has the feel of a fantasy property market, disconnected from the reality of life for the city's mere mortals and indeed beyond the budget of even many of the city's existing wealthy.

The extremity of alpha market prices and the opulence of many of the new developments geared to the rich have a somewhat ominous feel, perhaps because it may presage an approaching real estate crash, the proverbial canary in the mine, though such fears appear to have been allayed with the resurgence of Conservative national government. But another and more relevant concern is the danger of this transformation having a potentially destabilising effect, by inflating house prices as they cascade down into the wider property market. A more serious problem still, however, is the almost system-wide reallocation of housing development activity as it seeks out wealthy international buyers, rather than those on moderate incomes or those in need. When looked at soberly we can see the market in homes for the rich as a sign of urban malaise rather than a mark of global city pre-eminence.

The sale of homes generates a significant cast list of beneficiaries that includes governments (through taxes on house sales), private developers (through profits on sales) and estate agents (by mediating those sales). All of these groups benefit from the expansive circuits of consumption at the top of the city's property market. The trade in homes also brings new residents to the city – the more expensive the property, the more international the market. Sales also generate spin-off economic effects through flows of monies to developers, real estate agents, interior decorators and builders. In this sense it is not surprising that estate agents, developers and financiers are among the most vocal exponents of the city as a place that can and should attract footloose international capital.

Superhomes in alphahoods

For the international rich, one of the great attractions of London is its offering of classical Georgian and Edwardian terraces, squares and palatial homes. The dramatic growth in the number of the wealthy means that the traditional territories of the rich have expanded to include the city's inner and outer suburbs, a landscape increasingly filled with electronically secured cottages, mega mansions and multiplying enclaves with gates.

Many of the most important locations are familiar to the wealthy around the world. Chester Square (where nothing costs less than £10m), Eaton Square, Cheyne Walk, Grosvenor Square, Park Lane, Berkeley Square, The Bishops Avenue and Kensington Palace Gardens are key points on the prime London property map, but essentially they need to be understood as global addresses. These are the standout peaks in the mental maps of the global wealth elite as they compete to occupy the most advantageous locations. But these micro-worlds of the rich are not a single or uniform type of place. In reality they are formed of archipelagos of protected neighbourhood spaces and luxurious homes and are identifiable for the subtle differences

Patrician Heartlands

displayed by the different tribes of the super-rich. The preferences of these groups are defined by a number of key factors, including nationality, family structure, age and the particular path they have trodden to wealth.

The extent of wealth, the type of household, the presence or absence of children, and connections to existing social elites all play a role in steering the rich to particular quarters of the city. These factors in particular shape diverse rather than uniform tastes, including varying preferences in architecture, house type and urban or more rural locations. While rich Russians gravitate to the centre, they also have historical links to the inner north at Highgate and Hampstead where the Russian embassy used to be located. Arabs have enjoyed Chelsea and Mayfair for more than forty years, ever since their oil wealth generated incredible riches that opened the doors of central London casinos and clubs to them. Wealthy Americans tend to go for the inner West of the city or, if driven by schooling needs, to the outer suburbs and beyond. Wealthy Hong Kongers, Chinese and Singaporeans, as well as some from the Middle East, enjoy the lateral living and security of apartments found in the West End and waterfront areas. These are generalisations, of course, but they show the need for us to see the rich as a diverse group whose tastes and interests take them to particular alphahoods in the city.

Many of London's alphahoods and the stunning homes within them are desired for the status they appear to bestow on the buyer. Often their rarity makes pricing difficult, which can lead to substantial variations in final sale prices as multiple buyers vie to make the purchase. However, the search for one of the best homes in one of the top areas remains connected to everyday concerns that include the need for good schools, shops and services. For obvious reasons access to work is lower down the list, since many of the wealthiest do not work, rather their capital works for them. The underlying requisite is that locational advantages should be of the most luxurious quality.

These various factors mean that the preferences of wealthy corporate captains looking for a place to live will be quite different from those of oligarchs looking for a home in the city, or of super-rich royals from the Middle East looking for a bolt-hole to visit for just a few weeks a year. Such diverse motivations have helped create a variegated residential landscape, from the lively, cultured spaces of the well-heeled in South Kensington or Chelsea, to the apparently lifeless new apartment blocks and windswept plazas of much of the city's waterfront, notably at Vauxhall Nine Elms, which seems to offer simply a secure base from which to sally forth into the wider city. To understand this landscape we need a field manual that offers a guide to the varying tastes, nationalities and backgrounds that combine in particular areas of the city.

The alphahoods form a distinctive social mosaic in the city, each with distinguishing features based on the groups that occupy them. The first, and perhaps most pre-eminent cluster is what we might describe as the patrician heartland. This is the clearly demarcated space of the city's traditional West End, and what most will imagine when they think of London's rich. This area is the home of established wealth and the distinguished, but it is also a place of contest and change as newer and much richer groups have sought entry, with longer-term locals feeling as though they have been elbowed out by the new money. Its heartlands are the unambiguously magnificent districts that London's rich have long occupied, alongside ambassadors, embassies, charming restaurants, mews houses and unique expensive shops.

The West End is the long-standing territory of the UK's aristocracy, its landowners and its well-to-do, alongside, since around the 1970s, new groups from the Middle East, Europe and then central Asia, who began to challenge establishment dominance of these districts. The area's stucco terraces form the shell-like edges behind which one can find more intimate mews properties and comfortable back streets. These smaller terraces originally housed servants and horses but now accommodate some incredibly affluent households, if not perhaps the super-rich. Longer-standing wealth in the heartlands is also interspersed with a more complex geography of residents who bought homes when the area was relatively cheap, in the 1970s, and the legacy of this is that these areas are not simply the exclusive terrains of the super-rich. Many residents value this diversity, even if perhaps its range is sometimes overstated.

In the patrician heartland, the ambience is characterised by a sense of residential calm behind the key super-cosmopolitan and often very touristy streets of the Brompton Road or Sloane Street, or the more sedate areas like Mount Street and Berkeley and Grosvenor Squares in Mayfair, where bespoke tailoring, subtle perfumes and confident demeanours can be found in abundance. This is a London of the rich that many will recognise – often via visits to Harrods food hall or Fortnum & Mason. Here it is easy to find crowds that include selfie-taking tourists, the occasional fur coat, dark glasses, micro-dogs and bespoke fashion. Nearby one may see the chauffeured deliveries of the immaculately dressed to department stores, restaurants and hotels. Strike back just a street or two, however, and one will find an enveloping silence in many of the avenues, terraces and stunning squares.

Wandering these zones, one might find it hard to believe such streets are in the absolute heart of a capital city. The main sign of life is a persistent flow of service staff – delivery vans for food and all manner of household goods, window cleaners, cleaners, private security staff, butlers, servants, nannies strolling prams, locksmiths, interior decorators appraising new commissions, personal trainers running with clients, those who manicure hair, nails or lawns, dog walkers – all making up the vast supporting cast of extras needed by the wealthy to make life a little more comfortable.

As the ranks of the global and national wealthy have expanded, the movement of the new rich into this area has also had the effect of deepening its privatisation – Knightsbridge may throng with the world's rich but it struggles to fill the 'local' pubs that punctuate the backstreets to the rear of Harrods. Residents of Mayfair complain of empty homes next door and of having to look elsewhere in the city for more life. All of this gives the sense that neighbourliness is something that takes place among the more established but dwindling residents of this alphahood.

These areas accommodate new corporate chieftains, some in very expensive short-term lets, financiers, the self-made wealthy, the relatively few aristocrats who these days actually rank as super-rich, and the wealthier echelons of enablers including bankers, accountants and some politicians. The feeling generated here is of power embodied in stone and stucco. Eaton Square is perhaps the exemplar of this style and ambience, a place of symmetry and confidence and a sign of good breeding. This is what many of the world's rich have in their mind's eye when considering the purchase of a London property.

The patrician heartlands are interwoven with another alphahood, what we might call the ultraland. This is less a neighbourhood and more a series of islands formed of new mega-mansion blocks, the twenty-first-century equivalent of the older palaces built across much of London's West End. Despite them mostly being apartment blocks the prices are eye-watering. These properties are rather like stacks of palaces, nested within state-of-the-art medium-rise buildings that speak of money and the need for privacy and security. These newer buildings create imposing, luxurious splinters that stick out within the patrician heartlands. In many ways they are the particularly visible manifestation of the new super-rich within the traditional areas of London's rich. These new developments have been built on public land, or replace older large buildings that have been remodelled or rebuilt. Many have been built by maverick developers, often backed by international wealth. The brash internal excess is belied by often austere and sometimes almost bunker-like architecture.

One Hyde Park is a particularly good example of how this kind of development has been used to further the advance of the new wealth elites into the territories of London's traditionally wealthy areas. The story, as we saw in the last chapter, begins with the Candy brothers. Like a duo from a book of capitalist fairy-tales, the rapid ascendency of their star began with their meeting with Qatari Diar, the sovereign wealth fund assembled as a means of investing in global land and property assets to secure the future of a state built on fossil fuel supplies. The Qatari funders helped with the purchase of a site close to Harrods and Hyde Park that had been empty for several years. One Hyde Park is the house that gas built, which may sound unfortunate, unless you are sitting on the £1bn that the project reputedly made its developers. The cheapest one-bed apartment here would cost you around £4m; a night in one of the nearby hotels, around £600. Each residence (never call them flats) is shielded by bomb-proof windows, and street-level glass walls, the building's doors are guarded by staff trained by special services personnel. 'One' is also connected by tunnels and supply corridors to the adjacent five-star Mandarin Oriental hotel, so that bespoke services can be offered to its part-time residents.

The overall aesthetic effect of One Hyde Park has been described as 'junior Arab dictator'. Like many of these ultra-prime developments it comes with an array of services designed to compete with the public services and amenities outside – underground parking, a cinema, a spa, wine rooms, a conference/ function room, a golf simulator and the perhaps rather unlikely presence of a library. Some residences come with panic rooms. Throw in deliveries from Fortnum's and Harrods and one need never leave this gilded compound, staring instead from the elevated balconies overlooking Hyde Park itself. Taking out a mortgage to buy one of the most expensive apartments here for its reputed £110m price tag would mean monthly repayments of £469,000 (on a twenty-five-year mortgage at 3 per cent interest, assuming you have the £11m deposit). Simply living here for one month would cost you around £14,000 in service charges, which is just a little bit less than the national annual salary of someone earning the minimum wage (£15k). Such figures of course belie the fact that buyers come with cash in hand.

After the ultraland, the third alphahood is what is often referred to as prime London. This includes areas like Wimbledon, Hampstead and Highgate, the city's inner suburbs that originally formed its outer fringes as it expanded in the nineteenth century. While many of these areas have populations of established wealthy residents, the changes of the past decade have wrought enormous social but also physical changes. In these areas the significant impacts of sales to the wealthy have created the feeling of a city perpetually under construction, here and indeed in the patrician heartlands. This means constant flows of construction-related traffic and workers, noise pollution, and the creation of newly enveloped and buffed-up versions of the existing eighteenth- and nineteenth-century homes and townhouses.

Portland Street in Holland Park is a good example of prime London, though it is currently a mobile building site slowly extruding perfect residences as the front line of ultra-gentrification extends ever further. The street is awash with builders, finishers, carpenters and others working around the conveyer belts that lift soil and rock from below-ground basement excavations. Further up the road is a cluster of 'I saw you coming' shops, happy to relieve wealthy incomers of their cash. Reports of irritated neighbours checking for cracks on partition walls abound here, as in other parts of the city affected by a thousand other such excavations.

Although they now sit firmly atop the prime London hierarchy, Notting Hill and Holland Park have seen changing populations and fortunes over several decades. One might watch a film like Antonioni's *Blow-up* (1966) or his later *The*

Passenger (1975) and catch glimpses of these areas as the run-down backdrops for louche characters and art-scene aesthetics. Such popular depictions presented London as an exciting city of changing tastes and communities, alongside even more rapidly changing moral frames. The city's party atmosphere of today, after the entrance of serious money, could be presented equally well using the backdrop of streets like Lansdowne Crescent, whose hulking somewhat tatty upper-middle-class residences were featured in the films.

This is the same area that Wyndham Lewis once described as Rotting Hill. Its earlier decline seems hard to imagine when walking the same streets today. Now one sees dwellings renovated to the highest specification, muscular cars and casual but expensively dressed drivers, giving off the impression, as some see it, of a place rightfully returned to the heirs of its original owners. This process of class restitution and reappropriation initially occurred through processes of gentrification in the 1980s and '90s. More recently, the people buying into the area are those at the very top who have made room for themselves in what some describe as a process of financification. Massive homes, some as tall as seven stories, have returned from being sub-divided flats to single-family residences. Instead of David Hemmings in an open-top Jag casually stuffed with art, you are more likely to see only the faint outline of the driver of a Mercedes 'G class' jeep through its tinted windows.

In this and many other parts of alphahood London entire homes have been demolished and rebuilt to accommodate the art and lifestyles of the new rich – the sense of destruction and renewal is palpable. London is honeycombed with new and deeper basements and expanded spaces – for cinemas, servants, and even for cars. Attempts have been made to reconnoitre this subterranean landscape and the results have been surprising: nearly 5,000 basements created in the seven most affluent of London's boroughs alone.[1] One does not have to walk far through London's prime districts to find evidence of

Ultraland: Clarges, Mayfair

such residential, and indeed capital, mining. The digs beneath patrician London have been met in some cases with fierce community resistance from longer-term residents. Stories of inundation, subsidence, cracks in walls, noise and small armies of workers who might be set in motion for a year or more, make new basements a very visible indicator of the thick skins of many of the wealthiest, thickened further by security details, good lawyers and planning consultants to defend their ambitious plans for expansion.

To the city's inner north, one of the most notable clusters of the prime alphahood consists of the wealthy areas that bridge the Highgate-Hampstead ridge. Here the topography of the area has combined with the scale of homes to price out those on lower incomes. From the hills one can enjoy a view of the city as panoramic as it was when the area comprised a series of villages overlooking the growing metropolis below. Walking the ridge one finds mansions, parks and leafy residential streets interwoven across an elevated landscape. These sections of prime London have long been colonised by the city's upper classes, but they were traditionally, like their inner-city counterpart Chelsea, areas that made considerable space for the life of the mind, the arts and a host of bohemian characters drawn from the moneyed classes.

The attractions of the urban villages that constitute the prime alphahood is their proximity to the city, cleaner air and numerous large properties. Yet many of these have been remodelled or destroyed and rebuilt, much to the ire of longer-term residents and the area's conservation societies, which have sometimes engaged in protracted battles to prevent what has appeared as a kind of erasure of history by money. With the increasing internationalisation of the community has come the further securitisation of homes and streets by apparently paranoid arrivistes.

The apotheosis of these transformations can be seen in the centre of Highgate village where Witanhurst house sits, the product of the fortunes made from soap by Arthur Crosfield in the early twentieth century. As mentioned earlier, this massive house lays claim to being the capital's second largest residential home after Buckingham Palace. New money does what it wants, from behind imposing gatehouses or in large homes with private security staff, often appearing both to restore and destroy a property that is perhaps hard to describe as a home. This and other of the key alpha residences have the feel of warehouses for international wealth, 'fuck you' homes that highlight the fortunes of their owners while preventing either close scrutiny or integration into local community life.

Highgate has for some time attracted wealthy celebrities, including Jude Law, Kate Moss, George Michael and Liam Gallagher. What is interesting about many of the area's more famous residents has been their general reputation for being a visible and active presence in the community. New and international wealth has an altogether more private and discreet presence in the area, with many locals bemoaning its changing character as a result. Alongside the increasing wealth, there has been the loss of public assets, as with its student hall of residence, now sold to property developers. The result is what feels like a wealthy and privileged district slowly losing its cosy ambience and becoming a more withdrawn, less trusting and less socially engaged place.

Following the descending roads back to the centre of the city and the Thames, we arrive at the city's water riverlands, the waterfront alphahood. This is formed of an essentially linear development of the city that hogs access to much of the length of the river as it winds through inner London. This is arguably the most international and newest of the alphahoods, primarily home to what might be described as the middle- and upper-tier wealthy from around the world and a focus for anonymous purchases by offshore companies. At sunset the Thames is illuminated by the reflections of a hundred thousand plate-glass windows on the facades of these massive new apartment blocks, almost the sole architectural form in this area.

Walking west from the revamped Vauxhall underground station, one can see the emerging skeleton of the Aykon building with its fifty floors and 450 apartments ranging in price from one to three million. Adverts for the development boast that it is one of the first attempts at the branding of a whole building, in this case using Versace designers for all of the block's interiors. The building also has an entire floor devoted to a children's play room. Also known as the Jenga building due to its offset storeys, the Aykon publicity stresses its unparalleled offer of space and amenities that are, in reality, being supplied by many other developments in the area. The danger here is that a new high-rise city is being built without taking into account the ingredients needed for a community or a coherent sense of place. Such criticisms will no doubt appear

Riverlands' waterfront

naïve to those who understand that the true function of these new developments is to help absorb global investment capital looking for a secure place to rest, rather than a coterie of new residents.

Walking further along the riverfront we pass St George Wharf, a mixed-use development built in 2007 with around 1,400 homes. It may seem a little cruel that this was twice winner of the *Architects' Journal* worst building in the world award. The aesthetics of this section of the city have been increasingly shaped by the requirements of the capital flowing into it; it is more a place to invest and grow cash than one in which to live. The riverlands, shaped by the interests of super-affluent international investors, are a wellspring of modular steel-infused monoliths containing stacked super-cribs. In many ways this is a landscape built by the agents of the super-rich, run for affluent investors and those planning a city future that appears like a kind of evil paradise for capital. The result is an uncanny space pregnant with a sense of social absence, an ultra flightpath estate for the alpha folk leading the vanguard of a property-led urbanism.

Beneath the residences of St George Wharf we find chain coffee shops, restaurants and a 'London' pub in a concrete shell. One unit houses an international estate agency; a glance inside reveals a large neon sign with the Gordon Gekko-like mantra 'Property makes the world go round'. It is hard to disagree. But this iron law of city life has created a windswept and uneasy landscape that seems a world away from the kind of community life and vitality displayed on the billboards of many of the sprouting developments. The Wharf is not alpha territory perhaps, more the prelude to the new and more gauche entrants a little further along. The next mile or two, to Chelsea Bridge, is the epitome of riverland style – a high-rise alphahood with windy micro-climates the only feature connecting the buildings.

At 594ft, the St George Wharf Tower is the largest tower block that many will never have heard of. Its massive height is belied by a tiny footprint that encompasses the sweep of a short driveway behind electronic gates and a hole in the ground marking the entrance to its underground parking amidst its small but manicured landscape. Foreign buyers make up two thirds of the owners here, many of them absent for long periods, and many of the units have been purchased through offshore companies. Here the oligarch Andrei Guriev reportedly installed an entire Russian Orthodox chapel in his penthouse apartment.

A little further on, the showroom for the new apartments at Embassy Gardens is a huge space filled with large models, couches and several staff. Malt whisky or bean-to-cup coffee are on offer to prospective buyers. This will be a new and diverse community according to the development's brochures, though it is hard to imagine diversity with prices starting at £700,000 for a one-bed flat. With a new Dutch embassy near to the US embassy, the sales pitch here is the promise of a truly global neighbourhood, or what is sometimes described as a new geopolitical district.

This sense of prestige and place is stressed in some of the key features of the Embassy Gardens development, such as its 'sky pool' and rooftop garden – the kind of new spaces now being created as places of escape from the city, the rumpus rooms and walking circuits of the rich. The sky pool is made from super-heavyweight transparent acrylic and forms a liquid bridge holding a rather worrisome 50 tonnes of water between the two residential blocks, around 110ft above the ground – a cyclopean wet lens from which wealthy residents can survey the city below. The result yields a vision in the mind's eye of a partying class of the international wealthy on rooftops across a string of high-rise alpha-blocks, like something from an imagined filming of a Ballard novel. Here architecture is used to emphatically express the occupation of the city by a global, free-floating capitalist class.

These key alpha developments offer a private, club-like landscape filled with bars and meeting rooms, spas, cinemas and rooftop gardens. These amenities are frequently presented as spaces of refuge from the city, sanctuaries within which residents can circulate among their own kind. At Embassy Gardens the development's prolific features appear as antidotes to the sterility of the neighbourhood around it, perhaps also a response to the uneasy atmosphere generated by the heavily guarded fortress of the US embassy itself, with its submachine-gun-toting police patrols and visible CCTV pylons.

Continuing west along the river, one finds one's way barred by the perimeter of the Battersea Power Station redevelopment. Here the scale of the power station's carapace retains the capacity to generate a real sense of awe. Its towers and numerous cranes signal a returning wave of capital, washing back over the built environment, seeking out devalued spaces to reintegrate and generate value from the hot circuit of London property development. Yet this is also a zombie in the making, as capital reanimates the dormant structure originally designed to evoke a massive cathedral. This feeling is reinforced by the impression that many of the flats that were flipped in a frenzy before even being completed are either unsold or generating losses for those who dived in early. Now the development's rebirth as a luxury housing, retail and office complex gives the feel of industry with the symbols of Silicon Valley bolted on. It seems that those buying here are mostly people who have too much cash to care about the risk of a market downturn, which perhaps says as much as anyone could about the state of the city's malfunctioning property market.

Decommissioned in the 1970s, the power station building languished until 2011 when Malaysian sovereign wealth money stepped in; this was the last major prime development site left in central London. The future will tell whether the area will become the city's new tech valley – with Apple still pegged to be an anchor office tenant in the main building – or a salutary lesson in the folly of chasing foreign investment capital with bad timing. Of the 25,000 units in the district, only 600 were designated as affordable (itself a laughable token when pegged at 80 per cent of market rates), a number described as 'loads' by the former mayor Boris Johnson.

From Nine Elms one can look back to the East and be granted the grand reveal of the numerous new towers on the river's edge, a luminous glass wall that conceals pockets of public housing, railway lines, a few remaining greasy spoon cafés and the older terraced housing behind. Rather like dead mackerels the luxury high-rise developments shine but they also stink, the odour generated by investment-focused planning agreements and a housing system out of sync with the needs of ordinary folk in the city. This is the contribution that capital makes when unleashed from any sense of public mission or meaning, when plans and places for people are negotiated away by aggressive developers who see public or affordable housing as redundant when a dollar more can be made from selling at the maximum rate. The districts here combine the look of premium homes by a volume house builder with a dash of Dubai.

The final alphahood is the more dispersed geography of homes and neighbourhoods that make up the suburban exclaves, primarily those environs to the west of the city, among which Cobham, Esher, Gerrards Cross, and beyond, Henley stand out. Many of these super-affluent towns and villages are places of long-established wealth that have come to accommodate ever richer residents. They are commutable but more or less ex-urban districts in look and feel. Here are 'excellent' fee-paying schools, and a limited offer of clothing boutiques, wine merchants and bespoke shops.

The suburban exclaves are an enclosed and super-comfortable land of private golf courses, unfeasibly large executive homes, dinner party circuits and strings of gated communities to protect the more anxious among the super-rich. Alongside them live their more relaxed counterparts from show business and media, and a handful of the aristocracy in comfortable piles. This is a fragmented and socially diverse scene of old and new money, sometimes rubbing along in a fractious way due to disputes over home extensions and unfeasibly scaled reconstructions.

Suburban anonymous

Whereas expansion in the conservation areas of central London goes by way of burrowing down, an exclave home more often expands outwards.

In Cobham's town centre a small mosaic monument marks the historical presence in the area of the Diggers. It was they who in 1649 brought their vision of equality to the nearby St George's Hill, Weybridge. This feels like a jarring juxtaposition – between the Diggers' ideals of land and prosperity for all and the fierce enclosures of domestic space and private land that now make up this and the other super-affluent towns of the region. The exclaves could be described as London's Cheshire (or perhaps Alderley Edge is Cheshire's Cobham) – a place of wealth on show, enormous cars, sun tans, footballers, lottery winners and the international wealthy drawn to a simulation of rurality and community. More often this is an anxious landscape, conspicuously secured by gates and electronic eyes.

Gates across some roads open if one waits long enough, but the symbolic intent is clear – you don't live here or belong here. As a visitor it is hard to shake the feeling that one is being perceived as a potential risk. This is arguably the most private landscape of the alphahoods, with its standing guards, private security patrol vans, threatening signage and service staff being buzzed through the gates of large detached homes. All generate the feeling of a space designed to be out of bounds to the wider population.

Taking the West (End)

The impact of the rich on London's housing extends way beyond the homes they live in or buy each year. Their injections of cash, detached from any concern with economy or frugality, drive up prices in residential markets that were once generally geared towards the merely well-off, displacing the latter's offspring over time. This has an unpleasant trickle-down economic impact which can be quantified. One way to think of it is as a kind of stealth tax that few people know about but which all Londoners pay as a result of the over-heated and over-priced housing market. This has been calculated as amounting to around £30,000 on the average London home.[2]

The logic of owning luxury goods is not only that you deserve them, but that in owning them no one else can have them. Who indeed would wish to be second best? With unlimited wealth who would want to be seen owning, driving or residing in something that other people have? This is what is known in economics as a positional good; rarity or singularity confers a kind of social standing, and access to it is dependent on one's resources and perhaps a little luck in timing.

We must remember that many neighbourhoods have more or less stable populations, and in some of the most affluent areas properties come up for sale infrequently. This makes their status as positional goods even more emphatic – the fact that it is difficult to get the right house in the right place leads directly to the over-pricing of homes when they are sold. For the wealthy in search of status-conferring property, purchasing a rare, highly desirable home is key. There is only one Eaton Square, one One Hyde Park, one Witanhurst house.

Homes on the 'best' streets command enormous premiums compared with homes of similar sizes in other areas. House prices over the past decade – at first seemingly lost in the doldrums of a post-crash world and then rising rapidly in a resurgence associated with international buyer interest – give an indication of the degree to which the rich are prepared to throw capital at property assets. This was in large part generated by the curious fact that the wealth of many of the richest was not only untouched by the global financial crisis but was very quickly augmented by it. This meant they had cash to burn on whatever assets looked ripe for the picking. One of the notable stories that followed the result of the last general election was the almost immediate sale of a home for £65m in central London.

The internationalisation of the property market has connected otherwise sectional interests, spanning the political, property and finance sectors. Its effect has been to galvanise those involved in the different areas of construction, sale and financing of development activity, and the economic and regulatory environment that surrounds these processes. Property of course also generates returns to the class of enablers. The capture of the city operates here via the discreet ways in which the political administration works hard to create an investment and construction climate that will lure the rich and capital in general. Despite increases in stamp duty on property sales in 2014, London still has one of the lowest property tax environments globally.

Housing has been one of the primary means by which capital has invaded and taken over London. Without enough political interest in who is buying these homes it has been possible for the rich to generate an unchecked demand for property. With near unlimited resources the rich can purchase more homes and space than they need, an over-consumption that is reflective of both the gigantic returns to, and the newfound riches of, the global wealthy. But, more than this, their choices represent flows of capital looking for a safe bet. It is to these alphahood areas that capital is steered by real estate agents and the property buyers employed by the rich. Good money follows good and so becomes clustered in a handful of 'lucky' cities globally.

London's property system is, in reality, a politically managed operation designed to benefit capital and those who hold it, mediated and supported by a set of ideas that gives primacy to the role of markets and private property as the fundaments of a successful and vibrant city economy. Thus the hyper-consumption circuit of expensive homes feeds a subtle capture of the city by capital. Whether such a gravy train can or should continue is another question. After much uncertainty, the political direction of travel now points toward a lax regulatory environment, low property tax and a vision of the city as a place for investment and the wealthy.

4

Crime, Capital

There is something unsettling about London's aura. Its bright lights, opulent buildings and the almost unparalleled lifestyles of its wealthy are tainted by association with the darker operations of the global economy. Look no further than the city's role in receiving many billions of pounds' worth of criminally derived capital (to say nothing of its own multiple scandals and fines for malpractice in recent years). Much of this illicit wealth is owned by the super-rich and administered for them by their agents, who play the city's finance and housing markets as though London were a giant casino for capital. Bad money comes in bags to good places, spaces where investments will ripen quickly, where few questions are asked and reputations can be built or refurbished, to turn a profit down the line.

London remains a good place to 'cleanse' the money of the rich, and indeed their reputations and consciences. Many see it as the pre-eminent destination for criminal capital. The city offers one of the most advanced ecosystems for money laundering and financial crime. Since flows of criminal capital are barely addressed by the regulatory and policing authorities, the city as a complex political, economic and social system has effectively embraced criminal wealth as a means of underwriting its apparent vitality.

Backdoors for bolting horses

The global alpha housing market has been a backdoor for criminal capital for a long time, but revelations of the malpractices of the rich have only recently become an everyday feature of the mainstream media. It is now common to hear from investigative journalists about the shadier side of London's success. The luminosity of the city's alphahoods draws in the world's wealthiest, but it does so whether their cash has been obtained by fair means or foul. In fact, it is now clear that the laundering of illicit wealth underpins much of the excess of the alpha housing market and is part of the everyday running of the city's social, political and economic system. This means that when good money gets into bed with bad it becomes compromised and, as we will see later, the city succumbs to playing a role defined for it by the wealthy, and by wealthy criminals.

Take, for example, Zamira Hajiyeva, ex-wife of the former chairman of the state bank of Azerbaijan. Her wealth came from monies her ex-husband had siphoned out of the national bank, then used to buy a home in 2009 in Knightsbridge for £11.5m, via a shell company registered in the British Virgin Islands. One of the most newsworthy aspects of the case was the revelation that, over a ten-year period, she had managed to spend £16m in Harrods, at a genuinely impressive rate of roughly £100,000 a month. In 2018 her home was worth around £15m – a good investment alongside being an effective repository for criminally sourced wealth. There are estimated to be thousands of other such cases that have occurred over the past decade, and the fact we knew nothing of these only serves to highlight the silent running of a city designed to enable the easy flow of capital, whatever its origin.

As Noel Coward once wrote of London, 'The higher the buildings, the lower the morals', and perhaps never has this been truer. London's deep involvement in money laundering has not only facilitated the safeguarding of criminal fortunes but has also helped to drive and maintain demand for many of the new alpha developments across the city, while propping up prices in its established wealthy zones. Today, in the bars of fine hotels, it is possible to overhear conversations about the city's property market being built largely on such criminal capital. It has become an open secret that London has enabled the laundering of tranches of criminal wealth, but we need to consider the wider effects of this. What does it do to a city when a core component of its political and economic life is bolstered by the international criminal economy?

Laundering and malpractice in overseeing many property transactions have made London more akin to some outland bar in a Star Wars movie than the image of probity and tradition that many still cling to or promote in order to conceal the rottenness behind the facade. To fully understand the capture of the city by money we thus need to comprehend how the finance and housing systems enable the movement and concealment of vast amounts of criminal funds.

London offers what many experts now believe to be the most advanced system for money laundering and financial crime in the world. This happens because a range of enablers help rich criminals, as well as the criminally rich. Furthermore, the everyday business models of many city banks, estate agents and lawyers are also implicated in the process of welcoming wealthy criminals and helping them to hide their assets. In the story that follows, many in the city's political and commercial sectors are tainted by the scandal of its status as a repository for dirty money.

Most of the alphahoods contain substantial numbers of homes purchased through anonymous offshore companies, which are often used to conceal illicit wealth. Walk down any residential street in Westminster, for example, and you can be confident that, on average, every tenth home you pass is owned by an offshore company. This means that the source of

Offshore Investments

the funds used to buy these homes and the people who own them are unknown. Around £122bn of property in England is owned in this way, more than the value of every home in Westminster and the City of London.[1] According to government figures, offshore companies now anonymously own about 100,000 properties in England and Wales, nearly half of which (44,000) are in London – 134 alone on Cadogan Square in Knightsbridge.[2] Behind stucco facades in the city's West End and elsewhere lies the increasingly evident guilt of many of the ultimate owners of these properties.

In April 2018 a BBC *Panorama* report revealed that around £4.2bn worth of property bought with suspicious wealth was clustered within three miles of Buckingham Palace, particularly in the London Borough of Kensington and Chelsea. This juxtaposition of respectability and rottenness appears to be a common feature of the alpha city. Anonymous owners, empty homes and massively inflated prices are clear signs that the city has been a key beneficiary of criminal capital. Despite periodic displays of public and political outrage, the London-shaped gravy train of criminal capital has moved forward unimpeded, thanks to a lack of regulation and policing. Many, sometimes unwittingly, are on board this vehicle, including lawyers, bankers, accountants and estate agents.

One key effect of the waves of criminal cash rolling into the city has been the creation of an alliance of interests among those who prefer that as little as possible is done to prevent it. Even the state itself is arguably implicated in a system in which the massive public revenues generated by stamp duty taxes on house sales create an incentive for inaction rather than better policing. In fact action to police and prosecute rich criminals has moved at a glacial pace. Only in February 2018 was the first 'unexplained wealth order' (UWO) issued, in relation to two homes worth a total of £22m – not the most expensive of alpha homes but significant nevertheless.

Around half a million Suspicious Activity Reports (SARs) are filed each year by banks, lawyers and estate agents to flag that a buyer may be arriving with illicit or suspicious cash. Estate agents, however, appear less interested in issuing SARs. Of the 634,000 SARs filed in 2017 only a tiny 766 came from estate agents. In 2018 the National Crime Agency (NCA) said it was working on another 100 UWOs following the Hajiyeva case, but this barely represents the tip of the iceberg given estimates by some commentators that around four to five million buyers, sellers and those registering interest should be investigated. Clearly the apparatus to police money laundering remains hopelessly inadequate, while the idea that all investment is good investment, regardless of its source, persists in sections of the public imagination.

The beautiful oubliette

A city is a good way to hide misdeeds. The honeycomb partitions of London's alphahoods cloak the many illicit transactions used to buy homes within them. The city is like a beautiful oubliette, one of several go-to destinations for criminal capital when its origins need to be forgotten but the comfort of its owners is also paramount. The seduction of such a place is that the consequences and costs of bad money can be disremembered in an earthly paradise for the super-affluent. But those consequences remain – the city is a deep point of intersection for cash from a global elsewhere, McMafia-style criminal networks and massive expropriations of resources from numerous broken or corrupt states.

This background becomes almost invisible once cash has been evacuated and secreted in the real estate of the alpha-hoods. From Russia to China, the Middle East and the Far East, among other places, onshore finance has helped the rich to craft an off-world that is nevertheless grounded within cities like London. The city that emerges from this combination of offshore cash and local enabling actors is a complex automaton that is barely understood. The result is a system that has undoubtedly brought cash by the wheelbarrow into the city.

In truth, vast amounts of criminal wealth have been sloshing around London for years. But for a long time relatively few people knew about it, and still fewer appeared to care because of the money tree that the city came to be. More recently, in the era of Wikileaks, parliamentary hearings on laundering, and numerous independent investigations, a bright light has been shone into the murky operations of private finance and rich criminals. For example, work by Transparency International has shown that more than 700 UK companies have been impli-cated in fifty-two global money laundering scandals involving more than £80bn. Despite the growing sense that something is rotten in the heart of the city, successive governments have tended to see little reason to get too moral, perhaps in case this steady stream of cash in an uncertain global economy be switched off. If we were being cynical we might say that things only appeared to become a problem when the issue of launder-ing dirty money through the city's real estate became aligned with wider anxieties about the negative influence of Russia in the UK, in particular after the Skripal affair in 2018 when a former spy was poisoned in Salisbury. Yet even this political anger has quickly faded and the related parliamentary report, despite clear suggestions of Russian influence in British politics, did little to generate reform or improvement.

There have been many stories about fraudulent and criminal practice within the banking system in recent years. The gross total of fines alone handed out by the regulatory bodies over the last ten years amounts to more than £100bn. Episodes of insider trading, the PPI scandal, LIBOR rigging, to say nothing of the 2008 financial crisis that wrought devastation on lives and livelihoods, have seen few imprisoned or debarred from taking part in such activity. Meanwhile agents in good suits and efficient lawyers have helped protect the aggressive offshore industry from the law or regulatory oversight. Stolen money continues to be used to procure housing with minimal scrutiny or policing.

Laundering is the attempt to hide the source or destination of illegally or dishonestly obtained money. The source may be bribes, political contributions, untaxed wealth, the theft of corporate entities through organised crime, embezzled funds or the proceeds of various other crimes. If money can be successfully placed in property or other assets like artworks, then these can be used to store that capital, and access it later through a legitimate sale. It is hard to overstate the role of London's housing as a place to put illicit capital when around £100bn is laundered each year in the UK. The global scale of the illicit economy and the use of offshore tax havens are now being more closely scrutinised. In 2014, using land registry records of London house sales, the *Financial Times* found that £122bn worth of property had owners in secrecy jurisdictions across 36,000 homes in the city.

The impression of a city full of shadowy, criminal owners has not been helped by the revelation that so-called golden visas have admitted thousands over the past decade. Hajiyeva, who we met earlier, was one of these 'Tier 1' investors, bringing £2m or more to the UK, one of 3,000 (around a half Chinese, a quarter Russian), issued with passports by the UK government between 2008 and 2015. Despite their massively damaging effects (particularly at a time of naked hostility towards legitimate migrants and refugees), such programmes persist, and the laxity of efforts at policing problematic or criminal applicants reinforces the impression that possession of cash trumps a range of concerns about money laundering.

The value of privacy continues to be wheeled out to legitimate the use of shell companies and trusts. It is widely known that significant numbers of wealthy criminals buy anonymity in order to hide what is essentially stolen money. Such invisibility permeates what we might describe as the whisper market – trading in homes that are sold to clients directly using intermediaries who work hard to keep the identities of those involved secret. Often this is because a buyer may be, for example, a celebrity. This means that such properties are not advertised, while requests are sometimes made for Google street views to be blurred or deleted.

While much of this laundered money results from criminal organisations, another major source, placed in offshore investments and city property, is the super-rich themselves – those who have benefited from mafia state bureaucracies and corruption, or those fleeing unstable or intrusive states and prevailing tax laws. Referring to reports of a sudden surge in offshoring by the resident British rich, Donald Toon, director of the National Crime Agency, identified what he called the 'corrupt elite space'. By this he was of course referring to the culture at the top and the way that elites have been able to invest in assets using illegal sources of money. But the deeper point we might take from Toon's observation is that the city is now *itself* a corrupt elite space in physical as well as social terms – its new towers, homes, palaces, offices, alleys, buildings and the elites inside them form a zone deeply influenced by the ineluctable draw of money, whatever its source. From this viewpoint, the city appears as a place to which corrupt money flows, contaminating everyday commerce and the interests of those within it. Alpha city status confers the mantle of being a great attractor not only of the world's wealthy, but also of a good portion of the world's ill-gotten wealth.

Stories have been told of suitcases of cash being used to pay for property,[3] and of a lack of interest in who the buyers are or where their money has come from. In 2016 two investigative journalists set up an alternative tour of London whose route passed a string of mega-homes owned by those they had found to be involved in cases of grand corruption and the laundering of proceeds. Such 'streets of shame' tours have brought attention to the issues but have not yet led to strenuous action to remedy the problem.

The investigation of the luxury apartment block known as 375 Kensington High Street gives some sense of the extent of these practices. The block offers secure underground parking and a 24-hour concierge behind a rather austere frontage – a discreet place to hide. The development consists of 153 apartments, of which a fifth were revealed to have been sold to someone or some entity from a secrecy jurisdiction – in half of these sales nothing could be uncovered about the owner at all.[4]

The common feature of London homes bought with laundered cash, besides their frequently unearthly value, is that they are primarily located in the city's alphahoods. Commentators regularly discuss how properties are now used as places of pure investment and capital 'storage', more like a bank deposit box than a home. But for those with criminal wealth such storage systems only work effectively when their investments can be liquidated quickly to create ready cash. This means that high-priced and high-demand houses are competed for by the criminal wealthy, jostling for assets in the most expensive and popular parts of the city. One effect of this shady form of investment is that the value of these assets becomes heavily distorted as numerous properties are bought for high prices by those looking to dump as much cash as possible. Many now see this as the major contributory factor behind the enormous spike in alpha house prices over the past decade. This unchecked demand meant that bold pricing by agents was willingly underwritten by dodgy buyers happy to pay whatever it took to secure luxury properties in order to stash as much cash as possible in one go.

Assessments critical of rich investors, criminal capital and the London housing market suggest that property prices have increased across the board as a result of the demand expressed by the wealthy. For example, Transparency International has long argued that money laundering raises house prices while making it lucrative for developers to prioritise luxury housing. They also note how these processes have created what they call 'ghost communities' hosting many unoccupied houses (more on this shortly).[5]

The inflating effect of these vast flows of international and criminal capital on residential property prices can also be seen

A Secure Investment

as a hidden tax on house buyers in the wider city. London homes are simply more expensive as a whole because of the amount of cash flowing into the system. The investments of the rich, and of rich criminals, mean that buyers in general have to pay inflated sums for their homes – a kind of reverse wealth tax in which the wealthy impose a tariff on the city's wider population in the form of higher house prices.

These problems are shared by other cities that have seen significant investment by the world's rich. London's closest rival, New York, has experienced enduring problems of appropriation of property through offshore mechanisms and tower blocks left mostly in darkness by absent residents. By 2015 New York was seeing around $8bn each year spent on residences that cost more than $5 million each, more than triple the amount a decade earlier. Of these it was estimated that just over half were sold to shell companies, again meaning that their owners were untraceable.

London attracts the wealthy to its luxurious homes, streets, parks, shops and financial centre, but its secret additional ingredient is, in reality, more mundane. The city's stability means that it is a safe bet for investment. Criminal capital flows fast to the alpha city because it is seen as the calm centre of a global storm of economic uncertainty. Private money is often not scrutinised by agents or solicitors, nor is it often examined closely by the state. London's good prospects, built on global capital flows from both honest and dubious sources, have generated what some describe as a kind of hedge city, a good bet against the uncertain future of the global economy and regional chaos around the world. Many real estate professionals have long understood that global turmoil, organised criminality and dirty money flows have benefited the city by underpinning the demand for fine homes, expensive artworks and even public school fees.

Qualities of integrity and anonymity are overlaid with a frequent arrogance and neo-colonial sense of superiority among the city's enablers. There is the sense of 'us' having a strong law and respect for privacy which undergirds the ethos of the finance and property sectors. Yet these very principles became the means by which massive laundering and other criminal operations were helped to flow undetected while making many of the agents working in these sectors wealthy in their own right. There was a significant interest to be had in being disinterested about the sources of cash. This fact was highlighted in the Channel 4 documentary *From Russia With Cash*, which followed an actor posing as Boris, a wealthy Russian whose self-proclaimed rotten wealth is met with a very discreet, no-questions-asked service from many property agents.

Using the finance system to bring wealth to the city has long been a primary goal of managers of the Bank of England and Chancellors of the Exchequer. The need to assuage City institutions lies at the centre of much macroeconomic planning and receives enormous political prioritisation. But this unswerving pursuit of global capital, and the dominance of economistic and market-oriented ideas in the political domain, means that regulation has tended to be side-lined, along with embarrassing questions. The larger the fortune the bigger the crime behind it, as Balzac almost said.[6] This aphorism retains its force as a description of the situation in London today, where the many very large fortunes give serious cause for concern.

Laundering is a problem because much of it represents an evacuation of resources, primarily from poorer countries. There are also concerns about the funding of organised crime, as well as the facilitation of destabilising criminal activities. Often viewed as a problem 'over there', in reality it involves significant numbers of wealthy UK nationals as their money has historically used offshore havens to evade and avoid tax. These were clearly not issues that David Cameron wanted to discuss at the anti-corruption summit he hosted in Singapore in 2016. Yet the continued silence on such matters only highlights how the UK, as a former empire state built on overseas

adventures, arms sales, links to corrupt jurisdictions, and protected tax havens, is a massive hypocrite when it condemns
corruption elsewhere.

In 2015 an influential report emerged from Deutsche Bank
called *Dark Matter*. It suggested that around a billion a month
was flowing into London, particularly from Russian sources.
Despite growing public anger, the evident lack of interest in
criminal cash sources shown by real estate professionals is
particularly concerning, whether they are asleep on the job or
deliberately ignoring suspicions because of the potential reward
for not doing so. For example, in 2017 it was revealed that
only one in 300 property purchases by overseas cash buyers (of
which the total number was around 26,400 per year) had triggered 'red flags' used to raise suspicions about cash sources with
the National Crime Agency. This led the Agency to describe
London as the laundering capital of the world, after it was also
revealed that Suspicious Activity Reports from lawyers had
gone down by 10 per cent in 2017–18, while overall reporting
has risen substantially over the same period (9.6 per cent, to
464,000). Meanwhile the market moved into new and riskier
waters with some alpha properties being advertised for sale in
bitcoins, presenting the greater risk of untraceable movements
of criminal capital.

The reality is that much laundering lies undetected by regulatory agencies who are the first port of call if something
suspicious is suspected, or by law enforcement which has
frequently struggled to understand the problem. Despite the
massive scale of property held in secrecy jurisdictions between
2004 and 2014, only £180m of UK property was subject to
criminal investigation on the suspicion of corrupt dealings. This
was more or less nothing when set in the context of the gross
flows of criminal capital across the city during this period.

As London has become a city in which money is increasingly
no object, so money has itself become the object of increasing
anger and scrutiny. Yet there is still much that needs to be

done about the situation facing London. The most pressing need is for transparency of company ownership and, thereby, the removal of anonymity for buyers of UK assets including homes. A register of beneficial owners of property is intended to be in place by 2021, and in 2018 the so-called golden investor visa scheme was suspended, even as applications for visas by wealthy foreign nationals rose again. London also has an estimated 1,000 properties linked to what are known as Politically Exposed Persons – referring to people entrusted with a prominent public function. Pressure groups have been vocal in identifying a number of key enablers of criminal capital flows, with the cast list very similar to those who pave the way for and support the super-rich, including lawyers, accountants and company-formation agents (also known as Trust and Company Service providers).

It was recently revealed that a ticket seller at the Shinjuku national gardens in Tokyo had not taken money from foreign tourists for years, after becoming scared because he did not speak their language and so had felt too intimidated.[7] The story of the ticket vendor bears a striking similarity to how UK regulatory agencies appear to have responded to the problem of laundering and financial crime more generally – the sense that a somewhat retiring and insufficiently adept official is not fully in charge or keeping an eye out. For example, it is now well known that the UK tax inspector (HMRC) has been shy of tackling large corporations and rich individuals. It has admitted that it does not even try to take wealthy non-taxpayers to court. Instead it has relied on an unconvincing tactic of trying to worry the rich that court action might take place. While the release of the Panama Papers in 2016 resulted in seventy-one prosecutions by the state agencies in Germany, it generated only four arrests and six interviews under caution in the UK. One rule for the rich and another for the rest, rather like the admission of the American businesswoman Leona Helmsley that it is only the 'little people who pay tax'.

Necrotecture: The dead space generated by the market's invisible hand

In 2014 a *Guardian* investigation found that of the sixty-six massive houses on The Bishops Avenue in North London (also known as Billionaires' Row) only three were used full time. Urban explorers soon supplemented this data with uploaded videos of their illicit entry into derelict or slowly fading interiors in some of the most expensive real estate in the world. It is possible to find streets in London where, alongside palatial and immaculate residences, others appear apparently empty but well maintained, and still others sit, apparently rotting. The creation of what often feels like a dead residential landscape is another important feature of the alpha city. Taking the number 210 double-decker bus along The Bishops Avenue is a good way of observing this opulent and often faux landscape, since walking along it does not grant enough height to see beyond the walls and gatehouses.

We might call this kind of domestic space necrotecture, an architectural form generated from the needs of the rich to park their cash but not their bodies, literally a kind of dead space. Certainly the rich like to collect inanimate things. They have a fondness for the best of everything, in cars, jewellery, art, and, most of all perhaps, in houses as the most visible signifiers of their status. Properties are snapped up as signs of their progress and standing but often remain wholly or partially uninhabited. None of this would matter if dead things and spaces were not so damaging to the broader social vitality of the city.

Let's return to the facades of the riverlands alphahood, where laundering, international investment and development have combined to produce a spectacular verticality and emptiness. This area highlights the profound influence of wealth on the city, but also the capacity of criminal capital in particular to conscript the development process to its needs – homes for cash, not for people. The ribbon-like thread of developments along the Thames runs from Greenwich in the South East to

Chelsea's waterfront in the West. Today the city sees an ant's nest of activity in these areas, with more than 500 high-rise developments in progress. The scale of the construction represents an incredible acceleration of activity, equivalent to more than five times what was happening on the ground a decade ago. But almost none of it has been or will be used to generate affordable housing, and none of it will be social housing.

With the invasion of vast fortunes, both licit and illicit, some segments of the luxury market are only partially connected to the usual rules of supply and demand. Demand is not based on social need but on a desire in many cases to further expand capital by buying and selling as the value of these assets escalates with no work done at all. The rise of a ghost city is not an illusion or a myth of the left, used to galvanise opposition to the colonisation of the city by the rich. The emptiness of large swathes of London is open to calibration and measurement, as part of a wider, necrotectural look and feel to the city that, ironically, arrives at the very moment of its recreation as a vital, glittering, steroidal city-state benefiting from waves of illicit wealth.

As we have seen, in the Nine Elms development at the Battersea Power Station site many apartments were bought and resold rapidly before the project was even completed. Much of the new development along the Thames offers a mirage of community life that evaporates on closer contact, as thin as the billboards on which smiling alpha-hipsters dip their perfectly sculpted bodies into private spas and pools. The reality is a windswept microclimate generated by Ballardian high-rise monoliths. These dead spaces and dwellings, their lifelessness crucial to maintaining clean conditions in readiness for future exchange rather than occupation, are a key ingredient in the laundering process.

The emptiest and reportedly most laundered sites in the alpha city include One Hyde Park, One Tower Bridge, and Circus West at Battersea Power Station. All of these developments have seen the vast majority of sales going to clients from overseas, with around half to people or companies registered in high corruption-risk jurisdictions. Many riverlands developments have been particularly prone to being sold to anonymous owners and 'vehicles' offshore. Here the St George Wharf Tower in Vauxhall stands out, literally, due to its massive scale, but also because more than a quarter of its flats are held through offshore companies.[8]

Fine examples of the alpha city's necrotecture can also be found on many of the gated streets across the city, such as Compton Avenue in North London with its barrier and attendant guards, adding to the impression that such assets are intended to be hidden from public scrutiny.

In part the empty landscape is due to the globe-trotting of the rarely-at-home wealthy, but the lights are also out because empty property is an indicator of criminal enterprise at work. Of course the absence of owners does not always mean empty full stop, since many of the wealthiest retain a skeleton crew of household staff. Yet rounds of hyper-investment by the rich have yielded a landscape of such empty shells. The force of the wave of money that has hit London over the past decade has created spaces that are empty of corporeal presence and yet at the same time stuffed full of invisible capital. Neighbours complain of being the only ones left, of the loss of core shops and services and the general eeriness of living in a place emptied of many long-term residents.

The phenomenon of the city as a kind of latter-day necropolis has been given various names – lights-out London (with echoes of the response to the Blitz in the Second World War) or ghost neighbourhoods. One way to capture its scale is to look at census data which records who was home on the night of the survey. In 2011, the most recent census period which captures all residents and homes, vacant housing comprised around 3.5 per cent for London as a whole (homes where it was recorded that no one was usually resident). In the super-prime alphahoods the figure rose to 5.4 per cent, but in the most transitory and international 'alpha' areas 11.1 per cent of dwellings were vacant. For the City of London the figure was a quarter, in Westminster 19 per cent and in Kensington and Chelsea 14 per cent.[9]

London's planning authorities have permitted the construction of a further 26,000 prime market apartments,[10] roughly the equivalent of one year's gross housing supply in the city. The general picture provided by these findings is of a market very much alive in financial terms, while producing a landscape largely devoid of human habitation. Similar problems can be seen in other cities touched by the hands of the global wealth elite. In New York, for example, around 30 per cent of apartments from 49th Street to 70th and between 5th Street and Park Avenue are vacant for ten months of the year or more.[11]

It seems that the more money you have the less you are here, and the more this money comes from criminal and illicit sources the more this is the case. Yet ascertaining how many people are not using their London homes is not easy. One way to go about it is to look for homes where abnormally low or close-to-zero levels of electricity use are recorded by utility companies. One such study estimated that around 21,000 London homes are empty long term.[12] But this only scratches the surface since, according to the government's statistics agency, one in twenty homes in central and western London lie empty – and the more expensive the property, the more likely it is to be unoccupied.[13]

Nearly all new-build property in London consists of apartments (89 per cent), and between 2014 and 2016 around one in six (13 per cent) of these was sold to overseas buyers, many using offshore vehicles.[14] This figure rises to more than a third of buyers (36 per cent) in the 'prime' market areas of central London. In this study, vacancy was measured using transactional data to identify homes for which there is little or no financial or administrative paper trail. Using this measure, empty dwellings comprised half (49.5 per cent) of all prime residences in new-builds and 19.4 per cent of dwellings in the inner London boroughs more generally. Notably these figures rise along with the value of homes – 39 per cent of properties worth £1–5m are under-used, and 64 per cent of those worth £5m+. The figure for homes owned by overseas buyers was 42.3 per cent. Work by another team of researchers showed that half of all sales in central London between 2014 and 2016 were to overseas buyers and that Londoners were effectively excluded as tenants or buyers from 6 per cent of sales.[15]

The under-occupation of homes can be used as an indicator of the role of illicit wealth, since many such owners operate via offshore companies. Yet the demand for property expressed by such buyers still incentivises development – the result is a novel yet sterile playground for capital looking to hide or to grow. Despite this, one of the more curious points made repeatedly by some commentators is that without foreign capital investment many of the luxury housing developments of the past decade would not have been built. This rather odd line of reasoning is even more flawed when we consider the major role of money laundering in boosting the demand for top-end real estate. The argument is also strange because of course these resources have been occupied, not by Class War cells and squatters, but by the expanding foam of capital generated by the global economy in recent decades. Arguing that we need foreign investment to ensure that more empty homes get built is a bit like arguing that we need a monarchy because then we get palaces. The show will go on but no one other than the wealthy is benefiting from it.

The city that allows evil

Something of the London scene today evokes the moment in *Casablanca* when the eminently corrupt chief of police is compelled to investigate what's going on in Rick's bar. As its high-rollers are hauled away, he declares, 'I am shocked, shocked that gambling is going on here.' Feigned outrage is easily found among many of those benefiting from laundering in London's property circuit, to say nothing of white-collar crime and malpractice in other areas of elite life in the city. Few now would deny that London is a centre for money laundering and reputation washing, and a key destination for a good chunk of the world's criminal capital.

But what will be done about the link between wealthy criminals and the city's real estate market? While there is clear public anger about revelations of laundering, this has produced a surprisingly lacklustre political response. If anything, the debate about Brexit and economic chaos only produced more proposals to reduce taxes and create vehicles for shielding assets, such as the idea, mooted in 2020, of the creation of ten new Freeports where art, wine and other assets can be held without paying tax. As we have seen, it is clear that subtle interests and hidden networks help to deflect interest away from uncomfortable realities that sections of the elite are involved in one form or another.

The political establishment that enables those with real money power has shown little appetite to shut down, police or target criminal capital. This may seem too cynical, conspiratorial even, for some. Yet awkward questions are being asked about why a city like London should be such a major beneficiary of illicit investments and how this makes it an enabler of criminal acts and systemic destabilisation in other parts of the globe. Indeed, some of those challenging these practices come from within the political system itself.

Take for example the deliberations of the Foreign Affairs Committee hearing on Russian money laundering in 2018, much of which is worth quoting and all of which is worth reading. Here is just a flavour of how the Committee highlighted the way that wealth and the wealthy have affected the city and its politics:

As I understand it from what everybody has said today, there is a general feeling that British Governments of different political hues have tended to be rather reluctant to deal with the issue of dirty money in London. I note the nods. You could see various reasons for that – first, that we just think it would be too financially difficult for our economy; secondly, that we have not really noticed that there is a problem, which would be carelessness, or thirdly, that there are individuals or a political culture here that simply does not really care or has been inveigled into not caring by others.[16]

Inveigled is a more powerful word than it at first appears. It expresses something of the very effective system-worm of money and its capacity to bring into conformity a wider range of actors and institutions. While these groups often publicly throw their hands up in horror at the idea that the city has been used in this way, they nevertheless understand the 'logic' of capital and illicit wealth as massive subterranean drivers of its economy. The staff roster surrounding mega-wealth is very long indeed, and those on it often identify criminal capital as something to be taken, like a rather bitter but efficacious pill, for the city's financial health – and anyway, so runs the response of many enablers, if we don't, someone else will.

One argument in response to these problems is that we should stop pretending that tax evasion and criminal capital investment in the city are a cost to it and openly acknowledge that they are, in reality, de facto strands of its economy. If the city challenges tax evaders, para-criminals and launderers this will represent a significant and potentially existential threat to many of its real estate agents, solicitors, architects and developers. Interpreted in this way, we begin to realise that what might be seen as a crime problem is actually a morally flexible and pragmatic approach to doing business in the city.

As we are increasingly aware, many financial services and investment vehicles are established with the primary goal of avoiding tax and enabling criminal money to flow because it pays to be the banker in charge of these processes. By extension the city of London is the site in which bankers, facilitators and enablers live and work en masse. The city thus appears as a hive of criminal facilitation at the heart of a network of cities, institutions, island havens and offshore zones through which wealth and criminal capital are channelled. While many pretend that they would be appalled if they knew who they were dealing with, this is really the very point – why don't we know who owns properties in Mayfair, Knightsbridge and many other places besides? How does wealth that cannot be explained, because it would reveal violence, extortion, robbery and fraudulent practice, keep popping up around us? All of this makes London look rather bad, but this conclusion rather depends perhaps on the source of your income.

Many businesses, taxes and expenditure, all part of the lifeblood of the economy, have become interwoven with and effectively addicted to illicit sources of cash, from which both public and private purses benefit. This is less an argument for leaving things as they are and much more a word of caution about the kinds of interests that would be provoked if the issue were really taken seriously. Challenging the woman who spent £16m of criminal capital in Harrods over the past decade is a good thing, unless you own Harrods, you are one of the store's suppliers, or you are the government seeing lost tax revenues from such sales, and so on. Why be the principled masochist who suggests messing this up?

There are many for whom London has become a kind of magic money tree, a peculiar organism run by and for capital. But it is more than this because it is also in part a city run by and for *criminal* capital, as seen in the £100bn per year that is laundered through the City and London property. To give some sense of the scale of this activity we might compare this figure to the amount spent each year on defence (£45bn in 2017) or education (£39.7bn in the same year). But tackling laundering will mean cutting off a large branch of the money tree that the city sits on.

What we have seen for many years is the clever political stage management of a vast underground economy and associated corporate interests that have knowingly or otherwise facilitated fraud, market manipulation, the secretion of criminal assets and a range of other concealed horrors. This is because we know that, connected to the rich and their luxury developments, banks, lawyers and estate agents, are the muffled screams, the underfunded hospitals and schools, the housing crises that are the result of the damage violence and tax evasion cause in the lives of millions, both here in the UK and elsewhere globally.

Even those who are not part of the elite speak for the morally complex economy of the city because a number of key principles have an accepted place in public life. Financial journalists trained in neoliberal economics, the brightest of professionals who have chosen to make money in banking, those who believe in unfettered markets, that wealth creation for all is what elites do – all are part of this value system that extends well beyond the rich themselves. This is, in many ways, a rather rotten history, but it is at least also a distinctive heritage, and the pay is often rather good. This group of enablers, rather than the rich themselves, tend to be the most vocal about proposals for property taxes, wealth taxes and so on, because they see a threat to their business model, whereas the rich and their cash can simply float off to the next-best tax or city environment to invest in. This moral vacuum is not only generated by the property market. Following the Skripal assassination attempt, Jeremy Corbyn stated in Parliament that more than £800,000 in donations had gone to the Conservative Party from Russian oligarchs.

The city has been captured by big chunks of capital and, rather like at the time of the 2008 financial crisis, we don't really know which bits of this capital are good and which are bad. But precisely this inability to distinguish between good and bad is the city's ticking time bomb, because without more concerted action it runs the risk of a criminally funded bubble in asset prices and a legitimacy crisis in the political domain which is increasingly tainted as a distracted, ineffectual and corrupted space. Periodic claims of racism or an attack on wealth generators are sometimes thrown out as a way of obfuscating the sources and impacts of much of this wealth.

London has been addicted to cash with criminal origins for many years. Meanwhile many of the city's wealthy and its political and financial elites have become well versed in the use of trusts, offshore vehicles and 'tax efficient' investments, as uncomfortably thrown into the light by the Panama and Paradise Papers. Much of this activity is intrinsically linked to the expansion in the ranks of the global super-rich. But the city has not inadvertently been captured by this group; in reality it has actively courted and funnelled their cash for generations. London should be seen as an efficient machine for gathering, sorting and ingesting large amounts of criminal capital alongside more respectable sources of wealth.

It is revealing to observe the kind of voices periodically compelled to reject the need for more investigative and taxation powers. The financial press in particular frequently runs stories about how wealthy clients are preparing to leave the country or are moving their assets offshore, including the claim by the FT in 2019 that a trillion pounds of assets and wealth were being prepared to go offshore in the event of a Corbyn government. But perhaps, as the comedian Mark Thomas once said of a potential exodus of the rich, we will drive them to the airports. The Brexit-fuelled return of the Conservatives to government in 2019 presaged a Freeport-style environment in which the rich would be allowed to hide and where low taxes would be assured. The immediate bounce in sales at the top end of the London market also appeared to reveal the natural connection of government to an environment of property and finance driven wealth with little interest in social or even criminal justice.

Nevertheless, the fear of a loss of this wealth or of the rich themselves is real and helps to drive inaction. But the deceit here lies in presenting this as a *future* possibility when many of the UK rich have long used their offshore funds to evade or avoid tax. What the Panama and Paradise leaks revealed, alongside the *Private Eye* database on shell company holdings of UK property, is that the rich are at it every day – augmenting and securing their fortunes using banks, offshore funds or the family offices that work for them. They have been hiding, stashing, manipulating and investing their way for decades, aided by a proficient class of facilitators that include politicians turning a blind eye, accountants devising genius schemes for wealth concealment, and solicitors ignoring the potentially dodgy sources of house-buyers' cash.

5

Cars, Jets and Luxury Yachts

Imagine you are flying into London by jet, on the city's east-west flightpath. It may seem almost possible to touch the pinnacle of the Shard as it lazily slides past the starboard cabin windows. This feeling might seem more tangible if you now imagine that the jet is your own. But let's go still further, not to one of London's busy major airports but to one of its smaller private airports. From here a helicopter can take you into the centre of the city, where a powerful chauffeured car will arrive at just the appointed time before rounding off the journey to a residence in one of the city's alphahoods. All of this offers some sense of the speed, privacy, comfort and indeed power that undergirds the movement of the city's rich to and within the city.

London's accessibility helps to underwrite its alpha status. The city offers an easy launching point or terminus of travel to or from other, highly ranked locations around the world. The alpha city could not function without a sophisticated machinery that offers the rich the opportunity of rapid, comfortable and private modes of travel. This capacity for movement is tightly integrated into the life of the city's comfortable and private districts, but the depth of the integration and orchestration can be surprising. Cars are the primary lifeblood of this circulatory system, while jets and more leisurely yacht journeys extend the reach of the wealthy to far-flung destinations. Jet travel, much of it now flexibly chartered, but a sizeable chunk using personal jets, has increased substantially over the past decade. Private helicopter flights over the city peak in June and July. From the Middle East come billionaire boy-racers who fly in and then thrash their expensive toys around the West End before Ramadan. They compete for road space with the numerous S-Class Mercedes with blacked-out windows that form the workhorse, chauffeur-driven fleet of the rich. Spend time in Mayfair or Knightsbridge and these triumphs of engineering become almost boring to observe, while other, more expensive Bentleys or perhaps Rolls Royces may glide soundlessly up to dock at a previously unnoticed and unremarkable club or office doorway.

Though the city's social 'season' has faded, many spaces and events exist to enable parading and networking through cultural and sports events, festivals and political and corporate meetings that give cause for the rich to flock to the city at various times of the year. Family members, friends and associates join the throng in the summer months or at festive times, attending key events such as art shows, fashion parades, horse and motor racing or, more often these days, football. The city now sees multiple seasons, their circuits based around key families or new and criss-crossing alliances and social connections among the rich and their clans. These draw the well connected to balls, private parties, garden events, banquets and institutional dinners. Wealth brings a kind of hyperactivity, but it also fosters a private and sheltered view of the city around it.

The alpha city is not a bounded space for the rich. Rather it offers them a multiply-layered intersection that connects a series of premium highways by way of air, land or sea. The city's alpha transport network shapes an experience of the city that feeds the solipsism of the rich. For every single alpha-rich inhabitant the feel of the city is that of a place bespoke to them, a kind of ego-propping environment tailored to their every need and desire. This feeling of a place crafted for the wealthiest also

Getting Around

operates to remove the sense of cohabitation with the city's wider population or its more unsightly spaces.

A significant side effect of pronounced wealth is a hyperactive, carbon-hungry lifestyle. This is apparent to many perhaps, but a less well-noted side effect is the creation of a particular kind of physical city fabric into which is plugged the mobility system of the wealthy. London's notable districts form an unbroken world of wonderful spaces and spectacles easily connected or ported to other parts of the city and to multiple, attractive locales around the globe. Enabled by powerful engines, sophisticated technologies and clever infrastructures, the rich move at will – enclosed, cosseted and sliding from one set of wonderful experiences and places to another. Spanning these spaces a highly evolved rapid transit system makes life for the wealthy much less jarring than for the everyday folk of the city. Movement is made possible by the numerous helping hands – drivers, pilots, captains, staff – allowing the rich to experience the city as a place of ease and luxury.

Borders become more or less inconsequential; the city of the rich is a kind of smooth, continuous space in which rapid and frequent movement generates a distinctive but partial experience of the city. Their assisted mobility yields a world stripped of many of the difficulties of urban life experienced by its much less well-off. London gathers one of the largest clusters of wealthy citizens of the world together, yet this easy cohabitation denominated by cash yields little direct knowledge of or empathy with the city's troubles. The seclusion of the rich's movements might as well be designed to assist in building this insulated worldview, and in many ways, of course, it is.

Whether seen through tinted glass, over a personal driver or pilot's shoulder, from a first-class lounge or the window of a Gulfstream jet, the city is experienced from an extracted perspective. The methods of transport used by the rich generate a sense of isolation rather than an exciting foray into the rich diversity of the city. The resulting impression of urban social life is muted and muffled, experienced via a sense of ease, the feeling that one is at home wherever one is (and of course there are many such homes), while an entourage of support staff smooth out any risks or problems.

The paradox of wide-ranging elite travel is that it often adopts almost rail-like pathways that serve to sever the world of the rich from the city socially below it. At almost all times the rich are above the ground – in penthouses, planes, apartments, cars or lifts. To the rich an urban life of diversity, messiness, unpredictability and encounters with difference is replaced by one of privacy, luxurious sterility and meetings with people similar to them. Important aspects of urban life, the sense that other, different and less well-off people share the city, fade from view. For the rich the reach of their world is taken for granted. The globe itself is an unlocked space – without either barriers or the prospect of fatigue. For the rest, these discrete pathways and luxurious destinations are off limits or simply unknown.

The West End was in many ways designed to be a destination and to minimise the need for unnecessary or troublesome mobility. Here the rich could easily access the core social settings and institutions of empire and capital – places of power and influence as well as entertainment. The function of this space was to enable the society of the elite to come together. Opulent residences, palaces, places to eat, drink, socialise and be seen at formed the basis of a social circuit that had physical proximity at the heart of its organising principle. The West End was built to operate as a more or less compact urban space in which society could function without troublesome and potentially dangerous adventures across town.

Advances in transport technology had the effect of making residence beyond the city possible without foregoing its attractions or functions. The rise of the first-class train carriage, and later the private car, allowed a colonisation of the rural areas surrounding the city, the Surrey cocktail belt, for example, and the possibility of more rapid and thus more frequent movements between multiple residences. These changes extended the geography of the city's newer alphahoods to an extended archipelago of wealthy neighbourhoods, small towns, villages and gated estates. Despite these changes, aspects of the original distribution of key alpha places remains in many ways intact. Areas like Mayfair, Knightsbridge and South Kensington still give a sense of proximity to all that matters. But instead of the circuit of the court we find purveyors of material goods and consumption at the heart of this system – Harrods and Harvey Nichols, or the social roles played by Michelin starred restaurants, private clubs and nightclubs.

The experience of luxury in the alpha city offers a sense of lightness and comfort, and a place from which forays can easily be undertaken to similarly pleasant spaces. The two fundamental organising principles of alpha carriage and trans-portation are privacy and speed. These demands generate an enclosed, point-to-point system that operates between private homes, airports, shops, and underground garages at homes and tower blocks to similarly secured locations elsewhere. Many among the wealthiest do not want to be seen walking across a pavement from their car to the front entrance of their house. This is because it may represent a security risk or, more likely, a feeling of social exposure. Such a system speaks of a strategic relationship to the city, a place that is a comfortable home but nevertheless one with potential risks and discomforts that need to be managed.

The rich split the city into safe and more or less risky places. This viewpoint drives the creation of an increasingly complex infrastructure of tunnels, gates, locks, biometric scanners, bar-riers and cabins, car lifts, secured car parks at airports, and valet parking at sports and cultural events and hotels. The potential wildness of the central city is subdued, in a sense made *sub*urban, stripped of sociality and human contact while the

No Parking

management of mobility enables wealthy bodies to pop up or to disappear apparently at will.

Travelling with bags immediately marks out the non-alpha Londoner. This is because drivers and convenient secure parking allow the rich to travel unencumbered. First-class lounges, luxury cars and boats are connected via a complex of pathways, doors, gates and connecting modes of transport. These systems offer the sense of a new streetscape built for the rich. Meanwhile, at ground level, equally subtle systems are used, such as remote-controlled gates to cut off points of circulation, or, as with the Clarges development in Mayfair, remotely controlled rising bollards that prevent non-resident traffic while maintaining the illusion of an open, democratic streetscape.

Various resting points shield the wealthy from the potential hazards or tiresome social encounters that might be experienced at street level. Here comfort and privacy can be found in abundance. Hotels, airports, clubs, ports and gated residences form points on the mental maps of those inside the alpha world, places at which kindred others and smiling staff can be found. But the sense of freedom is also a kind of illusion, a simulation of unbounded living when in fact it is restricted on all sides because, outside of this comfortable world and its networks, there exists another world that cannot or should not be visited. Rather like a path through the gardens of a gated community that suggests a world beyond while leading only to a wall behind some shrubs, or a 'ha-ha' that marks the boundary of a stately garden with a sudden drop, there is the sense of adventure but within clear limits that prevent the possibility of real risk.

The alpha city is a kind of hyper-motion machine, but this movement also allows it to operate as a social sorting machine. The city's regular residents are separated and corralled away from the privileged. Such arranging and categorising is achieved via hidden portals and filtration systems scattered across the city – club doorways, underground car parks, retinal scanners, key cards, entrances to elite apartment blocks and hotels, all of which offer discreet barrier entrances. Like an uber-capitalist retelling of the rabbit from *Alice in Wonderland*, the rich are able to exit street level through these multiple anonymous doors or gates using keys, swipe cards or biometric locks, or else are ushered in by hyper-vigilant staff who switch seamlessly between demeanours of hostility to welcoming smiles depending on who seeks entry – perceived friend or foe. Such mechanisms create effective filters allowing the rich to enjoy the untroubled private spaces of first-class lounges, leisure clubs, luxury hotels and chauffeur-driven cars.

In reality those without the money required to ride this circuit often share the same city roads, airport terminals and lanes. Yet their experience is of a more glutinous, congested space that is exhausting to traverse. In this counterpart world, straining bodies are ensnared in traffic, or wedged together in train compartments, or choking on fumes as they cross the street. Overhead and overtaking these stifled masses, the rich move in a world of free flowing and delightful transports, along exclusive pathways subtly woven into the physical fabric of the city.

From the often lofty perspective of the rich, the city enables a feeling of simultaneous possibility. To be somewhere does not preclude being somewhere else very soon after. Such a whirlwind of mobility is underwritten by the demand that nothing should delay or impede. This generates a more or less enclosed landscape that enables the carefully timed movements and transitions of the wealthy. The simple mechanism for excluding others from this comfortable world is price. In this sense the system is perfectly democratic – with enough cash anyone can access these extravagant transports...

The world of first-class travel and luxury vehicle ownership is an experience as much as it is a mode of moving. The feeling it generates is of a world unfolding around the individual as potential barriers melt in whichever direction the ego chooses to go. But this world also requires significant coordination, which is provided by the guides and personal managers who make it so for the city's wealthy. Lifestyle management bureaus and staff in family offices help to stitch together the fine and intricate fabric of hermetic pathways that ensure the rich find everything within reach, on call whenever required. This may mean securing a premium ticket to an opera the next evening in New York, the delivery of luxury goods or foods from afar, the visit of a VIP entertainer, or a visit to an offshore art show-room at a 'freeport' adjacent to an airport (such as in Geneva, Dublin or Dubai).

The mobility of the alpha city's rich is facilitated by a Möbius-like remaking of city space. The lifeworld of the city becomes a kind of a continuous strip over which rapid movement can be made, stepping from one zone to another, or from one mode of travel to another. These characteristics are important because being on the move also entails a kind of vulnerability in terms of feelings of exposure, unwanted attention or the security risks that may be experienced, although the latter may be influenced by national background. For the super-rich, visibility is often seen as a problem. This is particularly so in an increasingly syn-optic age in which the many watch the few through social media, and where cameras, drones and mobile phones enable reports on the activities of the wealthy to be relayed far and wide.

The photographer Dougie Wallace highlights this unease in his series of portraits of the wealthy as they cross the last few feet of pavement – the vulnerable, somatic world of the street – from a private car or taxi to the environs of Harrodsburg (London, not Kentucky). Many of them appear startled or on the cusp of furious indignation as they stare into the lens. In reality it is the rarity of such invasions that has led many of the world's wealthy to love the city despite the worrisome possibil-ity of robberies and burglaries. The sub-tribes of London's rich have differing views on what is and is not safe, often based on their national background and of course on the particular tier of wealth they occupy. The discovery that they can feel safe in central London teaches many of the rich that it is possible to live in the city, even at street level, in ways that might not be entertained in their home country. For UHNWIs and billionaires such possibilities remain open but almost unthinkable.

This complex network of movement is a discreet co-presence in the everyday life of London – running alongside it while not being mixed with its more mundane rhythms and networks. With only a little training we can begin to recognise the signs of this world, its secret doorways and conduits, and the wealthy themselves as they traverse the city.

Own the sky

To paraphrase F. Scott Fitzgerald, the rich aren't like you and me. As well as simply having much more money, they use entirely different airports. The city's primary gateways for the rich are not really its five major airports – Heathrow, Gatwick, Stansted, Luton and London City. While Heathrow, the alpha city's largest airport, has the world's greatest volume of air traffic (a flight every 150 seconds), less than one flight a day is by private jet (only 400 of such flights a day are from the major airports). Of the almost 50,000 flights made by private jets and planes each year in London, nearly all occur at the private airports – Biggin Hill, Farnborough and Southend.[1] Of these, Farnborough, to the city's south-west, takes the bulk (32,522 private flights), and Biggin Hill, in the south-east, comes second (with 13,209). To the outer east, 'London Southend' stretches the idea of the city-region but is also popular with private jets, with around 4,000 flights a year.

We might say that time is money, but equally money buys the rich time. Each day thousands of them bypass the ennui and struggle that tends to mark the use of the city's major airports. Many rich people, business owners and corporate deal makers use the city's private airports to access European destinations for important meetings, for leisure pursuits or to visit contacts. Private airport facilities offer a standby time for their wealthiest clients of around ten minutes. This means that they operate more as gateways than waiting rooms – only here is it possible to be chauffeur driven to a waiting aircraft, with security checks made on the aircraft to accelerate the process still further. One curious effect of this rapid flow is that there is no need for a first-class lounge. Even waiting becomes the mark of those not truly wealthy or not sufficiently focused on where they are going.

The airports of the rich are designed with the understanding that the public presence or visibility of their clients is not desirable. One of the ambitions that underwrites first-class and private jet travel is not to have the flow of such experiences interrupted by the sight or intrusion of everyday folk. Such principles are written into the strapline for Heathrow's first-class lounge, which describes itself as a sanctuary away from the world. Here and at the other major airports the first-class lounges are bunker-like spaces separated via their own entrances, with their own car parks and taxi/chauffeur drop-off and pick-up points. Most travellers will not spot the entrances to these hidden zones, while those using first class will move invisibly from the lounge to a waiting jet using separate elevated gangways.

As a point of flow for wealthy business folk and jet owners, Farnborough, bridging the city and the gated communities and mansions of Surrey, is a key node. Its tagline – 'for business, for privacy, for London' – might have been written by the city's alpha elite. Notably, it has its own onsite customs facility and immigration clearance. This cash-enabled hopping of the barriers mere mortals have to negotiate has generated anxieties about the adequacy of security checks on flights from countries like Russia and various parts of the Middle East. Along with rapidity, control and discretion, private jets also offer the prospect of fewer questions and minimal scrutiny from officials. At Farnborough around one in ten jets were reportedly not checked at all in 2015.

The movement of wealthy bodies requires a perpetual motion system whose fuel is money, and an awful lot of it. The difference between even a standard return flight, from, say, London to New York, and first class is a ratio of seven. Or we might choose to go by charter jet, tomorrow, on our own. To Paris, one of the most popular destinations from the private airports, this would cost £8,000. While for the rich a flight can now be booked through an app like Lunajets or NetJets, for the super-rich the jet itself will be owned by them. Owning a jet puts you in a particular and coveted league. Buying one requires huge upfront costs (around £40m for a Gulfstream G650), but it also needs a pilot and staff, registration and hangar costs (£200,000 a year at Farnborough), as well as general servicing and maintenance, all of which means that a medium-sized personal jet costs over a million a year to keep.

The desire to travel at a certain speed is about time, but it is also a function of peer-driven anxieties about what being at the top means. Here the destructive logic of competition and narcissism feeds a culture of ostentatious display and, of course, an environmentally destructive reliance on massively carbon-emitting playthings like supercars and jets. Perhaps the ultimate sign of wealth in terms of mobility is the personal ownership of what would otherwise be mass consumer transport. Roman Abramovich has his own Boeing 737, a commercial-class jet capable of carrying about 140 people; his yacht, *Eclipse*, so named no doubt because it puts all others in the shade, approaches the size of a European ferry at 533ft in length.

Helicopters are another important feature of the alpha travel circuit, often used as the first or last step in movements across the city. Many private helicopter flights connect the private airports to final destinations in the city, or vice versa, or from those airports to residences and pads further afield – to the more distant alphahoods in rural and small-town England, to Sandbanks in Hampshire or to Alderley Edge near Manchester. In the time it takes to read the editorial in your copy of *Forbes* you can reach the centre of the city from Biggin Hill (six minutes); for those starting at Farnborough, a twelve-minute meditation is all that is needed to zone out for the journey.

While London isn't Rio or Mexico City in terms of helicopter traffic, according to the Civil Aviation Authority around 22,000 helicopter flights are made each year in London airspace. A little over two and a half thousand (2,643) of these are private flights. Given their cost, they tend only to be made by those with significant wealth. The key heliport in the city is Metro London, which describes itself as a 'vertical gateway' for VIPs, celebrities and business people. The pad, located next to the Thames for more than fifty years, sits in the city's inner West, which, while not the absolute heart of London (reflective of the fact that the central city airspace is tightly controlled), is as good as it gets in terms of leaving only a short private car journey to home, work or party. Its location does, however, put it very close to the riverlands alphahood at Nine Elms, where, no doubt, top execs at the new Apple HQ, as well as visitors to the US embassy, will find it useful.

Hot wheels

The opening shot of the 1957 documentary *Summer in Mayfair* looks down onto Hyde Park Corner, seen from the penthouse of the Dorchester Hotel. To the strains of an accordion ditty, the unfeasibly named McDonald Hobley plummily introduces us to the apparently common or garden central district of Mayfair. A handful of red buses and cars lazily drift along Park Lane, where today one finds a smothering blanket of fumes generated by a wall of traffic. But, of course, Mayfair isn't at all an ordinary place; it has always been the home of London's elite. Its enduring apex position can be attributed naturally to its location in the absolute centre of London, bordered by Piccadilly–St James's, Knightsbridge and Fitzrovia. But the opening point of this documentary of sixty years ago remains relevant – suggesting that even in a busy metropolis it remains possible to find a place that is warm, pleasant and friendly, to adopt Hobley's own assessment.

The key to understanding Mayfair's position and that of many of its neighbouring alphahoods is their ability to absorb and disburse affluent visitors and residents, among the best hotels (there are 3,800 five-star hotel rooms in Mayfair alone), in its fine vertical townhouses, and across its unparalleled offering of the arts, clubs, restaurants and shopping destinations. Here one can arrive via a chauffeured vehicle to parade the likes of Mount Street, dining al fresco behind glass barriers to create the illusion of experiencing the city at street level while protected at every step by the oversight of athletic doormen, serving staff and, afterwards, a waiting vehicle door.

Standing in Berkeley Square you are more likely to hear the roar of a supercharged car exhaust than a nightingale sing. This is the historical heart of many of the several premium car marque showrooms. One, the Jack Barclay dealership, seems to be a high-street retailer immune to anxieties about economic downturns or internet sales. Here we might stop a while to window-shop for Bentleys costing a quarter of a million pounds, so immaculate one might not dare dream of risking the melee of heavy traffic swirling around the large square outside. Here a number of smart and confident support staff curate a selection of the best motors for the super-wealthy person about town. Occasional exits are cleverly made through a turntable in the side of the showroom by test drivers and delirious new owners untroubled by the prospect of 16 miles per gallon, 'urban', on their Bentley sport convertible.

Summer in Mayfair reveals that even seventy years ago Mayfair's car showrooms were often decorated with the trophies of their competing cars in events on the new and private race circuits around London. These would have included the nascent circuit at Silverstone, which had been created as the first British Grand Prix circuit in the 1940s before going the way of most sports to become part of the highly financialised form of play and spectatorship by the wealthiest that it is today. Today the romance of motor sport is eroded, yet it is still the sense of history, prestige and mystique of marques like Aston Martin, Bentley (now owned by Volkswagen), Rolls Royce (by BMW) and Jaguar-Range Rover (Tata Motors India) that keeps these players in the game despite being traded as assets to boost the cache of the major brands.

Despite the apparently high cost of many luxury cars these toys represent only tiny investments for the super-rich. More importantly they are key components of the alpha life-support system, a vital means of secluded and safe transport around districts such as Mayfair and beyond. Air-con, in-drive entertainment systems and interior sliding blinds only serve to heighten the sense of privacy and comfort, but also the sense of distance from the city itself.

In neighbouring Knightsbridge, on the long drag of the Brompton Road, restaurants and cafés with outdoor seating offer platforms from which obligatory viewing is provided of the billionaire boy racers from the Middle East in their supercharged and money-pimped rides. Here cars are often found illegally parked, hazard lights blinking, or idling as drivers wait for their masters on double yellow lines, the price of a parking ticket an acceptable fee for the convenience.

More discerning buyers might instead choose a Maybach or a bespoke remodelling of a Range Rover by Overfinch, discreetly souped-up with even more powerful engines and luxury details. The interiors of such vehicles are more like a small, well-appointed hotel suite than a very weighty object that can nevertheless move its occupants from zero to sixty in four seconds. Just a set of wheels for one of these models would cost you more than £10k; the vehicles themselves between £70k and £250k. Overfinch also offer another tagline that might be adopted by the alpha wealth elite – 'capability, individuality and luxury'. The company produced the first armoured cars for UK government diplomats and heads of state in 1988. This may help to explain the increasingly aggressive aesthetics of some of these vehicles. New designs offer the more militarised, 'fuck-off' look that some sections of the wealthy seem to crave. But if the plan is travel to a game of polo in quiet luxury, or a place for the family to kick back with a tartan picnic blanket, then a more restrained version can be tailored for the client.

Despite the ranks of enthusiasts for sporty, dashing and highly obvious vehicles, others, often the wealthiest, seek to draw no attention at all. Stellar wealth is frequently a more restrained and hushed matter, particularly when about town. While a mirror-metal purple Veyron may appeal to a boy racer from Qatar, a seriously wealthy oligarch or UHNWI corporate chief is more likely to travel in a much more nondescript black Mercedes S-Class. It is all about horses for courses, and the central London circuit often suggests the need for a more cloaked presence given concerns about security and unnecessary visibility.

This doesn't, however, dampen enthusiasm for Kahn bespoke remodellings of Audis or Ferraris, or adaptations of the Defender or Wrangler by the Chelsea Tractor Company, vehicles that might look more at home in Juárez or Rio than a plush Knightsbridge street. Of course, even a price tag of a quarter of a million isn't enough to stop the hoi polloi, City boys or the merely wealthy from getting the keys to toys that flaunt excess. More recently, luxury watchmakers have jumped on the bandwagon to produce watches sporting car marques, such as the Richard Mille McLaren, Porsche's own range or Bremont's Jaguar model, allowing the wealthy to indicate what they own even while in a bar or dining out.

Having your own driver remains the mark of the super-rich. Personal chauffeurs are usually part of a wider staff presence, with the wealthiest households employing as many as fifty support staff. Of course, drivers can also be hired, as can a decent car for the weekend or a special appointment. This luxury-for-hire market is the preserve of the moderately wealthy as well as a new cohort of rich wannabes and hangers-on – individuals seeking access with temporary adornments of the necessary trappings. Gauging wealth by means of transport is also muddied by the rise of rental and pay-to-use models of access to luxury transport. Owning a jet or supercar is one thing, but a similar effect can be achieved by, say, renting an Aston Martin for the weekend for around £8,000. Similarly, premium Ubers can land you a fairly swish ride at a knock-down price, while black cabs remain the popular mainstay of bankers and hedgies about town.

At the middle tier of wealth, secure underground garaging of personal cars can be used to ensure a more discreet and off-street presence. In a number of secretive inner-city locations one can park in a climate-controlled car pillow for roughly the price of renting a flat in the East End. The benefit is security but also being able to unburden oneself of a vehicle in the busy city centre. The same principles also apply in many of the newer alphahood developments in which a driver and luxury vehicle are wrapped up in the service charge – a kind of communal taxi service. At 1 Grosvenor Square, £8m secures residents a two-bed apartment with a Bentley and driver at their disposal – one of several examples in the ultraland developments.

Getting around with a driver means drop-offs for shopping or beauty treatments, perhaps, and mobile-phone-coordinated pick-ups by chauffeurs in cars with blacked-out rear windows. It is a common sight in central London to see a waiting black Mercedes, hazard lights flashing to circumvent traffic regulations. Whereas a parking violation will attract a fine, a waiting driver can simply be moved on, often to land again at the same place a few minutes later.

Ensuring freedom of movement for the rich also requires the creation of a distinctive immobile environment. Many of the new luxury mansion blocks and towers are built with the kind of infrastructure that allows for an effortless escape from busy streets, enabling the wealthy to be enveloped by the safety of plush private interiors. Many alphahood developments, both new and old, will of course offer a concierge service or automated entry systems. At these and some hotels, double-door systems slow the passing from the public to private realm and enable visitors to be checked over before entry is allowed. On a closer inspection, the apparently open garage area on the ground floor of One Hyde Park reveals rising barriers. From this reception area owners are greeted and their cars absorbed into the fabric of the building, reaching underground parking via a lift. From there residents take a lift directly to their apartment.

Unlike the usual showy glass boxes, One Hyde Park's lifts offer a sense of enclosure and privacy, presenting a blank steel face to the street but with glass openings to see through the transparent spines of the building. What you will very rarely see are the residents of the building, not least because it is usually only at around a quarter capacity at any one time. A lift at Harvey Nichols whisks visitors to its champagne bar in a single jump from ground to top floor. Another at the Corinthia Hotel allows users of its presidential suite to go direct, avoiding the footfall of those on the way to its merely luxury rooms. The effect of these subtle systems is that the city becomes less a place of social encounter and more a private and controlled realm in which one is able to circulate among one's own, or indeed retreat from any form of social contact.

Floating worlds

In each of the past five years there has been at least one media-reported supercar traffic jam in London. The curious images of Lamborghinis wedged on Regent Street or Bugattis and Ferraris blocked around Piccadilly Circus highlight the sheer volume of wealth in the city. The traffic congestion that touches even the lives of the rich drives their desire for escape, and in particular the use of boats to do so. Many of the super-rich own large, bespoke yachts as well as smaller 'chaser' dinghies with massively powerful engines. The world of yachts and super yachts is truly one where money rules. Getting around the oceans by motor or sail requires near limitless resources. But the purchase price of many millions is only the beginning; crew salaries, port and mooring fees and unending maintenance costs mean a long-term financial commitment whose apparent recklessness is the sign of true wealth. Often this commitment is cut short by taste or changing whims. Around one in ten of the world's super yachts is registered to a British owner, but this statistic does not tell us a great deal because registrations are more or less unrelated to where the boats sit at any one time.

This is the great selling point of a boat: to be essentially wherever one wants to be or roam. Boats and yachts allow autonomy and privacy. The sea represents the realisation of a dream of total escape, the possibility of choosing almost any destination without control or imposition by state or society. Harbouring charges or the purchase of multiple permanent moorings enable visits at any time, even if this does not prevent the jams of clustering super yachts offshore at key times of the year.

London does see periodic displays of incredible floating wealth on the river, but it is less a key destination for the super-rich, as their boats are more often used to escape the city. While the Thames attracts some of the lazier traffic, London is no

Cannes or Antibes when it comes to the yachts of the super-rich. Why moor a luxury boat in the city when all this does is add to the sea miles needed to get somewhere nice? Much more likely is a mooring in the rivieras of France, Spain or Italy, which can be flown to and used as a launching point for forays around the Mediterranean. Off-world zones of luxury and seclusion, away from the masses, provide reference points for the wealthy, for whom knowledge of these places acts as a kind of secret handshake that shows someone is of the same monied club.

For the rich the world is a space without meaningful or troublesome borders – between states, between seas, and between the outside and the inside of perfectly manicured leisure and club spaces. This world appears as a menu of possible places and exciting new experiences. Often these are valued for their authenticity, while the loss of that quality is mourned as the same forces of global capitalism that produce the rich themselves also end up consuming and ultimately destroying many of the places they love (think here of what islands like Capri have become). This can be seen in the destruction of livelihoods and local economies in cities like Venice, or in the wildly distorting impact of the market on property prices in many rural districts and islands, where the local residents the rich seek as servants are steadily displaced.

The paradox of travel without checks or hindrance is that the prize of accessing remote locations becomes ever more valued and yet harder to achieve. The future of many such locations, as showpiece and impossibly beautiful places, will be as simulations. Often their colourful theatre is provided by imported 'local' labour and goods, allowing the rich to imagine that these fishing villages, rural idylls and mountain villages still exist as they did decades ago.

Better than home

The hotel network is a vital part of the seasonal life of the alpha city. London has the most five-star rated hotels of any city in the world (seventy-five); next in line is Dubai with sixty-one; New York has fifty-nine and Paris fifty-six. While many of the richest have homes that they may occupy for short periods of time, hotels offer a place for the visiting wealthy, for their family members or associates, and for those at the top of the corporate tree who may not have a place in the city but wish for uncompromising comfort. Such desires are pandered to by the hotels, but also become a self-espoused mark of success – the sense that in demanding only the best one has that indefinable quality required to make it.

The warmth on show in areas like Mayfair is primarily offered to the district's wealthy visitors and residents, who are met by the smiling faces of the many hundreds who 'help' – support staff, hoteliers, security staff and luxury goods vendors among many others. Such service is carefully stage managed to ensure a feeling of comfort and recognition among the wealthy, whether they are staying for one night or living full-time in the area. Traditionally, a handful of world-famous hotel names are associated with the West End. The old-school names include the Savoy, Dorchester, Berkeley, Connaught, Claridge's and the Ritz, which, when it was built, was looked down on by old money for its apparently brash, continental architecture. Newer entrants to the short-stay market cater to new money. The Bulgari, but a step from One Hyde Park and Harrods, is arguably for the blingiest clinging to some sense of taste; its multiple layers reach deep to offer a ballroom, cinema and even underground pools. In Knightsbridge, the Jumeirah Carlton offers a home from home for wealthy visitors from the Middle East; the Lanesborough, to the rear of Buckingham Palace, caters to an international set. Next door, and still under construction, the Peninsula's billboards display cringe-worthy colonial images of servants in pillbox hats, underlining its future commitment to obsequious service.

There isn't really a 'top' hotel as such, despite what some of them will claim. Rather there is the sense that different nationalities and sub-groups of the wealthy look for certain qualities or locational advantages in the hotel they choose – sometimes to be among fellow nationals, or to stay in a particular alphahood near to friends or family. The Dorchester and other purpose-built hotels like the Savoy, the Ritz (until recently owned by the Barclay brothers who also own the *Daily Telegraph*, now by a Qatari investor) and Claridge's were constructed to accommodate the growing numbers of the wealthy created by the national and then global economy from the late nineteenth century onwards. In some of these hotels the commitment to conspicuous displays of service has extended to remodelling hotel rooms to suit the whims of temporary residents, such as the installation of a Jacuzzi at Claridge's.

One of the core and earliest alpha hotels since it opened in 1812, Claridge's has often been described as an annex of Buckingham Palace – not because the royal residence is so very close but because of its connection to royal visitors. The hotel is now part of a group that includes the Connaught, also in Mayfair and near to the now closed US embassy (itself being converted into another luxury hotel), and the Berkeley, just south in Knightsbridge. Like the trophy homes of the rich, these super-chains of hotels are the jewels in the crown of corporate groups who trade off these collections.

Today, much of the luxury hotel scene is owned by international corporations and offshore vehicles designed to extract value from the city. The Maybourne Group, which includes the Connaught, Claridge's and Lanesborough, is owned by the Abu Dhabi Investment Authority, which often pays well over market guide prices for these positional goods. One learns what good taste is when entering through Claridges' hardwood revolving doors, stepping on its luxuriantly super-thick and sound-deadening domestic carpets, admiring its gold inlay, sculpture, carvings and paintings. Like many of the other key hotels, the sense of luxury but also understatement is heightened by a cosy bar, with its various nooks and crannies in which to meet, chat or simply hide. Two members of staff are dedicated to each of its roughly 200 rooms. The nearby Dorchester alone employs around fifty chefs. This apparent over-staffing is an important aspect of the alpha territories more generally – an essential means of meeting the demands of the wealthy, giving them the sense that help is on hand whenever one might need it.

When the Ritz opened in Piccadilly in 1906 it was considered vulgar by the city's elite, a kind of oversized emulation of one of Paris's most famous shopping streets, the Rue de Rivoli, adjacent to the Louvre. The hotel's bar is fitted with features that nod towards the luxury and romance of the carriages of the Orient Express. For a time the world's richest man, John Paul Getty lived at the Ritz. Twenty years ago, a group of comedians devised a sketch in which the hotel was sold to an oligarch. On arrival he tells an assembly of staff that there will be almost no changes to how things are done, save a small one: changing the hotel's name to the Titz. Such a ridiculous possibility seems almost plausible in a city in which new waves of money run wild, untamed by taste or restraint, a city in which money can buy almost anything – gold toilets, chrome push-bikes, gold-infused cocktails, football clubs or diamond-encrusted doorbells. Here in the alpha hotel zone even the traffic regulations can be broken; the road outside the Savoy is the only one in the UK on which one has to drive on the right.

Several of the alpha hotels are former palaces or stately homes. Metaphors of bunkers and retreats for the rich have a deeper resonance at the Dorchester, for example. The pale facade is due to its use of reinforced concrete, making it the natural site for General Eisenhower to set up base during his stays in London amid the Blitz. Like several other key hotels it is a former palace from the time of the nouveau riche, when many mansions were built from the new fortunes made in the Victorian and Edwardian eras. In the case of the Dorchester, the original building was Dorchester House built for the Earl of Dorchester in the eighteenth century.

The Dorchester today symbolises the established scene of the wealthy and powerful, its history displaying the absorption of new money into existing social structures and the city itself. Opened in 1931, its ownership shifted to an Arab consortium in 1977 under the Sultan of Brunei, then the world's richest man and friend of the 'new' owner of Harrods, Mohamed Al-Fayed. Al-Fayed, though a rank outsider of the British establishment, became the preferential bidder to own the luxury store after persuading the Sultan not to dump sterling at the height of the oil crisis, which would have risked plunging the national economy into further catastrophe. Al-Fayed's own massive resources and connections helped overcome the establishment's natural antipathy to new and foreign money.

Among the more recent contenders on the hotel circuit is the Mandarin Oriental, connected by aerial walkways to One Hyde Park so that residents in their own somewhat hotel-like apartments can be offered food and service. At the Mandarin, the penthouse suite beats all others in the capital at £42,000 a night. A journalist who stayed there described it as sterile, drab and vulgar, adjectives that some would consider equally appropriate for the 'banker chic' of the residences next door. The more serious point is that excess money erodes the idea of a home as a place of emotional attachment – how does one sustain a sense of home amid multiple residences? If one is profoundly wealthy what counts as home? Hypermobility blurs these distinctions. Yet for the rich, home is wherever one parks one's private jet, yacht or car. The idea of home becomes a portable feeling rather than a place; there is no need to ask which of one's homes is the best, which is where one's heart is most attached. Allegiance and ties fade. Why the need to choose when every home is the best possible, when any support needed or objects of attachment can travel by your side?

The hotel circuit is only one component of the market in prime spaces used for short stays by the super-rich. With the right contacts to help one organise it, there are multiple other options, including very short-term lets. Instead of the Mandarin suite one could, for example, rent an eight-bed house in Princes Gate for £40,000 a week, a seven-bed house in Belgravia for £20,000 a week, or a five-bed penthouse at One Hyde Park for around £40,000 per week, with access to its squash court and underground car spaces. These are examples of the many super-luxury rentals available from specialist agencies for short stays that offer the feel of home.

The hyper-mobility of the wealthy elite means that new kinds of home-like spaces are being created in the city. At 20 Grosvenor Square a string of new homes costing between £17m and £35m are on sale. The difference with these homes is that they are serviced by the adjacent Four Seasons Hotel, with staff who can provide laundry, pet care, babysitting and butler services, and with the seemingly ubiquitous offering of cinema, wine room and a 25-metre pool. These residences, in the former US Navy HQ, offer the ability to safeguard one's home while away, but also blur the line between what is home and what is hotel.

The aesthetics of this world are increasingly monoform. While the offer is always described as unique and lavish, the resulting feel of many interiors is cold and they are often very similar – a mix of metallic fabrics, hard surfaces, abundant chrome and washed-out palettes. But the lack of any significant difference between many of these staggeringly expensive apartments, hotel rooms, suites and residences serves an important function by enabling mobility without undue motion sickness. One might move between Dubai, New York and London, gliding through remarkably similar spaces – the non-places of the alpha elite. It is in the homes of longer-term residents, the wealthy rather than super-wealthy, that one finds more diverse and personal touches, somewhat less fashionable art, and unique displays of taste and signature interests. Frequent mobility, on the other hand, yields reassuringly similar environments, a kind of franchise space built around the need for flow rather than emotional attachment.

Hyper-mobility between residences, complex household and servant arrangements, and service staff kept in situ at a number of destinations all feature in the lifestyles of the wealthiest households. This may even extend to keeping duplicate wardrobes at each home so that confusion is minimised – the same shirt or dress in the same place, ready to wear whether one is in New York, London or the south of France. Such efforts at maintaining a sense of continuity reduce the feeling of 'friction' in a life that is so often lived on the move.

Shopping

The Beadles are the long-established private police of the Burlington Arcade, discreet, top-hatted defenders of the peace in an area not known for its disorder. Burlington Arcade is a string of luxury shops selling everything from shaving brushes to cashmere sweaters and vintage Rolex watches. Like several other arcades in the West End, it offers a sense of stewardship and service that acts like a magnet to wealthy shoppers. Emerging from plush homes and luxury hotels they can quickly step into shops with electromagnetically locked doorways, more or less secret and private spaces that enable unmonitored consumption. With sufficient purchasing power it is possible to commandeer the large private viewing room on the top floor of Harrods, as well as at several other shops and department stores offering bespoke facilities to wealthy customers.

A World of Fantasy

Walking Sloane Street on a sunny day one might spot a small temporary beach and beautiful flowers outside the royal jewellers Boodles. The area regularly exudes a sense of reinvention, a kind of theatre performed for the wealthy to keep them interested and happy. But the language of seclusion and security appears everywhere, even attaching to the pop-up kitchen at Chelsea Barracks – Hideaway. Even Rolex created a 'pop-up' store while its One Hyde Park shop was closed for a refit. The capacity to remake in order to entice the discerning client is ever present, while flagship stores act as a visible reminder of key brands.

Harrods is a massive meeting point of the forces shaping the alpha city. Its 4,500 staff cover all aspects of shopping, beauty care, estate management, real estate sales and catering to the wealthy. But being in principle open to all, the store also democratises the experience of luxury, even if many of its tourists and other visitors would not be capable of buying many of the items on show. For the rich the store retains a hold; butlers and staff shop here for their employers, while the rich themselves arrive at the back of the store to be guided direct to lifts and escalators immediately off-street. Here old and new money come together in a property now owned by the Qatari sovereign wealth fund, another national treasure reverse-colonised by the ability of money to triumph over what many still see as a national interest.

The city appears to have two hearts: one beats efficiently and propels its wealthy bodies around with ease; another, weaker organ struggles and sometimes fails to keep its public moving. The point is not simply to observe these segregated systems and pathways, but to reflect on the mentalities and values that are shaped by a world of such seclusion and privacy. At the very moments when we might hope to see the rich engaging with the city they sometimes call home, they remain isolated from it, their senses dulled by tinted windows, sound-insulated interiors and enclosed luxury cabins and lounges – a kind of antiseptic sociality, super-organised and untroubled by the real and messier city that sits immediately outside. This is a world unpunctured by signs of distress, in which a sense of social obligation and connection is uncoupled from the mentalities of the wealthy. Even on the move the rich do not see the city's diversity or troubles but are offered a kind of self-made simulation that masks its full variety and true life.

London acts like a machine of forgetting for its disconnected super-affluent denizens. Looking down from penthouses and high-rise apartments may induce a kind of social vertigo – a fear of the apparent chaos and social disorganisation below. Any sense of common inhabitation, reciprocity and altruism is inoculated against by this kind of city life. What do a hundred public housing estate demolitions, street-level begging, bedroom taxes, record stabbings, overcrowding, desperate schools and stressed public hospitals mean from the perspective of the secluded social circuits and bubble spaces of the city's wealthy?

Space matters. It shapes the subjectivities of the affluent and of those attached to them. This creates a curious psychopolitical formation that appears to give most people what they want while, in reality, creating an increasingly alienating and pathological environment. We cannot understand socially regressive planning decisions, public cuts and household displacement in isolation from the insulating architecture, narrow social networks and restricted movement patterns of the rich and the city's elites and enablers more broadly. Years ago analysts warned of the dangers of segregation, partly of course for its effects on the poor, but also because those with power over the rest of us live increasingly among themselves, disconnected from the consequences of the political and social choices they make.

In this sense, the mobile world of the alpha city erases the unwritten constitution of the city – its designation as a site in which encounter with diversity generates in its residents a knowledge of and empathy with other citizens. This kind of democratic and mutually connected city does not exist for the rich. It has been replaced by a world of super-fast cars, faster jets, private lifts and mega yachts that prop up and propel the bodies of the rich, between their homes, places of leisure and work. The idea of the public city gives way to an underground, overhead and in-between network of hermetically sealed pathways. In such a city the rich and their agents don't see, and much less care about, those who are not part of the spaces and networks they inhabit. The real city, the social kernel of struggling and underprivileged lives, becomes a wholly other space, unknowable and capable of being morally disowned.

My Own Private Stronghold

Wealth, as we have seen, can be an isolating force. While the alpha city appears to offer an open, natural setting for the rich, it is also their soft cage, a luxurious zone of insulated bunkers, fortress homes and gated communities. The city's wonderful spaces sustain but also confine the super-rich. Their captivity is driven by a contradiction that lies at the heart of the alpha lifestyle – with massive wealth comes irresolvable anxiety.

Anxiety and fear are key elements of the broader social fabric within which ordinary people are wrapped. The idea of a culture fixated on potential risks, uncertain futures and a deepening sense of precariousness is ubiquitous. Where the rich differ from the rest of us, however, is in the way they respond to everyday fears with enormously elaborate and sometimes disproportionate strategies to achieve a sense of total control and protection. In the end this creates an increasingly exclusive environment that is even more anxiety-inducing.

Studies of the lifestyles of the super-rich reveal that their worry is driven by multiple fears – of intrusion, breaches of privacy, domestic invasion, the loss of property, fraud and impersonation, embezzlement, and even the possible loss of life. As we saw in the last chapter, the rich are particularly able to use certain strategies and technologies of movement that engrain this kind of evade/connect pattern of engagement. So while there are recognisable aspects of these patterns that overlap with those found in more everyday lives, the intensity with which risk is mitigated operates at a much broader level. Massive personal wealth generates the feeling that one is different or a potential target. This can result in the kind of confinements that we have already seen, with a concerted effort to secure property, bodies, minds, homes, staff and, of course, money.

If you drop in to the Banham security shop on Kensington High Street you'll get a sense of the attention to detail and security in London's alphahoods. Here you'll find a busy scene in which wealthy owners jostle with the servants of other owners for the attention of staff, amid comforting displays of steel-braced doors, safes and gun cabinets. Many such devices are sold to create the illusion of an everyday home while concealing the use of bolstered doors and shatter-proof windows in a domestic space designed to turn into a trap for the soon-to-be-confounded burglar.

But such subtlety is not always the name of the game; many owners seek features that shout at ne'er-do-wells not to chance their arm. Such measures include the use of overt cameras, video entry phones, steel grills, and signs warning of rapid response units should the trap be sprung. Such are the common trappings of the alpha fortresses in many of the streets in these districts. One walks out of the shop with the mind's eye focused on a cast of innovative burglars and tooled-up intruders who might take advantage of any home less than medievally fortified.

London promises, particularly for nationals from riskier countries, a low-risk environment, or at least one where external risks can be mollified. The rule of law and the low risk of crime are reassuring qualities, teaching the rich that wandering through open public spaces is possible. Yet despite the feeling that this place offers a site of shelter and safe harbour, the idea of not planning for and strategising against risks is seen as foolhardy. As the old joke goes: a man sprinkling powder on the ground is asked what he is doing; he explains that the powder is elephant-repellent dust. The questioner, thinking him mad, points out that there are no wild elephants for thousands of miles. With a smile the man says, yes, effective isn't it?

The array of visible and less obvious security arrangements in the alphahoods gives the impression that paranoia and fear are never far from the imaginations of the rich, a concern with possibilities never likely to eventuate. But it would be a mistake to think that they sit trembling in these fine cocoons. Security is generally a delegated matter, something for someone else to install and manage. Seamless transitions between places, spaces and vehicles, the employment of drivers and other staff, enable a sense of ease rather than fear, but there is nevertheless a sense of lurking danger that undergirds these complex arrangements and infrastructures. There are always just enough stories of domestic burglaries, hotel hold-ups, jewel heists and violent robberies to make precautionary measures appear necessary. To stop worrying might invite disaster.

Protecting one's house with locks is sensible, but for the rich this is a minimal approach to home defence. Their security regimes involve personal guards, panic rooms, motion-sensing cameras and bio-print door entry systems, among an array of other expensive extras, staff and bespoke products. These muscular responses to risk have a wider impact – the domestic security arrangements of the wealthy do not stop at their front doors or garden walls. The security labour and infrastructure that protect the rich and assuage their anxieties generate a more pervasive aesthetic and atmosphere that now inflects the life of the city more broadly. These efforts have changed the feel of traditionally open streetscapes and of homes designed with total security in mind. In many cases it is no longer possible to reach the front door of such homes.

A number of quite visible symbols index the deeper play of negative emotions and fears that seem everywhere in evidence across the alphahoods. These include CCTV cameras, guards behind shop doors, blacked-out car windows, the large electronic gates of many homes, the employment of large numbers of household staff, booms across roads and signs denoting private roads. Yet such efforts are also designed not to impede on the lives of the wealthy or to generate unnecessary concern. The result is an aesthetic that seems to combine special ops with Italian tailoring. Security details in hotels or shops, often fronted by athletic young men in black suits and earpieces, are part of a chain of potentially escalating responses to threats. An initial impression of openness can quickly change depending on the nature of a threat, whether it be from those inappropriately dressed (diverted to another, more suitable venue), rowdy behaviour (quickly calmed or challenged), or an attempt at robbery. Rows of fine townhouses can quickly be shut down by domestic security systems or swarmed by rapid response units from the police or private security personnel.

One of the fundamental challenges of being very rich is knowing who can be trusted. But the process really begins with another question – who can be trusted to tell who can be trusted? Wealth arrives with risks lurking in tow. Being a member of the city's wealth elite makes one a potential target of burglars, fraudsters, cyber-criminals or the very real prospect of potentially untrustworthy personal staff, money managers and accountants. Myths and stories are traded among the rich about whom to avoid or to engage. Trust itself is a hard-won thing when the gap between personal staff, the general population and one's own wealth is so immense.

The possibility of being duped is thus a constant worry and a frequent source of potential embarrassment. In an acquisitive, materialistic and media-saturated culture of display, excess and the flaunting of symbols of achievement, the position of the wealthy is coveted. The rich themselves know this and act accordingly. An awareness of envy and possible ill intentions behind the broad smiles motivates the use of well-paid and long-term staff wherever possible. These may include a family office of wealth and personal advisers, trusted butlers, and, less often, bodyguards and security personnel. Among the wealthiest, entire household retinues can be found, many of them retained during the owners' absences to ensure both continuity as well as the maintenance and security of a home. But the gnawing possibility of employing someone on the take, or with risky connections or just a lax approach to security, demands that one keep a close eye on who gets access to the home, to the children and of course to one's bank account.

Safety is not just a matter of how one gets about or the security features of one's home, it involves a much more encompassing set of strategies for ensuring a safe place to invest, to educate one's children, to live and to socialise. The principle of staying safe is extended and expressed in the desire for seamless movement between the eyrie-like spaces of fortified homes and the protected and cocooned spaces of private clubs, galleries, schools and exclusive shopping destinations. The desire for safety also relates to the wealth accumulation strategies devised in the City, connections to offshore and secrecy jurisdictions, and the role of land and property in offering a safe investment in a world of economic turmoil.

The net effect of this operating principle is to combine diverse aspects of the city in the pursuit of protection and security – the absolute core of how the rich relate to a city that remains in their imaginations a place of safety, democracy and rule of law that allows the unperturbed use of public space. For a group that may feel some anxiety at their lofty position, these are immensely valuable aspects of alpha urbanism.

For the city's rich, however, everyday life is limited to safe zones and uplifting spaces; it is lived in an urban setting akin to a spectacularly comfortable open prison. The resulting impression is one of a privileged group in a distinctive and highly manicured habitat – one in which the wealthy can roam, but ultimately with strict boundaries. Like a large gated community, the city's alpha quarters offer the illusion of having everything that one needs, belying the reality of a bounded space disconnected from the threats and irritations that might exist outside its limits.

At first glance this will seem a bold assertion given the immense resources and hyper-mobility of the rich that we have already witnessed. Yet in reality the daily pathways and tracks laid down by and for the super-rich are repeatedly travelled in quite fixed ways – from one secure node or safe space to another. The idea that privilege brings with it a gilded cage is no doubt one that many among the wealthy would vigorously deny, yet it is clear that like-with-like association among them is the driving feature of many of these everyday social circuits. Despite their magnificence and opulence, it is the same clubs, communities, leisure spaces and homes that are the recurring stamping grounds of the elite.

The alpha securityscape

A subtly securitised look and atmosphere permeates the city's alphahoods, varying according to their location and the composition of their households. The range of their defensive strategies is split particularly between old and new residents and between suburban and central city locations. Another key factor at work is both the extent of the wealth and the national background of the rich themselves; notable groups like the Russians tend to be more security conscious, Europeans and established Britons generally less so. Yet new money brings with it the sense that status is also about defence, and in this sense the alphahoods form a series of micro-territories, bubbles of security over which control can be exerted and threats repelled or expelled as and when the need arises.

For some years London has increasingly securitised its streets, privatised public spaces and installed an almost total surveillance system in its centre. Much of this effort stems from the city's experience of domestic terrorism and a series of bombings in the 1970s and '80s, leading to the massive deployment of advanced surveillance technologies, particularly CCTV. These provisions have since been directed at unruly citizens or used to guard against the kind of spectacular shocks that terror has brought to the city more recently. These broader changes in the look and atmosphere of the city compound the sense that anxiety is the key organising principle of an alpha urban order, born of massive inequalities, techno-responses to risk and an emphatic intolerance towards any form of disorder.

London's capture by the rich is in part expressed through this almost wholesale transformation of many areas organised around the principle of security. There can never be too much of it. Its unwritten diktat states that this logic will extend to include any homes and environments not currently attached to it, for to fail to do so is make oneself or one's home a more vulnerable target. Ever-expanding security systems take in affluent homes, peri-urban communities, city neighbourhoods, villages and even towns that have become integrated in line with these principles of protection.

The precautionary principles and dedicated planning for security that underscores the life of the alphahoods produces territories; spaces that can be defended. The potential for aggressive countermeasures surrounds notable homes, gated communities and key streets protected by private security outfits and surveillance systems. Walking the environs of key alpha developments, such as Belgravia's squares or Chelsea's quaint townhouses, or suburban areas like Cobham or Gerrards Cross, one will feel like a trespasser simply for not being a resident. Being challenged feels like a constant possibility, and indeed will come swiftly after entering a private road or even passing close to the gates of some residences.

In many such areas one of the standout features is the number of service staff running the homes, cleaning the streets, patrolling the boundaries. When the urbanist Jane Jacobs talked of the desirability of having eyes on the street to help communities to be safer, she did not envisage this super-secured landscape of wealthy neighbourhoods and armies of suspicious helpers. These numerous staff now represent paid 'eyes' undertaking surveillance and security on behalf of the rich, rather than members of the community looking out for each other. The overall impression is of a search for safety in the absence of community or indeed, in some places, of residents.

In the central London alphahoods aggressive and strategic planning is translated into a corresponding physical form. The trick here is to ensure that antagonism towards potential threats is as subtle as possible. The miniaturisation of cameras means that surveillance often feels unobtrusive, but in many of the new developments security guards sit inside the reception area examining a bank of screens. In The Bishops Avenue in Highgate there are homes with guard boxes at the front gates, while others have gates and walls that cannot be seen over.

Until the late nineteenth century, London's West End had around 150 private barriers, used to prevent noise and traffic as well as access by the general hoi polloi. In some cases these were open during the day, but at the Bedford Estate tickets were required to gain even daytime access. The inconvenience and anti-democratic nature of these gates generated massive public resentment and then agitation, which finally resulted in the London Streets (Removal of Gates) Acts of 1890 and 1893.[1] A little later, the London Building Act of 1894 also prohibited any post, rail, fence or bar across a street. During this period the threat of occasional riots rarely touched the West End, but nevertheless provoked the formation of associations to protect property. Today, once again, a perceived deficit in control over space and property drives private residents or entire neighbourhoods to use their combined resources to purchase additional layers of security. In these areas the perception that state-run policing and security are not enough is rife.

In many ways the central London alphahoods manage to combine the need for security with a vibrant street life, particularly on larger roads. But this geography of security and residence is complex and changes quickly. In an area like Knightsbridge one finds a kind of 'shells and yolks' patchwork in which softer, interior streets feel cosy and protected. Here an almost village atmosphere can be found, with small pubs and shops sitting alongside modest mews houses (often belying their quite staggering cost). These relatively inviting spaces are juxtaposed with areas where embassies, ambassadorial residences and the mansions of the super-rich create a more intimidating, harder-edged atmosphere. Here one may bump into security guards walking Alsatians in the streets or encounter guards in pillboxes manning the gated entrances to some streets. In nearby Kensington Palace Gardens there are patrols of armed guards and police, and the street's gates can be closed if security is at high alert. Signs dotted along the Gardens prohibit the taking of pictures, though, curiously, it is possible to park one's car using one of the meters along this wide street.

These observations underline an important point in relation to the contemporary look and feel of the West End. Here the many and varied spaces of the wealthy and super-rich, hypersecure nodes of homes, hotels, mansions, apartment blocks, stores and banks are almost lifted out of the city by their technologies and security apparatuses. These infrastructures enable the control and coordination of residential life, filtering out non-residents or unwanted individuals at one location while including them at others. Yet immediately alongside these zones one can find an unrestricted and open street life as one moves from areas of lockdown and suspicion to others of everyday encounter and porosity.

For some among the newly arrived rich, a highly desirable aspect of London life is the provision of safe houses from which excursions can be made to equally pleasant and secure homes, venues, clubs, restaurants, and sports and cultural events. At the former Lever mansion in Hampstead, which has been subdivided into a luxury enclave apartment block, guards with dogs patrol the gardens. Non-residents at the gates are asked their business via a videophone entry system, and all around are signs warning of the dogs. These new developments continue a longer history of urban fortification that includes streets with barriers across them and guards to prevent casual entry.

The construction of new alpha developments, like The Lancasters, One Hyde Park or St George Wharf, enables key security features to be more easily embedded into the infrastructure of the building from the outset. A strong case in point is the hyper-secure development at Embassy Gardens, which overlooks the new American Embassy. Well-heeled but casual coffee drinkers are checked-over by plain clothes officers. Baristas, receiving dollars and euros in their tip jar, are briefed on what to do in the event of an attack. Here, even the wealthy are brought into the orbit of an even more powerful security regime, and almost every piece of street furniture looks like it might have a camera embedded in it. At One Hyde Park, external glass walls offer the impression of openness while belying their use to divide non-residents from residents; cars

Canine Patrol

are accepted or rejected at ground level, and all post is X-rayed before final delivery.

In many alphahoods, security systems are also embedded in the shopping and commercial infrastructure. Jewellers and prestigious hotels have been the sites of robberies and attacks. In 2014 a single scooter gang made a series of attacks around the West End, smashing cabinets and stealing jewellery from cases in the lobbies of the Dorchester (which saw two attacks in the same year), the Jumeirah Carlton and another two jewellers before being caught. Notable robberies have also occurred at Boodles, Yves Saint Laurent, Selfridges and Tiffany's on Sloane Square in recent years. In 2018, in the space of only three months, watches worth more than a million pounds were stolen in central London. All this talk of crime, the risk of robbery and the audacity of criminals of course reinforces the setting of priorities around continued security and perhaps also the feeling that with wealth comes the lurking possibility of moments of lawlessness and violence.

At the flagship fashion stores the subtle filtering of unwanted social elements is achieved by the symbolically intimidating presence of luxury as well as guards on the doors. Where security is needed in abundance, at jewellers and banks, it is not uncommon for the doors to be locked until prospective customers have been vetted, or for double-doors to be used that enable customers to be placed in a kind of very temporary off-street isolation. The tension is thus that between a desire to appear open to all, enabling a feeling of seamless transition for 'legitimate' users, while ensuring a tight protection of assets.

If we move out of the city back to the suburban exclaves, we find an even more secure alpha zone, a place that elite property agents will often direct wealthy buyers to if they want total control over their property. Here ample space gives greater latitude for installing more extensive systems and controlling domestic borders. London's adjacent counties have seen significant expansions in the number of executive mega-homes and both large and small gated enclaves. These areas have an increasingly urbanised and highly securitised feel that is some-what alien to a region once tied to agricultural and feudal relations. This apparent leap out of rurality is also accom-panied in many cases by the impression of a curtailment of freedoms – blocked paths and highways appear everywhere, and historical rights of access on public footpaths are set in conflict with the desire of new owners to maintain total privacy.

London's outer alphahoods have the feel of a pseudo-rural space – a place of security guard boxes rather than chocolate box cottages. This is an often conspicuously enclosed, electroni-cally eyed and, in many cases, unfriendly landscape. From one enclave to another, guards patrol in their vans and service staff are buzzed through the gates of large homes as powerful cars fly past. In some cases the trappings of security are purely sym-bolic: wait a short while and the gates of some roads will slowly open; but the intent is clear – you don't live here or belong here. The only sound of life in many of these areas comes from the wind, the traffic and the slow whine of airliners appearing almost suspended above as they glide into Heathrow.

Economics has long operated as an important means of maintaining the social prestige of wealthy areas, resisting the construction of public and affordable housing that would diversify such communities. Affluent neighbourhoods create hermetically sealed spaces that keep out the poor through high house prices and rents. The changes in these areas have a longer history, and again we can find continuities as well as intensi-fications of the trajectory towards greater privatism and the retreat of the wealthy elite behind walls and gates. In many picturesque villages farm-worker cottages have been gentrified, while nearby gated lanes open onto new housing developments tightly integrated into established woodland – an attempt at ensuring privacy as well as concealing the scale of develop-ment and indeed the massive size of many of these homes. It is possible to pass through many places with little awareness of their extensive security arrangements or any real knowledge of the extent of this new and exclusive scene. The weaving of new boundaries, cables, infrastructures, lanes and homes gives the impression of a kind of synthetic rurality tinged with a semi-urban feel that brings to mind Stepford lives.

Private security details, powerful cars and secure enclaves mark the new residential landscape of the city, while bunkers and complex surveillance systems appear to further the sense of paranoia among those who have 'made it'. These zones of gun-toting security personnel in the grounds of mansions, control rooms and dorms provided for security staff, and panic rooms in hotels for super-affluent visitors, mark out a highly suspicious, twitching residential landscape of curtains, cameras and guards. As we will see, all of this generates the impression of a self-governing zone which administers its own rules and boundaries.

The fortress home

For the rich the key defensive position, the place from which all other bets and adventures are hedged, is the private home. If we were to build a composite archetype of an alpha city home it would be a large townhouse, with perhaps six bedrooms, in the patrician heartlands of Knightsbridge or Mayfair. One would be greeted by the regular signatures of sturdy locks and a video entry phone, sometimes with pin code entry. This is a kind of buffer zone in which traditional connections between home and street are made fuzzier, the intention being to create a higher degree of control. Above the door will likely sit a small CCTV camera, operating in infrared to enable night vision, relaying a live feed to a screen inside the house or to the owner's phone so that visitors can be vetted remotely. Reinforced glass windows will be installed at ground level, and when residents are away for extended periods some homes may display security grille shutters that prevent access even if a window is somehow broken (unlikely when many are treated with tough polymer to prevent breakage). The front door will have two steel deadlocks and, while seeming to be made of solid wood, will often be reinforced with steel (or made bespoke to an even higher specification). Doors made of hardened wood that will flex under impact to prevent fracturing are one of the more or less standard features of homes that feel increasingly fortified.

The typical home of London's super-rich is a high-tech security apparatus, threaded with layers and cables of infrastructure. It has been estimated that the average cost of securing a central London mansion is around £50,000 a year. At the top end numerous additional security features can be added to homes, and the results are in some cases spectacular. Verging on paranoia, the list of extras begins to sound like a Bond villain's wish list for securing their bunker. They may include the installation of collapsible steel gates on the inside of windows, gun cabinets (subject of course to applications for firearms licences), the use of DNA 'water' systems that spray burglars for later detection, as well as ingenious 'fogging' systems that flood rooms with a high density mist making it impossible to see what might be stolen.

With significant resources one can install rapid automatic shutters to block key rooms after an intruder alert has been triggered. A related system uses electromagnetically sealed doors which can be remotely shut to trap intruders. Sensors can be employed to monitor various aspects of the life of the home. It is now possible, for example, to fit vibration, temperature (to prevent damage to artworks) and even weight detectors (to establish that it is the owner who is at home). Even further layers of detection can be installed using, for example, acoustic detectors to pick up on the sound of breaking glass. Infra-red beams are the standard fare of burglar alarms, but multi-layered intrusion detection beams can also be used to ensure that a cat burglar doesn't gain entry by hopping over or avoiding beams.

The list of security devices is long, and numerous providers are engaged in the profitable business of offering advice, support and installation. Fingerprint locks are now beginning to make an entrance onto the market, while safes can be used to trigger intruder alerts, with one code used for normal access and another to alert that it is being opened under duress. Panic buttons are of course linked to the rapid response unit of the security system provider, and portable versions, a bit like a small walkie-talkie, can be carried around the house. Various companies will offer a key-holder service with rapid delivery by motorbike if one is lost, highlighting the web of supporting services and personnel who are there on a just-in-time basis.

In many cases, owner absence means that it is staff who are left to keep properties secure (in gated communities this is less of a concern). This again highlights the importance of high-trust relationships developed over time and of employing staff on recommendation. Staff maintain and secure the house, and also check on the often numerous companies offering services when the owner is away. This also means that homes will still appear to be in use.

In alpha apartment blocks and large homes key cards can be used to allow timed and restricted access to parts of the home by servants (such as preventing bedroom access at night, or the wine cellar in general), with only owners or the 'master' of the house being given access to all areas. This ability to restrict staff access increases the sense of a stratified and untrusting domestic realm. The possibility of monitoring both staff and potential intruders is built-in to devices like smoke detectors and thermostats which can be provided with cameras installed – making it possible to watch a nanny with a child while away from the home, for example. In some cases the demand for security has driven planning applications to extend already large homes in order to accommodate domestic staff and even personal bodyguard units. While London is not rife with bodyguards, particular groups of nationals and others with specific concerns do of course use them. More common is that the simple accompaniment and chaperoning of a driver, who may have some basic combat training, doubles as a source of protection.

In many of the key housing developments even more advanced systems are installed. At One Hyde Park they include iris-scanning security access and bomb-proof glass in the apartments. Guarding the front doors of the development are reportedly special services trained staff. If one really wants to add style to security the possibility of installing the Elite Crown Jewel doorbell might seem appealing. For only £72,000 this 18-carat gold entry system includes diamonds, sapphires and a 1080P motion-sensing video camera. One might even feel better at the prospect that Elite will make a donation to support schemes that help reformed criminals to re-enter society.

The Crown Jewel is a bling form of security, a strangely stand-out device in a terrain largely governed more by subtlety and inconspicuousness. But it is possible to find other high-tech examples that offer an insight into where these markets and technologies are moving, with the development of cameras capable of learning and distinguishing between the faces of residents, known visitors and new 'unknowns', whose images are then sent to the phones of owners. The camera systems deployed at some of the larger and most expensive gated communities are additionally connected either to a private security firm or, in limited cases, to the police, such as at the nineteen entrances of the Wentworth estate in Surrey which operate live police cameras and number-plate recognition systems.

Monitoring can be provided for intruder and fire alarms, but also to deal with the failure of freezers, or checking for changes in the ambient temperature of the home to protect artworks that might be damaged. These highlight more domestic concerns perhaps, but they add to the ability of owners to leave their homes unoccupied for lengthy periods of time. All of this brings with it a sense of reassurance, and few of these systems have any real impact on comfort – one can live in luxury surrounded by devices that are hidden or require little preparation or maintenance.

The risk of burglary is not by any means an unthinkable possibility. Rates of burglary are lower in the very wealthiest neighbourhoods, as heavy use of security makes entry more difficult, but the general impression is that danger is out there at all times and must be prepared for. A domestic security arms race has led to innovation on the part of burglars, who use contemporary tools of the trade such as Google Street View or photos in online property profiles – the latter often include ground plans which can be used to plan entry and escape routes. In response to these strategies elite property agents now special-ise in listings without using the internet, passing paper details direct to clients who are vetted as genuine buyers first.

In some cases the celebrity or wealthy owners of significant homes have taken steps to have themselves taken off the map. Some owners seeking anonymity or celebrities who may feel at risk from stalkers have been known to use shell compa-nies to buy homes to prevent themselves from being identified. Other efforts at retaining anonymity involve requests to avoid online mapping – areas like St George's Hill, to take one very obvious example, cannot be explored using Google Street, having prevented access to Google's camera cars. More recent concerns include the use of drones to scout properties, and burglars using prestige cars to gain access to expensive streets or gated communities without raising the suspicions of guards or residents.

Perimeter security is a particular concern in suburban loca-tions. Here it is possible to find staff with dogs patrolling larger areas. More common are passive measures including high fences and remote-controlled gate systems. A simple but effective strategy for concealment and privacy, as well as secu-rity, is of course the use of gates, commonly at a height of 8 to 10ft – sufficiently tall to obscure views. These have become de rigueur in such locations and are easier to deploy in suburban environments. Here the tricks and traps are more evident as a means of putting off potential intruders, including pole-mounted CCTV cameras and 'trip wire' infrared systems across driveways. Buyers with sufficient resources will also select homes that are not located next to public footpaths, choosing secure estates like Wentworth, St George's Hill, Burwood Park or a property on one of the private streets in the city that have guards and barriers, as at Courtney Avenue in Highgate.

The beating heart of the most fortified homes is the so-called panic room. This can range from being a fairly simple box room to a much larger interior space, often concealed by false walls or a bookcase. Panic rooms come with a wide array of options, but essentially they are a super-secure space in which to hide in the event of a home invasion. At the top end, they come with bulletproof doors and can be fitted to provide light and air-conditioning with a backup power supply if the main power source is cut. Panic rooms have also been installed in the most prestigious hotels.

Reports suggest that nationals from less secure contexts, notably Russians and Eastern Europeans, tend to favour the use of perimeter security and armoured cars. Officers with dogs can also be hired to escort worried citizens back to their homes. Of course architecture and design can be used to help promote the sense of concealment and relative invisibility. It has become popular to use tall fences to conceal homes or to 'submerge' them via basements, rather like icebergs, so that the full extent of a luxury home is barely on display – what has become known as stealth architecture. The general message is that wealth should be hidden rather than flaunted.

Physical intrusion is only one anxiety for the super-rich. One increasing concern is with cyber-criminals who may target affluent individuals, monitoring emails over months, and collecting important information that might then be used to access accounts. High-tech approaches extend to the use of GPS jammers in cars to prevent them from being followed, the fear

Going Down

of abduction or assassination being a not entirely unjustified concern for some of London's wealthiest citizens. An encrypted mobile phone is essential to prevent conversations being intercepted, while tracking devices are used in case of kidnapping. All of this suggests that no security can be seen as superfluous, and that, in many cases, the more visible security practices and infrastructures are sported almost as a kind of status symbol.

The fortress city

Many of the alpha city's homes have taken on the look and feel of personal fortresses, a trend that is only amplified by the increasing use of gating and boundaries around entire neighbourhoods and small enclaves. There are now well over a thousand such gated communities in England, but the bulk of them are in and around London. In the city itself there are hundreds of small estates and developments that use gates to control access at street level, and many thousands of homes also have underground parking, remote-control electronic gates and CCTV systems.

In Surrey alone there are around a hundred gated 'communities'. Often very small developments involving a handful of homes, they create a sense of privilege as well as insulation from potential risks. Appearing in many commuter-belt towns, gated communities represent a radical break in the British planning tradition, helping to seal-up what were, even in the most affluent neighbourhoods, largely porous spaces open to the public. There is something particularly affronting to the British sensibility about these spaces, premised as they are on the ability to pay for heightened security.

As we have seen, the earlier attempt at gating the West End in the nineteenth century provoked a popular reaction that resulted in the barriers being removed. In many ways this was both a practical as well as a class-based antagonism, since the denial of access to certain squares and streets increased journey times for the general public. The triumphs of well over a hundred years ago have, however, simply been displaced by a series of contemporary gated suburbs. These new elite neighbourhoods have become the means by which a cocooned and faint presence in and beyond the city is maintained by many of the wealthy. Gated communities also offer the opportunity to bring the resources of affluent households together, producing a securityscape and leisure space that rivals the provisions of the world outside. The larger of these developments have almost sufficient facilities to secede – sports facilities, shops, health centres, restaurants and bars.

Gated communities have become more ordinary and everyday aspects of a city that has historically prized its openness and social diversity. There are of course many gated developments and private streets in Knightsbridge and South Kensington, but other examples can be found, such as the conversion of the former Tate mansion, built on sugar money in 1874, next to Streatham Common. Some of these changes are driven by a fear of crime or plans to design it out. But gating is also born of a desire to protect second homes or residences from which owners may often be away for long periods of time. These patterns fit with what many observers identify as the desire for displays of prestige emblazoned onto the residential landscape – a lord of the manor syndrome, rescaled to fit the executive home developments in many of the rural-urban fringes of the city. Thus gating fits into a broader pattern of residential development in which buyers work hard to achieve a sense of privacy while outwardly displaying their inaccessibility. Of course, in many cases these efforts only succeed in generating further interest in who is resident, how to get in and what riches might be available if entry could be gained.

Why are these kinds of developments appearing in a city with one of the lowest crime rates globally for a city of its size? Much of what is at work here connects with the desire to present a public-oriented facade of the kind that Deyan Sudjic has called 'the Edifice Complex', whereby the self projects to the outside world an image of prestige and inaccessibility.[2] Also at work are deeply ingrained fears that, while the city itself may be safe, burglary remains a real possibility, as well as, for some individuals, the threat of organised criminal activity. Where security is seen as paramount, the retreat is both to the home and to largely hidden suburbs which offer a firebreak from contact with crime and social difference. Streets that were open are, over time, seeing again the installation of booms, then metal gates and cameras.

The resulting impression is of armed staff in fortified homes, within gated neighbourhoods – a kind of Matryoshka doll of nested security arrangements devised in order to maintain a significant distance from and control over contact with the outside world. In some of the larger gated estates there are even subdivisions with further gated communities within them. The days of rock stars buying a pad in St Georges Hill are long gone, replaced by a more private, status-conscious and often fearful class occupying a paranoid landscape. Today it is the rich who build the barricades.

By 2018 the dream of endless capital investment in the city had soured. The turmoil generated by the agonies of the Brexit deliberations was one factor, but another was the series of stories about money laundering and the attempted assassinations of former KGB staff by foreign agents. For a time there was fresh momentum for action against laundering as concerns about criminality became entwined with a wider geopolitical angst. The Litvinenko assassination (a dose of poison administered via a cup of tea in the Millennium Hotel on Grosvenor Square) and the Skripal case in Salisbury are only the most well-known of a string of cases of overt or suspected murder by the Russian state on British soil. It has been estimated that the Skripal attack was likely the fourteenth of its kind, most of which have occurred in London (a further nine high-profile cases have been recorded around the world since 2016). The attack soon led to a Foreign Affairs Committee hearing at which a string of investigative journalists laid bare the feudal workings of Russia's oligarchy, the sloshing of illicit wealth in the London property market, and the so far futile attempts at dealing with these issues.

Litvinenko's billionaire friend Boris Berezovsky had apparently committed suicide in a small estate near Ascot, but his friends believed assassination was the more plausible explanation. Berezovsky himself had occupied a Surrey mansion fitted with security cameras, bullet-proof windows and reinforced steel doors. Associates of some oligarchs have also been victims of suspected assassinations, notable examples including that of the property developer Scot Young, who may have been thrown onto the railings below his Montagu Square apartment, and deal-broker Stephen Curtis, whose helicopter crashed on its way to his castle near Dorchester.

Where did the Skripal case take us? Perhaps most of all to a very dark and unsettling world in which assassinations across national boundaries were continuing, in which an impression of living of a safe life could be easily overturned. Perhaps also to the impression that life at the top is sometimes lived in a more or less lawless state. The stories of attacks on Russians in London go beyond the protagonists, yielding the sense of an anarchic space in which key actors use private security in lieu of the general inadequacies of British security. The message seems to be, we need to look after ourselves. Traction on laundering in general and Russian money in particular proved to be a short-lived thing, and the destabilising impact of criminal capital on the city has largely continued.

The effect of Russian nationals on the ambience of some neighbourhoods has been notable. Longer-term residents in some of the alphahoods now complain that new residents who bring guards or security details have minimal interaction with their neighbours. But they also raise concerns that the overt security measures might bring risks. The Russian cases highlight the fact that the rich can be a vulnerable group, as their wealth brings unwanted attention. What some see as paranoia others see as essential and necessary preparedness.

The Litvinenko and Berezovsky cases feed both myths and real fears among ex-patriot communities, who note the reach of foreign agents and the inability of local police forces to resolve matters relating to key trading partners as well as international bullies. More broadly, the impression of an overlapping of underworld and upperworld periodically arises, often through court cases as well as newspaper reports. When the Candy brothers were recently involved in a court hearing, one of the things revealed was their fear of falling victim to the schemes of kidnappers. One of their associates, an accountant, had suffered serious injuries when armed men broke into his property; he jumped out of a first floor window and fell down a ravine outside, breaking his spine.

The principle by which more layers of security and technology must be added only brings more and more areas into this defensive landscape. Money appears to drive the construction of a hostile, uncanny and, in many cases, unnecessarily protected streetscape. Beyond the entrance halls with timed releases of subtle perfumes, the dining rooms with ambient lighting, the personal cinemas and cigar rooms there is the sense that this excess is built on unfair gains and, in some cases, on criminal enterprises. The world of finance from which so much wealth has been generated is frequently revealed as a world of malpractice in which the system is gamed by clever financiers, a world built on the use of offshore funds to evade or avoid local taxes. It takes a degree of psychic armouring to deflect the kind of public anger now being directed at the rich, anger which is regularly given new vigour by newly leaked papers or investigative journalism. All of this may give us the sense that the security arrangements of the super-rich are connected, to varying degrees, to a shadowy world of intermediaries, threatening agents and illegal practices.

Money power has transformed many parts of the city according to a more or less sterile vision of sociability, security and partial residence. Yet this panorama is also strangely cloaked – few have cause to visit these districts and even fewer to build connections with their residents. Nevertheless, their effect is to create an unsettling and often hostile ambience and the loss of open access and walkability. Many longer-term residents decry the extent and speed of these changes and lament the loss of a more comfortable, open and cohesive form of community that now appears eclipsed by the more privatised modes of living of the American, Russian and other foreign nationals who buy many of the larger and more secured homes in these areas. Here the kind of urban planning once used to create fine districts while undermining the working class's capacity for revolt is put into reverse in a new anti-urbanism. Now we find an invisible revolt of the elites – a kind of insurrection physically expressed through the barricades erected in defence of the anti-urban zones of the super-affluent.

The alphahoods of the city have been secured to meet the uncompromising demands of the wealthy. But we have also seen how their paranoia is in many ways a latent aspect of alpha life, a fear of something that in the vast majority of cases does not and will not happen. This fear is a variegated thing, particularly in relation to the different national groups, but the effect nevertheless is a super-securitised landscape in which the gains to the few give rise to feelings of distrust and anger on the part of the many. The paradox of alphahood security is that despite its regressive impacts on the city, it still continues to offer the appearance of a more or less open, cosmopolitan and safe city. These qualities, as we have seen, form the basis of London's long-standing attraction for those originating from the globe's more insecure and damaged regions.

But we can also understand security as an essential requirement of those involved in or vulnerable to criminal and para-criminal activity, who are by necessity determined to protect themselves from state and regulatory agencies as well as competing criminal actors. Some of the most unsettling aspects of the landscape we have surveyed in this chapter relate to Russian and related networks as they have sought to protect themselves. The notable cases have thrown a spotlight on murky activities and generated the sense that little can be done to counter determined efforts to attack targeted individuals. But these cases and the defensive repertoires employed do have a deeper and wider effect on the feel and operation of the city.

The use of overt security measures including street-level guards and security details creates the impression of a simultaneously securitised but also vulnerable zone within which wealthy individuals feel the need to bunker themselves. This is not a cityscape of open pathways, cohesive neighbourhoods or happy communities. As one architectural critic once said, form follows fear, and this is certainly true of the residential landscape that has developed in the alpha city in recent years.

Life Below

The decision to convert two of the most symbolic tower blocks in London from local authority to private residences is a sign of how much the city has been set in service to the needs of capital and the rich. The idea that there is no money left, and that therefore any public assets must be sold to the rich, or converted for use by them, is highlighted by the example of Balfron Tower in the east of the city, or in high priced sales of former council flats in Trellick Tower in the west. Both buildings were designed by the architect Ernö Goldfinger as public housing, rather than as the affluent lairs they are soon to become. In the absence of sufficient state support, the most profitable use for such spaces becomes the sale of high-quality apartments to the well-off – social housing appears unwork-able under a dwindling financial regime, compromised by the waiting users and cash streams that can so easily be found. The fate of these towers, motifs of the desire to tackle housing need in the socially equalising post-war years, and their subsequent decanting of tenants to make way for rich buyers, say much about the state of the city today.

While inequality has become a pivotal political issue, con-cerns about poverty and lack of opportunity barely register on the social radars of the rich. Life below has become a kind of urban hell, while the wealthy continue to extract ever-greater resources and enjoy easy lifestyles. To be sure, an urban under-world exists. It is made up of renters, precarious workers, marginalised young people and the diverse multitude who rely upon rapidly withering public services. For the most part, the rich and their enablers don't notice the extensive hardship of those they share the city with.

Most people see or experience difficulties around them. Daily media coverage, political and community groups, myriad academic surveys, and the political machinery of the city remain entangled in debates about how poverty, exclusion and inequality remain enduring features of urban life. These issues are well understood, and inequality and poverty can be found in abundance in other alpha cities whose economies are defined by the presence of large financial sectors and wealthy populations. Yet the gritty realities of city life remain concealed from the wealthy themselves in a kind of urban theatre whose curtains, entrances, exits and trapdoors enable insulated worldviews shielded from social suffering. In many ways the city structures and influences the imagination and mental world inhabited by the rich. In this context, arguments for reciprocity, common purpose or social cohesion break down – to make it is to escape such stifling bonds. How can an ethic of care be sustained among people who know nothing of scarcity and have no contact with those in need?

London is a city of gross inequalities. More than a quarter of its households live below the poverty line.[1] This stark figure is all the more alarming when we realise that half of all the wealth in the alpha city is held by the top 10 per cent of its residents. Since the global financial crisis, there has been a significant change in the way this inequality is understood by the city's elites. Capital has become so entwined in the alpha city's land market, its housing market and its politics, that this has not only overwhelmed but also obscured its many poorer residents. Capital, as flows of finance or of the bodies of the rich themselves, is doing something that we have not seen before.

It is well understood that the city is implicated in reproducing the divisions between rich and poor, but how has this malaise deepened alongside and as a result of the management of the alpha city? While the poor were supposedly once recognised and cared for by the city's elites via welfare and housing systems, the dismantling of these supports since the crisis has been enabled and fuelled by the alpha ascendency. Here London's receptivity to capital is hand in glove with the denigration of its poor and a shift in its social politics to one altogether more callous and uncaring. As a result, life below becomes more akin to the fate experienced by the Morlocks in H. G. Wells's *The Time Machine* or the sweating workers in the underworld beneath the streets of Fritz Lang's *Metropolis*. Such parallels are worth making because, while they may appear extreme, they sum up how many see and understand the contemporary city to operate. But the pursuit of the wealthy and capital forms part of a wider process that has significantly undermined the state's role in mediating the worst excesses and inequalities of an uber-capitalist city.

The gulf between the wealthy and the urban poor shows that, rather than becoming an advanced and enlightened metropolis, the London of today takes on the excesses and poverty of its Edwardian and Victorian counterpart but without the sense of social mission of those times. Few among the seriously wealthy see, and even fewer comprehend, the city of want and exclusion from opportunity that exists outside the alphahoods. Their social networks and locations structure and reinforce a worldview that sees poverty as unfortunate, inevitable or indeed as a threat.

To understand this disconnect between rich and ordinary citizens we must try to see how the life and physical fabric of the city conceals social distress, neutering what might otherwise be an imperative to confront and tackle these conditions. An integral part of this processing of people and places is the way in which the social problems of the city become an invisible substrate. This 'underlife' of the city occasionally surfaces in the form of people sleeping in the streets, or in news reports of homicides in the city's dangerous districts – close-by yet elsewhere, unknowable and happily avoidable.

Among the rich and their enablers, the goal of private enrichment without social benefit, including the continued side-lining of the city's working population, is increasingly evident. The direction of travel is ever further towards the creation of a private city in which land is chewed-over and fracked by capital, while the cost of providing essential services and infrastructure to citizens is reduced as far as is politically possible. While money appears as a measure of the city's success, it is also a force driving the displacement and diminished social futures of many in the city.

Un-homing the poor

Beyond the alphahoods exists a city of poverty, homelessness, revenge evictions, defunded state schools, displacement from gentrification, bedroom taxes on the poor and perpetually rising rents. Such a city becomes a kind of massive centrifuge, spinning out its dizzy and sickly poor to regional centres beyond its boundaries. Overcrowding, under-policing, cramped and delayed public transport mark the everyday experience of many. Yet it is to the question of housing that attention particularly falls, since it is in this domain that hardship is perhaps most evident. Indeed, the city's poor and stressed housing conditions more broadly appear to be linked to the plans made for accommodating the international wealthy and their cash.

Five hundred new towers are being devised for the rich, while over 100 council estates are marked for demolition to make way for more investable homes. The home is the pivot point around which daily urban life is organised; when domestic life becomes strained or is made impossible through demolition or prohibitive costs, everything else breaks down. This form of breakdown has become an increasingly pervasive element of alpha city life today. Yet as the city and its political and economic value system increasingly celebrates the home as a kind of investment, trophy or reserve currency these core functions are forgotten.

London's housing crisis is in many ways central to the questions of material inequality and human insecurity, generated by the switch towards finance capital and the rich. It is in the area of housing that we see most clearly the antagonism between capital and the needs of the city's workers. Of the 3.3 million households in London, around half own their own home, a quarter rent from a local authority or housing association, and the remaining quarter from a private landlord (the national averages are 63 per cent owner occupied, 19 per cent private rented, 17 per cent housing association and local authority). We could say London as a whole is pretty good at reserving a place for those on low and no incomes, but the geography is uneven and it is changing for the worse. In the city's alphahoods only around 4 per cent of households are in social housing, highlighting the stark contrast between these areas and the wider city.

One significant consequence of the political handling of the housing system is the condition of much housing and the insecurity of many of those in it. Private landlords, the bulk of them individual investors looking to make money from others, have grown substantially in number in recent years – millions of tenants effectively finance the pensions and investments of their landlords. This highlights an enduring problem in the political management of the housing market in which homeownership and landlordism have been encouraged and supported. This remains problematic for many in the city given that one in six homes in London falls below the decent homes standard, and this rises to a quarter in the private rented sector (15 per cent and 12 per cent for social rent and owner occupiers respectively, 2015 figures). Those renting from a landlord also tend to suffer overcrowding, which affects nearly one in six council tenants and close to one in ten private renters, while the figure for owner occupiers is only one in fifty (2 per cent).

Here the pressure points really start to show. The sense of predation extends beyond extortionate rents to multiplying stories of evictions by landlords angry at the temerity of tenants complaining about the condition or cost of their property. Such revenge evictions are an indicator not only of the depth of the housing crisis but also of the sense of power that comes with owning property in the city. Private landlords are responsible for nearly all of the attempts at eviction in London. Alongside stories of 'sex for rent' by predatory landlords we can see how vulnerability more generally runs along the fault lines of ownership and tenancy. To rent privately in the alpha city is to confront the sense of being a resource for others while facing perpetual insecurity and continually rising housing costs.

Economic planners and politicians might describe the city as a kind of super-efficient engine, allocating resources effectively and generating opportunities. But perhaps a more appropriate image might be that of a steam train. In housing, as in other areas of social need, the city operates as a sputtering contraption whose fuel and exhaust is the raw material of the very lives of its many vulnerable citizens. The property machine is, if nothing else, an excellent sorting mechanism for generating winners and losers. Some of the most obvious material injustices can be identified in relation to the way that market and public housing opportunities are distributed.

Public housing has been steadily sold off for the last forty years, but there is a growing sense that such sales amount to a cannibalisation of core housing resources. This is because many housing estates have been demolished to make way for market and 'affordable' housing. More than fifty have been disappeared through redevelopment in this way,[2] ushering capital into spaces reserved for those on low and no incomes precisely because markets persistently fail them. Such policies, often adopted in Labour-controlled boroughs as the only means of generating new homes in cash-strapped times, have resulted in transferring land assets to corporate and private investors.

The programme of estate demolition represents an absolute betrayal of the primary mission of public housing to provide a place for those on modest incomes in perpetuity. Dressed up in narratives of opportunity, community building and new futures for all, a massive programme of gentrification and household dislocation has been unleashed. Increasingly long waiting times for 'council' housing have been worsened by the sale to date of 300,000 (5 per cent of the national total) of such homes in London since 1981. Over the same period councils were only able to build 62,000 new homes, one for every five lost. Despite widespread criticism of the right to buy policy, it was reinvigorated in 2012 as discounts were further extended to encourage council tenants to buy. While some steps have been taken to encourage the construction of affordable housing, the ability of such programmes to defuse the perfect storm of low

Destruction, Then Creation

investment, the open courting of capital, and the interests of owners is extremely limited.

One of the most evident injustices in London's housing landscape today can be seen in the continued sale of council homes while the poor are kicked out and left without support. Many London councils have seen the contentious sale of homes that have then simply been flipped into more profitable use by incoming private landlords – capital enters and gains as the state graciously defers to it and exits. One result of right to buy and the hunger for investment property in the city has been that many homes sold to tenants at discounts have then been sold on to landlord buyers – including wealthy Conservative MPs.

Around a sixth of London homes sold under the right to buy scheme are now rented privately, 54,000 in total. Many of the tenants of these homes require housing benefit to cover the rental cost, yielding the perverse result that many London boroughs now underwrite the profits of private landlords to the tune of £22m each year.[3] Today a quarter of a million households languish on housing waiting lists, while around a third of those deemed to be homeless have been 'exported', either outside their home borough or to the regions – the London centrifuge spins ever faster while drawing in ever greater volumes of investor capital. In what might have seemed a fabricated story it was revealed that the typical waiting time for a council house in Barking and Dagenham, on the eastern edge of the city, now stood at fifty years.

Those seeking a private rented home face intense competition with other citizens, and, if they manage to find one, often a herculean struggle to hold on to it. The options for those pushed to the limits of the system have also been radically restricted. Reductions in eligibility for housing benefit for young people, and the imposition of a bedroom tax (reducing housing benefit for those with an 'unused' bedroom space), have prevented many from being able to remain in the city as rent levels have been capped and higher paid prospective tenants jostle for a place. While vacancy rates for some super-prime developments often sit at around 75 per cent, those trying to stay in rented housing are hit by measures intended to incentivise them to move out into a bear pit of a market that few will navigate successfully.

One result of such measures has of course been an increasing amount of homelessness, on the streets but, more often, concealed among friends and families or in temporary accommodation that offers a moving twilight zone for some 56,880 households in the city today (more than half of the total for England as a whole). The city now has more than eighty homeless hostels and record numbers of street homeless – around 8,855 rough sleepers in London every night (nearly a quarter of the UK total).[4]

Between a decent home and the street a new set of alternatives has emerged in response to the opportunity to gouge the city's vulnerable: temporary informal housing, consisting of small units described as 'beds in sheds', is provided by opportunistic owners acting as landlords renting out sheds, garages and hastily built structures. In 2017 it was conservatively estimated that there were around 6,000 such 'sheds' housing tens of thousands of desperate tenants. Unsurprisingly, this is seen by many in the alpha city not as a sign of the dog-eat-dog conditions at the city's ground level but rather as a problem of lost council tax revenues and the potential concealment of 'illegal' migrants. This kind of wilful misidentification of the root cause of London's evident housing problems is one of the more obvious examples of how a property-owning plutocracy manifests its views. Despite this, to many commentators, such problems highlight the degree to which the city now operates as a playground for capital, supplemented with aggressive measures that dispossess or leave many households vulnerable.

*

In 2019 it was revealed that the new Duke of Westminster was planning to demolish the Cundy Street and Walden House blocks of flats in Belgravia, where many tenants have lived for decades, in order to build the Cundy Street Quarter. Such examples highlight how naïve it is to think that the market provision of housing might be enough to address London's housing needs. In most new private developments there is no affordable or social housing, and where it is included, as is intended with Cundy Street, the maximisation of profit trumps social goals and needs. Even after social housing has been built it acts to sort the poor from wealthier residents. This can be seen in the clever segregation of low-income users by 'poor doors' or the boundaries used to prevent poorer residents from accessing play spaces or green areas. In any case, even housing described as affordable has been demonstrated by analysts to be well out of the reach of most citizens.

In the winter of 2018, the *Guardian* ran the first of several reports on new developments where the children of social housing tenants were unable to play with those of their immediate homeowner neighbours because the blocks had been built with segregated play spaces. Similar stories followed the attempt to rehouse some of the survivors of the Grenfell Tower fire in the Kensington Row luxury development, where apartments cost between £1.3m and £7.2m. Here the social housing tenants were forced to use an access door next to the bin storage. This emergency attempt at tackling human need had the effect of revealing deeper attitudes to social diversity as residents and commentators questioned why low-income tenants were being placed in such an expensive development. The inescapable reality is that a rising tide drowns those who cannot swim quickly enough to keep up with it. This wave of capital and investment in London has inflated housing costs while dictating that those on lower incomes should not be catered for – if you cannot afford it you should not be here.

The Heygate Estate in Southwark was one of fifty public estates identified by the elite estate agency Savills in a report for the Cameron-led coalition government.[5] The report made proposals for the demolition of 400,000 public homes. The rationale went that redeveloping these spaces could bring higher density, better urban design and for existing residents to be re-housed there. Yet Elephant Park, literally an empark-ment of the area akin to the removal of villages around many eighteenth-century aristocratic homes, would ultimately provide a scant seventy-four social rented flats after demol-ishing nearly 2,000; 500 flats would be 'affordable' under the definition of 80 per cent of market rate.

Taking a walk around areas like Elephant and Castle, home of the former Heygate Estate, after just a few years leads to a sense of disorientation. Massive changes are revealed among the new forest of tower blocks, re-routed roads, shops, bars and coffee shops. Established areas that provided for lower income citizens have become nascent alphahoods. In reality these are newly created places for capital investment, ushered in even by many of the city's apparently left-of-centre local authorities over the past decade or so. But before the wave fully crashes you could grab a cuppa in the café of the soon to be demolished Elephant and Castle shopping centre, one of a dwindling number of affordable options for the area's lower income residents.

Soon the erasure will be complete however, with the bingo hall one of the few services likely to be retained in the replace-ment shopping centre. Almost next door is a maquette of the new buildings that are about to re-make the area. Slightly nervous looking staff employed by the developer wait to fend-off irate questions from those about to be displaced from the public housing blocks nearby. It is an affecting experience walking an area where so many residents live on notice, soon to be removed in the name of housing that will be affordable only to those on high incomes. The section of the city that has already been lost here does not even have the ghost of a pres-ence, with most of its residents having been displaced to other parts of London or beyond its fringes.

It doesn't take a rocket scientist to do the social calculus – massive net losses here and in many other parts of the city where plans to build again reveal few or no opportunities for those living in housing that had been designed to deliver in perpetuity. To say this is unfair risks sounding simple, yet it is this and more – a social injustice wrought in the name of profit and a capital-led clearance at heart. In response to such ill-considered projects a lot has been said about state-sponsored gentrification in the alpha city, much of which has been carried out by local authorities, notably Labour councils, in coalition with developers. Some commentators, tired of stories of displacement by affluent in-migrants, suggest the story has somehow been told too often. This rather misses the point that these processes continue to impact on tens of thousands in the city and will do so for many years to come. Gentrification has moved from being a localised neighbourhood phenomenon touching just a few areas of London in the 1960s to a massed flood of capital whose path has been paved by local authorities and central government planning rules.

There is something to the idea that this has happened because all of the areas that were ripe for being gentrified have come and gone; new sites must be found to feed the machine. For capital to grow new spaces are needed, like that at Nine Elms, or old, as with the cannibalisation of existing public housing neighbourhoods. This search to maintain profits has underpinned new plans while gifting new opportunities to the property sector. Cameron's plan to knock down and start again in 100 sink estates was premised on the image of a city with pockets of immorality and danger that could be swiftly erased and rejuvenated by letting capital rip through these spaces. This plan alone was credited with the loss of 7,000 socially rented homes. Such plans have revealed how representatives of capital, along with estate agents and politicians, became the means by which wealth influenced the development process, mediated by the development sector and local authorities who were either unwilling or unable to wring more from the changes for poorer communities.

The outcome of a single-minded focus on the poorest and most vulnerable areas has generated a catalogue of social distress. The number of people displaced by the lack of a right to return for tenants has been estimated at between 150,000 and 200,000 since 1997, with nearly 54,000 public dwellings demolished or slated for demolition still to come.[6] These figures are likely to be significant underestimates given the difficulty of locating and tracking those affected. Currently a further 118 sites are undergoing or facing regeneration and of these eighty are to be fully or partly demolished. This will involve a further net loss of around 8,000 public homes over the coming decade. The social injury involved in these transformations has been enormous; displaced tenants, tracked down by researchers, have talked of the stress of inappropriate and distant options provided for them or of mental health challenges and suicidal thoughts. New developments, like that at the Ebury Estate in Pimlico, have seen renewed resistance to plans for demolition. The weight of the evidence suggests that promises that tenants will be able to return after the creation of new and greater numbers of social and affordable units simply do not materialise as the interests of developers triumph those of social need.

Even the city's alphahoods have not been immune to gentrification. In some areas, the super-rich have come to compete with or supplant the merely rich – the switch in the economic profile of residents from poorer to richer can occur in Knightsbridge as much as it can in Peckham. Our hearts may bleed less for those with more resources, but the deeper issue remains vitally relevant to the city. If even the city's wealthy are being dislocated then something is badly wrong. What binds these disparate processes is the way that land markets operate as perpetual motion machines for capital, enabling inflows of capital and outflows of value by evacuating established residents to make way for new rounds of investment. Alliances

Rotten Borough

must be created and a stronger, cross-class consciousness developed in order to help people to see how nearly everyone is being screwed by the sale of the city to capital.

The ongoing gentrification of the city has involved a massive physical transformation comparable in scale to Napoleon's redesign of eighteenth-century Paris as a capital for his empire. London's plans, however, involve a more complex alliance between real estate, the state itself and investors – an empire of capital whose only commitment is to whatever re-making and social displacement might be required to extract future rounds of value for capital.

Perhaps the changes afoot are better described as a kind of logic or imperative, rather than a plan as such. Instead of the micro-level and organic changes that yielded the new ciabatta zones of Islington or super-hip Notting Hill we now see district planning targeted at the areas where the state can act as a coordinating agent in terms of its own public housing. Combined with austerity, scant opportunity, and changes to welfare conditions, means that the city's poor and those on low and moderate incomes face a bleak future. In spite of this, many of the estate renewal packages that removed thousands are proclaimed as great opportunities for London and its communities.

The accelerating death of the public city

One key symbol of the decline in living standards for London's 99 per cent has been the transformation of its high-rise buildings from being places accommodating those on modest and low incomes to being the homes of the rich. But this is only one element of a broader set of transformations in the city that speak of a continuing privatisation and loss of social support. Today even many of the streets of the city are now privately owned. In 2017 the *Guardian* was able to plot more than fifty public spaces in which private landowners and security staff now owned and controlled the streetscape at ground level. These revelations generated significant anger and exasperation at the kinds of changes sweeping through London. The public city, with its infrastructures and institutions that so many citizens rely on, now faces an enormous, perhaps irreversible, set of challenges. The idea of a beneficent and provident state is increasingly seen as a kind of anachronism. The logic of the market and its efficiencies is trumpeted while, in reality, public resources and assets are diverted or effectively gifted to private pockets and providers.

The urban world of communities, public services and mutual support is straining, falling apart in many cases. The death of the public city has been brought on by a regime of political and private interests that have marketised, defunded, privatised, demolished, repaved and displaced in order to cut a path for capital. Those who have the misfortune to be in some way reliant on social support face enormous challenges or the prospect of simply trying to get out. Yet it remains the case that many forms of social support are provided to and needed by the absolute bulk of the alpha city's population, covering all those institutions reliant on public funding and infrastructures of one kind or another – police, roads, fire service, schools, hospitals, social care providers, libraries, care homes and so on. The parlous state of this shared world is evident to all, but the deeper risks of not offering a more inclusive future are not.

The city is now the site of a fading form of citizenship which now hangs by a thread. The austerity cuts since 2010 that have stripped social support to the bone have also enabled a kind of clarity in terms of how we understand the internal workings of the city, the way that it so evidently operates in favour of capital while supporting those in need as cheaply as possible. The cuts enacted during the rise of the alpha city have further enabled the killing of the public city, the loss of the municipal and the shared. Exhortations addressed to those who have least to muck in together, by politicians who can retreat to the home counties or a *pied-à-terre*, highlight the rationale that lies behind the changes afoot – sort it out, we are off. Outside the alphahoods, ideas of a right to the city, to its support, to safety, to health and to learning are becoming subject to negotiation.

London is in essence a more private city than it has been for many years. This exclusivity does not operate only in the sense of gated squares reserved for the rich or the absence of state provision. The situation is of course more subtle than the proposition that the city is purely for the rich. Rather what we see is the increasing sense that the city and its administration works for wealth and the wealthy. So what's new, you may say. What is at least partially new is the very particular meanness of the situation, the sense that the massive new round of wins by the wealthy elite has not yielded wider benefits for the city, and that those few who have benefited do not care about its inability to spread its prosperity in a more just and diffuse way. The progressive social gains wrested in the post-war period (in the areas of health, education and housing) have been all too quickly undermined by the application of market mechanisms and the denigration of those who require support.

When London councils regenerated slum housing in the city in the post-war period, the role of the state was one that would bring investment, improved living conditions and stronger communities. Now the meat axes wielded by planners and developers simply cut away the communities that had managed to find a place in those spaces from when they were newly built. The vision of the city offered by government and corporate players offers little that is socially inclusive or progressive. Instead we see a large number of local authorities struggling to identify their role in the absence of sufficient government funding and with an increasing competition for globally footloose capital: austerity makes a fine beggar of the city, and when bad times come the rich get what they want. If there is an underlying vision, it is that of following whatever pathway leads to the money. It is this search that comes to define what is best for the city and the course required to achieve it.

To really understand the alpha city as a unique place where the rich are abundant and inequalities thrive, we must grasp the way it is both nested within and benefits from the global economy. The deep connectivity of the city to other places and to larger and powerful forces, drives its distinctive local social and physical form. It is what makes London London, and indeed what makes it an alpha city. As we have seen, however, this distinctive constellation, with the market as its most cherished organising principle, generates longstanding divisions, social conflicts and scarcity among its losers. And without welfare safety nets, social support and adequate public services, those losers are further beaten down or excluded even further.

Large sections of the alpha city's citizenry are now denied the palpable benefits that a finance and real estate urban economy might deliver. World-city status rings hollow for many of its residents, yet its connections generate a distinctive culture and related assumptions about how the city can be used to the maximum benefit of capital. This market focus comes at the cost of turning a blind eye to the needs of communities and those in need. A daily phantasmagoria of news dispatches highlights how bad the city has become at providing decent work, education, health and personal safety for many of its own citizens. It now has the worst income inequality of the UK regions, high rates of poverty even among its working citizens, and spectacular levels of grievous injury and lethal violence in many communities, all occurring alongside the increasing unhoming of the city's less well-off households.

Many alpha citizens have been deeply affected and damaged by the long drift towards the city's hollow global pre-eminence. One of the clearest signs that something has gone wrong can be seen in Trussell Trust data which showed that 166,000 three-day food bundles were given out in the last year – but this was from only one such provider of food aid, and there are now more than seventy food banks scattered across the city. Commentators point to the Dickensian conditions implied by such services. Despite this, cold-hearted politicians continue to defend the austerity cuts that have led to the need for such services. There is an increasing devastation being wrought upon the city reliant on public spending.

The loss of this public city can also be measured by the closure of core key facilities and amenities. This includes the roughly twenty public swimming pools lost in the past decade, many sold to developers; the closure of libraries (more than fifty across the city) and playing fields (fifty-four lost in the period 2009–18); and the loss also of thirty hospitals and several care home sites, most of which were also sold to private developers. The continued sale of public land by the state, local authorities and land-holding public institutions such as hospital trusts continues, providing temporary cash windfalls on a path to the apparent eventual removal of all forms of public provision.

Another indicator of social stress can be seen in the quarter of secondary school pupils who are now eligible for free school meals. Furthermore, the classroom has often become a place of contention rather than education. The average teacher in inner London lasts less than five years after completing their training, highlighting the stressed conditions within them. Core areas like social and youth support services have been notoriously affected by public funding cuts. In the wake of the significant rioting of 2011, the number of youth clubs in the city was halved before the decade was over. All of this raises an urgent question: how can younger, poorer, elderly, sick and minority groups survive in the alpha city?

Perhaps the clearest sign of the move away from the city as a social space is the spectacular rise of violence. Aside from debates about the role of music and social media, the core issue is the relationship between the changing political management of the economy and its tendency to create social conditions that generate higher rates of aggression and violence. The decline in support for conditions that ensure stable homes, good jobs, schools, and strong forms of family and community life comes at a terrible longer-term cost. A decade of cuts alongside a wilful lack of understanding of these social conditions has made many in the city less safe, while many young men are either exposed to potentially lethal violence or become caught up in it. A drug trade, much of it exported to middle-class communities in other parts of the city and beyond, has galvanised gang identity around turf and territory, alongside an increasingly hardened youth masculinity.

The wider changes cementing these problems come in the form of social and mainstream media that reinforce materialistic values and a search for respect through aggressive codes of conduct (which ironically connects many disadvantaged young men to their assertive alpha counterparts in the City). London's violence also increased at the same time as the austerity cuts hit law enforcement. But violent robberies were not escalating simply because street-level policing was increasingly absent;

it was primarily happening because of a collapse in the social core of the city that was simultaneously being filled by ideas of notoriety, the lure of easy and abundant cash and displays of male bravado on social media. What did matter about the fall in police numbers was that the capacity to respond, prevent, detect and reassure was radically constrained. These functions have of course suffered heavily under the massive cuts, with policing often reduced to an emergency response model that only distances police officers further from the communities they need to support them. In 2018 there were only 3.3 police officers per 100,000 people in the city, where eight years earlier it had been 4.1. The Metropolitan police force dropped in size by 40 per cent over this period, reaching its lowest strength for twenty years at 31,390 officers. Meanwhile, the steadily rising numbers of those injured in knife attacks stood at 4,700 in 2018, a rise of more than a third on the figure a decade earlier.[7]

In numerous ways the alpha city has brought with it a much deeper malaise by coordinating a collapse in support for those in poverty and those reliant on state functions more broadly. The orientation to rivers of prospective gold has stripped the social city, leaving an essentially anomic space. This means that those key social institutions needed to guide and maintain lives now struggle and are able to offer little in the way of a legitimate narrative that has widespread buy-in. The wider population thus drifts without a sense of direction or a future, particularly in relation to housing. The slow crushing of social bonds and opportunities brings with it a rising enmity within the population, an anger without an object to focus it on – raw material for a more populist politics to exploit perhaps. This is the inevitable outcome of a statecraft that pursues a vision of the economy detached from the idea that such activity should ultimately be in service to the social domain.

Without a more effective rationale the legitimacy of expanding inequality cannot be justified, yet we may well continue to wonder how much wider this gulf can be made to yawn. The powder keg of underlying social conditions seems assured by the sense of stress and grievance that many now feel – a depressive discontentment with the kind of future being mapped out in glass and chrome around us. Despite this, the city continues to support measures that advantage its well-off without seeing or recognising the profound social consequences in the city around them.

Cuts don't *cause* community violence, but the loss of core funding lays bare the institutional and communal structures that gave young people a sense of recognition, support and a future. Few people apart from the really wealthy will be able to fully protect themselves from the wider costs of these social conditions, as street robbery and anti-social behaviour further spill into gentrified and traditional middle-class areas of the city. Stories of mob robberies of wealthy footballers and the adoption of group tactics in burglaries may presage a more worrying future trend in this respect. Of course, this broadening of the negative impacts of an unequal urbanism may yet generate the seeds of social reform. For now though, the city's middle classes and the poorest bear the brunt of the social crisis, and few except the rich are immune from the deeper ambience of insecurity that pervades large sections of the city.

Highest and best

How can we begin to understand a city machine whose politics and economy are so increasingly adapted to markets as their dirty fuel? One way to develop the necessary mechanical knowledge would be to recognise the centrality of the housing market. This centrality is not simply about house prices, homeowners, estate agents, developers and taxes – the logic of property and market gain is hardwired into the culture of the city and the dispositions of those who inhabit the world of real estate. What this means in practice is that an unassailable logic of highest and best use is lodged very deeply in the minds of those running, planning and profiting from the city. What place for social housing when more expensive homes could be developed? What prospect for the poor when they live in areas where house prices are now among the highest on the planet? What place for principles of social diversity or cohesion when a buck can be made? So it comes to be that property under-scores the functioning of the local economy while undermining arguments for retaining and providing for the public city.

The property economy includes homeowners seeking increases in the value of their homes, estate agents taking com-missions on sales, developers building to sell, landlords (many of them individuals) letting out houses or rooms, and politi-cians seeking to stage manage this property-based economy. This is an encompassing phenomenon, as other forms of eco-nomic activity have been squeezed out of the city or killed off entirely in the regional hinterlands. And it feeds a deeper set of assumptions: that all decisions regarding development should be dictated by the pursuit of the highest and best use of property or a piece of land. This matters hugely because the embedding of these values in the mentalities of urban managers (planners, developers and so on) comes to subordinate social and community needs to the pursuit of profit.

The principle of social diversity in neighbourhood plan-ning has been challenged by the triumph of land and housing market values as the primary means of assessing social value – it is good for the community if money can be made because this represents investment. But it does not take a huge leap of imagination to understand how narrowly the idea of commu-nity is being framed here. Without some kind of intervention, we will continue to get the kind of monoculture that is already taking over many parts of the city. Rising prices and rents block opportunities for younger and key workers, leading to extended commuting times and businesses struggling to find workers. In other words, markets will tend to benefit certain sections of the capital machine over others – good for the property sector, bad for those running outfits that employ or make things. The machine has different components and these are by no means fully in harmony with each other. Meanwhile low income households are progressively sieved out of the city through the unchecked operation of the housing market and lack of public housing. This is a clear social injustice, something that can be linked to the apparent gains to the national economy from the finance sector, which ultimately appears more like a curse on the city and a boon to a select few than it does a nest egg for this and future generations.

We either believe in the principle that all in the city have a right to it or not. The attachment to profits over people has resulted in the kind of proposals to destroy entire communities that have wracked many of the larger estates described by David Cameron as sink estates. This defamation of the weak in powerful political narratives has been an important part of the methods used to unseat the urban poor, and has helped capital by appearing to clinch the argument that new investment will create better places and, hey, even the people originally living there can return. But in reality this apparently happy possibility of redeveloping places for all has not happened – plans to rebuild public housing have proved to be an illusion conjured in order to help push such proposals through.

The new primal law of the alpha city is that if significant money can be made from the erasure, construction or sale of property or land then this must be applied to any area of the city. The role of affordable and public housing in this context becomes deeply problematic and compromised. Suggest to a developer that, say, 5 per cent of housing on a new prime site could be allocated to social housing and look at the expression on their face; it isn't pretty. Worse is the fact that this market logic is underwritten by lawyers and planning consultants who fight hard to justify the lack of contribution to social objectives, part of an entire machinery devoted to the denial of social need in the city. This denial comes in various forms, such as arguing that any provision of affordable housing would damage the value of other homes being sold, or that the high cost of maintenance fees in the development would prevent lower income residents from living there – put it somewhere else, don't put it in at all if possible.

Housing is now used for capital and wealth accumulation more than it is for ensuring we are all comfortably and safely accommodated. This outcome appears either as self-evident fact or depressing reality depending on your politics, relative wealth and probably on whether you own your own home or rent it. Whether a city run according to these principles is ultimately worth living in for the bulk of its inhabitants is rarely considered. The excitement, energy, diversity and possibilities of life in London (and indeed Berlin, Paris, New York) perhaps two or three decades ago is something to be slowly mourned and forgotten, while claiming that the new chunks of super-prime real estate, increased philanthropic patronage of the arts and better coffee are signs of urban vitality.

If you ask someone whether they want no new homes, or new homes that they will not be able to afford, the falseness of this choice is immediately apparent, yet this is precisely the logic that has undergirded much of the shallow renaissance of large parts of the city. Many commentators have argued that without wealthy investors many of the new developments would not have been produced. This is a bit like being given a cake and then watching someone else eat it. Inevitably the argument is made that increasing supply will help offset prices and bring new opportunities. But London is not a closed system; it is, as we have seen, very much an international market and an investment market in nature. This means that without some restrictive covenant on use or purchase, assets can easily be snapped up by capital. Much of the foreign investment that has hoovered up the high-rise and other developments in the city's alphahoods is identified as a boon to the city by some, but it is not clear who or what is benefiting from this activity. Similar claims underwrite the estate demolitions as well as the socially regressive attitudes among the enabling class who deem the city's poor an expendable opportunity rather than part of the citizenry of the city – I work hard, why do they get to live here for free… Of course the reality is that 'they' work incredibly hard too.

Perhaps the main role of the less well-off is to help create areas that become ripe for capital investment once they have been displaced. Massive hikes in land values over the last decade have also incentivised many *social* housing providers to sell up, arguing that offering such housing in other locations retains their mission. A side effect of such strategic decisions is that these sales come to benefit private developers, to the utter dismay of those looking for housing options in a hot housing market that seems only to incinerate the ambitions of poorer working households.

We can approach the housing crisis by looking at questions of cost, availability, crowding and quality, but we cannot understand these questions in isolation from what has happened at the top of the market and to those who govern and orchestrate that market. The housing market is overseen by the local and central state, which are themselves shaped by enormous vested interests in the form of the developers, bankers, lawyers, real estate agents and financiers who profit from the creation and sale of homes.

Digging below the superficial differences, many of the wealthy in the city's west have more in common with social renters in the city's east and south. Their situation is characterised by a sense of loss and disorientation as they feel less at home in a city so imprinted by wealth and the guiding role of money. This feeling is referred to by some as a kind of housing alienation in which many are now excluded from the core resources that they need in order to live any kind of meaningful existence.

One sign of the rise of anomie and alienation in the city, and perhaps the one most can easily relate to, is the loss of both social rented and owner-occupied housing, which have fallen by 8 per cent and 12 per cent respectively across the city over the past decade. Private renting now dominates many of the city's poorest areas, while AirBnb pits residential use against flexible and tourist uses for many homes. We have already seen that part of this story involves the sale of council housing to sitting tenants, alongside its frequent resale to private landlords. Another aspect of the sense that housing in the alpha city is disconnected from human need is the fast retreating possibility of ownership, particularly for the young and precariously employed. The very real problems in the private rental sector – dismal conditions, intrusive landlords and crushing costs – make ownership more attractive than ever at a time when its realisation appears ever more illusory.

So far, in order not to undermine the profits of builders and landlords, the government has simply thrown cash at more affluent buyers to help them buy new homes (even though this has simply helped inflate prices and drive developer profits). The Help to Buy scheme has already cost the government around £12bn, and has primarily operated as a subsidy to more affluent buyers, particularly so in London. All of this means that the real salvation lies not in a market let loose even further, but rather in the planning of genuinely affordable housing, either as private housing for owners or as secure public housing for rent. But this cannot happen when the market principles that benefit the existing constellation of property interests persist. Even here, however, there is tension as different factions of the capitalist class display contrasting interests – bodies lobbying for London business, for example, support more affordable housing so that they don't end up having to pay higher wages. On the other side, developers and real estate agents clamour for less regulation and lower property taxes to help keep the market going.

Another key factor underlying the widespread feeling of estrangement among residents from their city stems from the new kind of environment being produced – the many thousands of empty and under-occupied apartments bought by investors stand as symbols of a broken housing system and the creation of an increasingly unfair, almost Hobbesian society. In an alpha city it is easier to find a Brazilian billionaire to fund a phallic viewing platform in the shape of a flower stem (The Tulip, as it became known) than it is to retain desperately needed social housing.

One of the really stand-out features of the development sector over the past decade has been the steadfast meanness of the single-minded pursuit of profit above offering a more socially equitable legacy to the city. But this is of course what the private sector does if unchecked by government regulations, and to think otherwise is to imagine that the fox will not eat the chicken it carries across the river – the fox is not bad, it is just hardwired to be the predator it will always be.

Measures to ensure diversity in new developments are persistently challenged. For example, in the super-affluent borough of Kensington and Chelsea developers contributed 15 per cent of social rented or affordable homes across ninety-six schemes between 2010 and 2017. So-called viability assessments are an obvious sign of the way that injections of capital into the city have thwarted ambitions for the city to be inclusive. In line with the law of highest and best, many developers use these market assessments to offer exaggerated underestimates of profits so it can be shown to planning authorities that the inclusion of affordable housing or other community contributions would make a development unprofitable. Many developers have long been at this game, but local authorities have also been incredibly lax in policing these viability assessments. The overall result of this negotiation of contributions has effectively been a privatisation of the redevelopment of the city. Using 'tax efficient' vehicles and complex rules, these forms of investment have also been allowed to extract value without social contribution.

Victorian and Edwardian London saw enormous investments in infrastructure that benefited the city as a whole. This took the form of philanthropic housing, parks, the embankment of the Thames, new sewers and public spaces; later, the post-war city saw publicly orchestrated social housing construction. Today's waves of private investment appear only to dissolve the city's role in providing for all and in particular for those on low incomes. The question is how resources can be fairly unlocked to deal with a new crisis when the wealthy and their enablers appear to remain blind to the consequences of their policies.

The highest and best logic can be seen in operation as public land and institutions have been sold to private developers. Further evidence of the rise of the private city can be seen in the number of public resources that have been transformed into new real estate assets. Notable among these was the sale of the last state-run care home in Kensington, which was turned into a super-luxury variant named Auriens in Chelsea, and the sale of the Queen Mary Hospital site to become the future ultra-prime development Hampstead Gardens. The same process can also be seen at Barts Square – a scheme of 236 apartments, office, retail and restaurant space on land previously owned by Barts Hospital in the heart of the City. Countless examples are now given in forensic detail on numerous blogs, and the reports of activists documenting a death by a thousand cuts through sporadic sales of housing, land and buildings across the city.

These processes are often attributed to a lack of state resources, but it is equally clear that many local authorities have become willing partners in supporting speculative investment activity, and that this role is now tacitly understood to be part of their mandate in the leaner and meaner world of city politics today, one in which the rule of markets is understood to be the way things are. Whether the city has experienced boom or bust, not enough has been done to extract contributions from capital. While hay was being made and the sun was shining little was stored or invested in what was really needed. At least it might then have been possible to argue what a wonderful boon to all that international capital and the super-rich were for the city.

The politics of poverty in the alpha city

A city run to capture mercury-like flows of cash is unlikely to identify its mission as one of accommodating those on low incomes. Neither will ideas of welfare, education or healthcare appear as important. A 'highest and best' mentality is also one that thrives on notions of personal success and wealth as things that are won or wrested by the individual, not things to be shared or divided. The kind of politics that rests on such ideas likewise sees wealth as a private matter; indeed, it also sees public assets as a means of bolstering that wealth – ostensibly in the name of creating a better city while, in reality, promoting a land grab whose beneficiaries are the usual cast of the alpha city elite and shady offshore investors.

The extent to which many lives are laid bare and neglected is increasingly striking. A household on a low income would do better to move to Birmingham than eek it out on a high-rent flat in the East End. A prisoner leaving an institution is more likely perhaps to be looked after by the profits generated by sales of £70,000 video entry phones at Selfridges than they are by the probation service.

The needs of capital and the wealthy are second-guessed and engaged while the social city burns up under the heat generated by a financialised housing economy. It requires close inspection and the assembly of diverse sources and perspectives to appre-hend the deeper influence of these processes. But the result is a city that superficially appears to be thriving while covering up its deeper pathologies and the callous treatment of its less

Untenable Inequalities

fortunate citizens. Rather like the mostly empty first-class rail carriage on an otherwise packed commuting train, the benefit is restricted to a few users and, of course, those providing the premium service who can charge handsomely for it.

London has increasingly become more like Paris, shipping out its poor like human freight to suburban and regional centres, leading to charges of social cleansing. At the same time as these households are waiting to be rehoused, it is possible to purchase a single six-bedroom house in the city costing £200m.

The alpha city's decision makers do not wish to plan a future city for all. Such visions are truncated by a desire to be the city that pays its enablers well, a city of and for capital. Such a city can only thrive on these terms when less well-heeled neighbourhoods are made to disappear and when the voices of those within them are ultimately dismissed soon after being consulted. In this context, poverty, exclusion and desperation are understood to be rooted in a mass who choose not to engage in the city's abundance of opportunities, or cast as an inevitable feature of city life – the poor, like the rich, will always be with us.

Many who rely on public services and support have been left wanting and desperate as the cuts kicked in during the alpha decade. The result has been a kind of social decimation, enacted by a political elite that actively fosters the denial of its impact. This doubling down on what this elite sees as a kind of underclass has involved an attack on substandard living conditions that comes in the form, not of repair, but of removal. All capitalist cities inevitably generate inequalities and spatial divisions, but these problems have only been amplified by the coordinated raid on key assets of public life (urban, housing, health, education, law and policing).

The yawning gulf between conditions among the few and the many continues to be met by the claim that the cupboard is bare. The grand deceit of this position is highlighted all around by massive gains to capital, to corporations, to investors and to the rich themselves. London's wealthy and poor may be isolated from each other spatially, but they remain connected in other ways. Of course they share the same city, yet their citizenship is unevenly weighted as politics arbitrates continually in favour of capital and the wealthy.

An alpha city therefore needs to be understood as a distinctive and powerful conjunction of economic, social and political interests. It is a capitalist city in a capitalist global economy, and the logic of money, markets and finance binds these scales and forces. Today the city's position is tied to its place at the vanguard of a system whose logic and interests have helped the wealthy to capture fortunes by enabling an environment of low taxation and corporate freedoms, ignoring forms of tax avoidance, reducing tariffs and regulations and by making state systems (particularly in relation to urban and housing policies) work for capital. London is understood by the enabling class to dominate and benefit disproportionately from its role within this global capitalist economy. But the illusion of this advantage is felt within the concrete reality and daily routines of many in the city, particularly in those homes, communities and neighbourhoods which are now worth too much to be left to the poor as new rounds of displacement and clearance kick in.

The political domain and the kind of psychology shaped by the economic life of the city and its plush new landscapes have been fashioned and smoothed by the arguments of financiers and by business. In the process, the ultimate rationale of economic life, to serve human need, is lost from view among a sea of triumphal new skyscrapers. Whichever way you cut it the city is a confluence of powerful interests, bound to a political system based on a clandestine logic designed to enhance the take of the winners, while maintaining its losers as cheaply as possible. Seen in this way the city is a kind of extended Drones Club (for young and workless rich men, as described by P. G. Wodehouse in many novels) – an unproductive system, contributing little to the wider vitality of its communities while enabling a good life for the few that is closed to non-members. The ambition to form such a club can be seen in the former mayor Boris Johnson's talk of the rich as tax heroes, of the bundles of good things that would come as a result of attracting their investment (affordable housing, garden bridges and other white elephants), and the general pro-business bluster that disregarded the contribution of the working city below.

One response to the city's current problems has been to argue for even more open markets, freeports, lower taxes and deregulation so that investment can flow in and downward to benefit those languishing in the city. This is arguably insulting given the evidence showing that waves of deregulation have primarily benefited capital and those who wield it. The kind of pathology that emerges in such a city is the curse of an over-developed, politically dominating finance sector. The goose appearing to lay the golden eggs is in reality a significant drain on social resources in the city. A number can be attached to this curse, estimated at £4.5trn in costs to the British economy by its fixation on finance between 1995 and 2015.[8] The free-flowing oil of high finance and international capital investment brings with it burdens on citizens, such as rising housing costs to meet the demands and spending power of well-paid workers and managers in the finance economy, and of course the rich. This finance curse is ultimately an expression of the diversion of human activity in the economy towards methods and mechanisms that build value for the already wealthy while giving too little to the wider population. Yet, despite this, many believe that the city isn't working as best it might because it is not sufficiently open to investment. And post-Brexit, many political and corporate actors among the enablers have already suggested it will need to offer an even more pro-business, promoney environment to secure a viable economic future.

Interests and entitlements in the city have historically been framed around the idea of citizenship and the responsibility of the state to provide. What was powerful about the compact between the state, people working for a living, and the middle/upper classes was the tacit understanding that ultimately all would suffer if investment in public services and infrastructures was not maintained – from rising crime, poor health and social care, de-policing, pot-holed roads, and so on. Today the situation is not so simple, as the rise of an increasingly exclusive city generates a stronger defence of private provision as well as an evasion of the consequences of a withering or damaged public domain.

Worried about NHS hospitals? We don't use them. Crime? We live in a gated community. Standards and safety in statefunded schools? We don't use them either. In practice this situation of gross inequality and the stratified use of core services increasingly offered by market providers creates a kind of immunity, a form of social insulation among today's wealthy who do not feel that cutting social support will impact on their lives. The argument for social investment as the mainstay of progressive social thought is weakened by the spaces, institutions and systems of the alpha city. With the emergence of a more private city, problems become the preserve of the poor and those of moderate means. With money one can access a wide range of private services, including clubs of security in gated communities, clubs for private healthcare, for private policing, an archipelago of private-school providers, all stitched together by powerful and discreet mobility systems that skip over the shadow zones of the city containing its poorer and anxious citizens.

All of this breaks asunder the compact that was commonly expressed in the idea of citizenship entitlements and responsibilities. Market logic and accompanying austerity measures have ultimately created the conditions for an increasingly fatalistic social politics. Among those desperately worried about their future the question 'what instead?' is met with a shrug of the shoulders. Austerity has disciplined and made compliant many local authorities, social service providers, charities, arts organisations and urban communities. In this strained environment arguments are made in favour of rich philanthropists sometimes defending their money even if it comes from a morally dubious source. Meanwhile, those needing the support of state services find a hard shoulder, a locked door, or a bus to the north of England.

*

Is London really a kind of evil utopia of the rich in the way that this chapter suggests? Many will respond by saying, look, this city delivers, in spades. It employs hundreds of thousands in a finance sector that is one of the mainstays of the national and global economy. It is a cosmopolitan, vital city that offers opportunities for anyone prepared to engage. It is one of the best, most exciting, hyper-diverse, historically rich places, accommodating more than 8 million people, and many others want to be at this party. For many with a college degree and good family fortunes the city is indeed a place of opportunity, excitement, social engagement and diversity. From the window of a powerful car or the café at the Houses of Parliament it is indeed possible to see London as a place of opportunity, possibility and abundance. But this very construction, this perspective tinted in rose, is given form by the comfortable spaces inhabited by the city's most privileged elites. Such worldviews are the offspring of beautiful places and of people confident in the beneficence of the world around them.

Beneath this cossetted lifestyle another reality lies. Space and society intersect in this city in ways that allow the lives of the rich to appear benign when in actuality they help to unleash a kind of violence upon others in the city. These others include the quarter of the population living in poverty, the still present yet disappeared, holed up in low-grade rental accommodation, surviving defunded school environments or awaiting eviction by landlords. For many such people, London offers only a daily nightmare to be carefully navigated, mitigated where possible, and ultimately endured. This is the ignored but enduring kernel of city life that the rich and many of the elite will never see or understand.

Too Much

For more than a decade London has been a 'fuck you' city – the kind of metropolis built from class arrogance, bucket loads of capital and a lucky history of financial pre-eminence. Such a city appears to sit above all others. But this standing is not based on national power or military might. Instead it is founded upon the alpha city's centrality to the global, capitalist economy and its primary beneficiaries – an expanding wealth elite who command enormous influence as a result of their fortunes. The ambience of this city is pervaded with an air of aggressive confidence and a more general feeling of self-importance. These qualities are generated by being one of the greatest single concentrations of the world's rich, resulting in a maelstrom of investment activity and the good times that arrived with it. Yet in reality much of London's wealth is based upon its offering of a safe harbour to capital and the capitalist wealth elite in an increasingly destabilised world. The idea that city greatness can simply be measured by wealth rings hollow.

The construction of a city for the rich and their investments has occurred alongside a deep crisis in the social life of the city; wealth sits alongside poverty and exclusion. But the choices and actions of a compliant political, economic and real estate elite have also been an important factor in generating these outcomes, privileging property and money above all else. The gains of the alpha decade have been underwritten by the attractions of the city's history and culture, but also by attaching a monetary value to any asset or site that might bring a bob or two from footloose wealthy investors. In chasing the potential victory of being the number one city for the rich, London's achievement ultimately appears as a chimera.

The contemporary city is a vision of status without sight or recognition of social consequence, a place of glaring inequalities that no one at the top needs to care about. The place looks great to the extent that a significant social mass can simply be forgotten. The mission to attract wealth and the wealthy has become detached from the role of combating the enduring exclusion of many others in the city. The city's elites have appeared all too relaxed about excessive personal wealth, alongside the very real suffering of its poorer and, indeed, many among its middle classes.

How should we read such a city and can we begin to divine its future? London's mood since 2016 has been, perhaps temporarily, more sombre. Stellar house prices became merely stratospheric amid the instability generated by the unending Brexit deliberations. Expensive apartments took longer to sell and the prices of mansions were cut to attract buyers. Yet these falls were simply met with renewed interest from cash-rich buyers sensing bargains – there is always money out there, waiting for the right moment, the point at which the price is right.

The early days of the new national government highlighted that the past alpha decade may well be the model of the one to come. A celebration of the wealthy, low taxes, privacy and unfettered capital are its clear principles. The arrival of Brexit has been met with a sense of relief at some kind of stability. This stability and overt signals to investors have quickly restored interest in the city and revitalised sales at the top end of the property market as champagne corks fly in the elite real estate agencies. We seem to be back to business as usual as discussions about tax evasion and Russian influence on the Conservative party and general election are put on ice.

Meanwhile the schmoozing and interactions between the city's political and wealth elites suggest that much of what many found so abhorrent about the alpha city will become a resurgent feature of its management in the future. What some worried would be a low tax, low regulation city, necessitated by being located in a national economy pinned to finance capitalism, a kind of 'Singapore on Thames' model, appears to be precisely what is again taking shape.Where estate agents and developers suggested that falling prices might be indicators of an incipient city decline, it seems unlikely that 'beta' status will approach anytime soon. Despite the froth of some market signals and anxieties about the future, the fundamental structures of the alpha city's political and economic system remain intact – the city retains its role as an epicentre of global finance, its post-colonial position as the world's banker, and its more or less duty-free regime for the super-rich in a discreet business environment may help to assure this outcome.

Yet this, of course, is the problem! London's centrality, its sustained planning for growth based on finance and open borders for money, will help it retain its alpha position while the 'social' city and its public life continues to fade and struggle. London's locational advantages allows it to maintain a retinue of long-term wealthy residents and a liquid flow of cash from offshore locations, and it continues to be hugely attractive to overseas buyers and investors. While the sense of political crisis and austerity-driven ruin lie all around, architects and the wealthy elite's enablers continue to help build a city that offers a conduit to, and the very embodiment of, global capital.

If there is any sense of allegiance, it is to wherever the next pound will come from; a kind of nationalism defined by alignment to capital and capitalists, rather than by attachment to a state territory. The richest are supported by political enablers who increasingly act less for their own country and more in consideration of their retirement, or the revolving door between public service into private business.¹ Every choice and step becomes a move towards cashing out rather than to public service and common cause.

What does London mean to the rich? Experiences and motives clearly vary, but for many it is in multiple ways the best place to live, to consume and to be seen. Many still view the city as a place to cement social standing, while simultaneously being a centre that helps to process and expand personal wealth. Wealth has brought a subtle but deep-running force capable of remoulding the city's built landscapes while redrawing the parameters of what may be considered politically or ethically possible. The foreclosure of alternative ideas, driven by the dominance of market and finance principles has helped to deactivate a concern with the rest of us, encouraging a neglect of social investment and any measures that might create a fairer city. Principles of equity and social benefit are thrown out as those who mediate the power conferred by capital. Here money is seen as the primary metric by which success should be measured.

How can a city that produces such enormous inequalities be defended? How does it continue to enrol such wide support, even from some of those whom we might count as victims of a machine that delivers such skewed rewards? How indeed is criticism from dissenters faced down and diluted?

To answer these important questions we must look further than the enablers and the cheerleaders of the market to see how the sources of the city's success appear rather like a giant tap of capital, a faucet that should remain open and unimpeded if the city is to benefit. This apparent root of prosperity is often identified regardless of divisions between left and right; many on either side of that boundary understand that the society of the city and the cohesion of its communities are being washed away by this flow. But beyond the occasional complaint from city and local politicians lies a deeper and more aggressive logic – the compelling force by which money is simply understood as that which binds the urban economy together, the thing that there should always be more of.

London's elites understand that the economic vitality of the future city will be fundamentally tied to global flows of capital, whether licit or illegal. Many who cast themselves as economic realists will insist that, whether we like it or not, this is simply how it is. Those who seek to tax or intervene risk wrenching the tap shut. There is a common position espoused by the city's enablers and those seduced by the logic of money – that no one will benefit from turning off this flow. Yet in reality, the flow from this tap offers only selective irrigation, filling the bowls of the already wealthy and spilling over only to those operating the finance and real estate economy which dominate the city.

In his influential book *The Power Elite*, C. Wright Mills asked: 'The little cities look to the big cities, but where do the big cities look?' The biggest cities today, measured in terms of their raw economic power, can only look down perhaps with a degree of trepidation. Their fear of falling down the league tables, of losing wealth, only generates more arguments for keeping the tap open. Such fears compel city leaders and influencers to act like barbarians employing a winner-takes-all strategy, with the result that the public realm becomes a place to be plundered.

But do the rich capture the big cities, or do those cities seek to ensnare the rich? In many ways what some see as a kind of seizure by a class defined by wealth is, in reality, a kind of willing submission. The very tap itself is fashioned of the laws, political groups, finance wizards, enabling intermediaries and a shifting opportunistic political class. More than a set of clear rules, a constitution or a plan, it is formed of unspoken values and assumptions that comprise a model of how the world can work to advantage the already wealthy. Of course, some will say this is simply what capitalism is, that this is how it comes to be embodied in the winning cities around the world.

The alpha city is now characterised more by the purchase than the creation of great assets (whether these be galleries, museums, public spaces and infrastructure projects) by its wealthiest residents. Such purchases also include massive homes, major corporations and football clubs. The resulting culture of the city rests upon a distinctive mindset, one that is unquestioningly allied to the needs of capital. Here the idea of city capture operates via an urban system devised to guide, manage and attract money into this safest of harbours. But to understand that system and its consequences we need to dig a little deeper: we need the means to conjure a macroscopic impression of how this 'thing' fits together and works.

A better class of person

The rich see only beautiful places and people – extreme wealth brings with it a kind of tunnel vision that is blinkered to social consequences. The ebbing of social life that the city has seen over the past decade is more or less invisible to an alpha elite enclosed in a luminous world that puts all else into a darkened background. Being lifted into this world not only generates a sense of wealth and comfort, it also conceals all sight or sound of the pain that exists in the city beneath and beyond. A rising sense of anger among the multitude can be largely ignored by the few, or their moral outrage dissolved by the sedatives of occasional philanthropic crumbs.

Free-flowing wealth on the one hand; poverty, exclusion, desperation and violence on the other. This is the Janus-faced nature of the alpha city. Yet these two sides remain, ostensibly at least, connected by a political system that is supposed to mediate the excesses of capital and the losses to the social. Instead the political domain has become one of the key spaces through which the rich infect the rest of the city, validating the laws according to which winners take all, markets are

New Barricades of the Rich

freed and open competitions are offered to secure core social resources. This ethos is now widely seen as a self-evident good. Ideas of capital and markets have not simply been imposed by some all-powerful elite, they have come to colonise and influence newspaper editorials and comments sections and the minds of a large number in the city, both those in power and those who would like to be. Yet it is evident that wealth floats upward to those with the most, while stagnation and anxiety embitter the city's middle classes and shit rains down on those without.

The enabling class express hostility towards anything that might upset the foundations of the city's economy. Anger and indignation is frequently targeted at the usual bogeymen: any proposal to increase tax; any regulation that might be an impediment to trading conditions; and, inevitably, the crude straw man of 'socialism', regularly pulled out and then set on fire (some mention of the 1970s is often made at this point). This simplistic attitude splits the world into a good land of market freedoms and borderless capital flows and a bleak shackling of humanity and opportunity that would ensue were any attempt made at wresting more from capital and the wealthy. These ideas often underlie the lobbying efforts of powerful corporate interests and actors through political funding, gifts to politicians and planners, newspaper op-ed pieces and the funding of think tanks and reports. They also lie behind the offering of passports to rich investors without due attention, turning a blind eye to laundering, giving knighthoods to billionaire para criminals, facilitating the construction of towers and homes for investors, and offering a low tax and tariff finance and investment sector. Taken as a whole this is an industrial level of effort, a juggernaut of opinion formers and influencers set in motion to misdirect anything that might resist or upset the dominant economic narrative.

Political support for the rich and the economy that produces them has helped undergird a nitro-injected decade of fortune-building among the wealthy. This followed a global financial crisis that initially appeared to threaten those fortunes but which capital and politics quickly dealt with to the benefit of the elite, creating a mindset among many in the city that the rich and foreign investment would help to supply the tap of capital during this period of economic uncertainty. That uncertainty continues, but so does the view that the rich and offshore investors 'saved' the city and, indeed, will now help to insure its future. This line is still regularly trotted out without considering how the benefits of this apparent rescue were enormously selective and have done little or nothing to redress the decade of cuts and state withering that went alongside it. The only 'success' accrued to the same group of beneficiaries that have popped up throughout this book – the lawyers, advisers, lobbyists, think tanks, estate agents, wealth managers, corporate chiefs and politicians riding the wake generated by the rich.

One of the greatest mistakes made by some members of the political establishment has been their use of the presence of the wealthy as a yardstick by which to measure the city's success. If money is the measure then London is the best city in all the world... Yet this is ultimately an empty proposition. The alpha city is like the person who thinks a fat bank account, good clothes and the car he drives are not only symbols but proofs of success. This deficient logic shapes the culture of the city's movers and shakers, who owe their allegiance solely to flows of cash rather than to any idea of patronage, altruism or paternalism – values that once underpinned the legitimacy of the city's rich and powerful.

In 2012 the comedian Ross Noble led a fox hunt to the top of the Shard. This surreal chase was followed some years later by protests at the base of the tower by Class War, a group who suggested occupying the unsold, empty residences of the tallest tower block in the city. These apartments, like many other super-prime properties, could be seen lying empty at the same time that survivors of the Grenfell Tower disaster remained unhoused years after the tragedy, alongside many others home-less in the city. It would be too crude to suggest that the rich themselves are the architects of these awful juxtapositions. But what is increasingly clear is that wealth has yielded a city that operates as a kind of unfeeling and multiplying disaster zone for the poor and even for those on relatively good incomes. In seeking out the wealthy the enablers have helped create enor-mous inequalities, a city of two speeds in which green lights are granted to cash and the cashed-up and red lights for its poor and excluded.

Neoliberalism has empowered the powerful – helping to justify the sense that they are a floating class disconnected from social need or a sense of obligation to the cities and societies upon which they nevertheless rely. They are less citizens of nowhere and more destroyers of the idea of citizenship itself. Their relationship to place and society is frequently seen in contractual terms – expressed in instrumental links to others, to companies and capital, to the places where the returns are best, even in rights to citizenship that is simply purchased.

The neoliberal directive is to commit to markets and the idea of the unfettered individual. Such ideas blend well with the codes and lifestyles of the urban rich as they disconnect from city society and use their membership of nations, clubs and corporate vehicles to access preferential tax regimes, beautiful places and advantageous social networks. The lie that wealth is somehow self-made only underscores the principles of a gliding elite who touch down around the globe at those points of maximum advantage and where sufficient state largesse and tax incentives are offered. Yet, as Mills suggested, without their structural position in the economy or society, key members of the wealth elite are ultimately nothing. There is little that is intrinsic in the individual to explain their own rise and position when set against the talents of so many others around them.

A city that has long been wealthy now sees the wealthy taking and colonising its primary resources even further, while others are pressed by the property market and the absence of collectively provided services. But what is interesting in this is that the straining social contract generated by the city's inequalities has also become a concern among some of the city's wealthy enablers. Only a few years ago (2013) a senior financier wrote an op-ed in the *Financial Times* expressing anxiety at the massive increases in house values and the growing disconnect between a wealthy capital city and its poorer regions. The subtext: social cohesion is damaged by a global super-wealthy class who are driving the city ahead of the needs of the many losers in society. This feeling has been given further form by the inclusive capitalism movement. These vanguard causes appear to be trying to restore the legitimacy of capitalism itself by seeking to address the conditions of those at the bottom. It seems likely that these new moves by the privileged are ultimately efforts at diverting attention from the systemic roots of inequality.

Stagffluence

The hundreds of new towers, thousands of basements, water-front starchitecture, gated estates and new mansion blocks of the alpha city speak of a more hermetic wealth than the city has seen in the past. This is a more emphatically private wealth, born of a period of global excess rather than some local economic miracle, and even more detached from a sense of social or national contribution. While many of the rich who live in London love the city above all others, this can be a stifling form of affection – one that risks strangling the object it is attached to. Their money has a deadening influence over the city, a kind of plutocratic necrosis. Similar arguments have been made in relation to other cities and jurisdictions in which the pursuit of capital has led to the reduction of other economically productive sectors, such as San Francisco or Jersey among many others.[2]

Sure, London has the most billionaires, the most five-star hotels and the biggest finance sector, and is one of the largest beneficiaries of offshore tax evasion and organised criminal funding. But beneath this dazzling canopy of the city's economy and its high society there are massive social problems, as ordinary lives in the city are actively eroded by the lack of opportunity, punitive welfare regimes and stagnant housing opportunities generated by the political management of the economy in favour of the city's winners.

Many on the right will argue that these are unfortunate but disconnected outcomes: poverty is a regrettable but an ever-present problem, but the last thing you want to do is frighten footloose capital investors or the rich with talk of raising taxes because then what are you left with? To which some might reply: a fairer, more innovative and diverse economy, in which the wealthy pay their due. But no. We are often told by many enablers that the finance and property sectors are major boons to the urban and national economy. So we are compelled to ask an awkward question: Is this economic dynamo something that can really help float all boats or, as many now believe, an extractive set of industries, actors and elites that has sought only to make a profit for itself, evaded or avoided taxes, and used monopoly positions and low tax regimes as the means to make even more money?

The alpha city has been sufficiently agile to allow it to attract new rounds of winners from the global economy, making and breaking ground anew in order to realise the benefits from the flows of capital it is addicted to. Yet talk of a near-future crisis or the fleeing of capital should be treated cautiously – we need to take a longer term view than the one offered in the ebb and flow of monthly reports of sales of high-end homes or in panicked assessments of a potential exodus of the rich or bankers. Whether prices and sales rise or fall, the rich remain positioned to benefit, often holding a vested interest in the kinds of crisis conditions that yield temporarily depreciating prices. When we set aside feverish commentary the substance and structure of the city's position is more clearly revealed – a stable economy built around land, finance, rent and invest- ment, a city exemplifying global capitalist forces. Beyond this core of the urban economy we also need to understand how the culture and society of the city help to ensure that its alpha- hoods will always be the heartlands of large numbers of the world's wealthy – places where the rich want to be above all others, whether taxes rise or not.

This is the curious position of a city whose affluence has been counter-intuitively responsible for a broader social depression, that we might term 'stagffluence'. The city contin- ues to build and to embrace the dominance of its finance and property sectors. In the face of declining demand a zombie market in high-rise apartments persists, with 541 new tower blocks planned or underway, an acceleration of construction even under uncertain economic conditions.[3] Despite these developments appearing to suggest an economy firing on all cylinders, the reality is an underlying malaise – a growing number of the wealthy, a languishing middle class, and a large number of losers whose labour and spending helps to line the pockets of the few who own the city.

In the boom decade little was done to enable the wealthy and their investments to contribute to and benefit the wider city. Gains from development were neglected by weak or complicit national government and city boroughs, while the absence of a competing vision for the city's steroidal finan-cialised economy facilitated the creation of a beggar-takes-all approach to economic development and planning – rooted in the profound sense that attracting the rich and offshore invest-ment was the only possible game in town. As we look to the immediate future such a game seems even more likely to be set in place as a recipe for boosting the city's economy. This will involve the continued creation of a charming place to be if you are rich, while austerity and inequality will continue to scrape away at core services and to fuel inter-class tensions.

Now even the city's middle classes feel pinched and let down by those who seem to look after their own bank balances by chasing those of others. The result is a local politics charac-terised by the dawning realisation of just how unfeeling and damaging money can be – destroying homes, communities and green spaces in even the leafiest of neighbourhoods. Too late comes the understanding that the genie is out of the bottle, or that the cash is leaking out of the bag.

The idea that the wealthy make a disproportionate eco-nomic contribution to the city drives the defence of riches, according to which large numbers of taxi drivers, interior dec-orators, builders, estate agents, art galleries, bank staff and chauffeurs would go out of business without the patronage of the rich. But the contribution of the wealthy seems shakier when one walks past empty luxury monoliths, or when one sees social housing, old people's homes and hospital grounds being cleared to make way for super-priced housing. What the rich give with one hand is more than taken away by the other. That which is valued for its use comes to be destroyed because of its greater value in exchange.

Money not only has the power to corrupt people, it also tears up the unwritten mission statement of a city. London's story today, its alpha position, is experienced to varying degrees by many other cities around the world – including Vancouver, New York, San Francisco, Paris, Berlin, Lisbon, Amsterdam, Singapore, Tokyo, Hong Kong, Taipei, Melbourne, Sydney. We tacitly understand cities to be places of diversity in which all who inhabit them are accorded the same rights, the same access to services and a place to live regardless of their resources. This definition of citizenship is

Rent is Theft, The Tower

threatened by the secretion of market mechanisms into multi-plying aspects of daily life. Money represents a form of power that has the capacity to incentivise or destroy those lured or confronted by it. Many politicians, estate agents and those working in finance are animated by it more directly. But where does this ultimately get the city and those who call it home? If you are wealthy, or adopting a strategy to become wealthy, who cares as long as you are on the winning side?

London's alpha status is ultimately a mixed blessing, involving what has been described as the curse of finance. This is because, like those countries apparently blessed with natural resources such as oil, the gift of high finance brings with it large economic and social costs. In this sense, the 'best' places are also hostile spaces for lower paid citizens, even as the wealthy remain reliant on them. How far can we go before either the pips squeak or that they are simply crushed under this jugger-naut of excess? While many businesses are concerned that a lack of affordable housing leads to a demand for higher wages, for other sections of capital, notably some real estate agencies, some politicians and those working at the core of finance itself, the answer is more often – let it rip.

A decade ago, at the beginning of the alpha ascendency, Alain de Botton offered a somewhat cryptic warning in Knight Frank's 2009 World Wealth Report. He cited John Ruskin who had emphasised the need to celebrate life rather than the vacuous display of riches. De Botton was subtly suggesting that, when asked by an elite estate agency to discuss what real wealth means today that measures of money and property fail to capture the things of most worth to humanity. Today such sentiment seems lost in a culture that psychotically celebrates material gain.

Part of the reason for the staggering gains of the rich is the architecture of systems designed and structured to facili-tate the extraction of value through rents, low pay and other favourable macroeconomic conditions that allow the wealthy to proliferate. These folk may not be bad people, but personal assessments entirely miss the more substantial point – a system that produces such staggering and unjust disparities is problematic and requires rethinking. The city that is both the product and maker of such a system also needs significant re-evaluation even if such thoughts are unlikely to be prominent in future political administrators of the city and national economy.

The benevolent billionaire is a key myth, particularly in a city like London whose rich patrons give up so little of their wealth. As the 'die in' at the Victoria and Albert museum in 2019, organised by artist Nan Goldin also highlighted, the sources of philanthropic wealth are often questionable. Should a city rely on crumbs from the tables of the wealthy as a means of addressing social problems? Aspen, Davos, Caiman and Mustique men, and indeed some women, need to think beyond, and help rework, the system they live in, and to take much less. What kills a city, what really destroys its social fabric, is a situation in which losses are borne by the many, gains go to the few, corporate pay is unchallenged, the ranks of the wealthy burgeon and the poor are cut loose by a state antagonistic to what it sees as an underclass. Yet this remaining social rump highlights the failure of the state, markets and corporations to bring sufficient opportunities for all.

Capture the city, capture the world

It is hardly surprising that London has been compliant when faced with the profound wealth of those who have won playing the world economy. But their influence has also permeated the city's economy, politics and society, making it one of the most unequal cities in the world and creating a land apart from the one it sits within. The display of the power of money can be seen in the recreation and extension of the fabric of the city and the almost subconscious alignment of policy and corporate elites. More tangibly it can be seen in the sovereign wealth fund purchases of key real estate sites (the Shard, Harrods, One Hyde Park, Battersea Power Station, the Walkie Talkie, Heathrow airport, Canary Wharf towers, Grosvenor Square, among many others) and in the increasing presence of big money on the political circuit, with concerns about hedge fund managers and wealthy Russians funding the Conservative Party and billionaire funding of the 'Leave EU' campaign.

The process of capture can be evidenced with data showing the scale of changes to the built environment and by examining the narrative constructions of the city's future offered by media commentators, politicians and corporate representatives, many of whom see security and economic vitality only insofar as footloose benevolent capital can be attracted. Examples of the inveigling logic of money can be identified particularly in relation to the redevelopment and sale of parcels of the city. Consider the case of the chair of Westminster borough planning, who was found accepting gifts from developers and then systematically waving through a series of proposals. Many of those managing the city appear to do so in line with their own interests and the interests of those whose money they court. We might be reminded of the film *The Ghost Goes West* in which a young Scottish laird sells his ancestral castle to an American plutocrat only to see it transported brick by brick to America. The Westminster case threw some light on what many intuitively felt – that the rich and those brought into their sphere of influence have formed an alliance of the self-interested with no concern for the everyday life and strains of the places they monopolise.

The super-rich have had an almost alchemical effect on London. The raw resources of land, brick, concrete and steel have been animated, mobilised and given form by the power of capital to reshape the city. Yet the wealthy have not only bought up tracts of London housing, their demands have become absorbed by the culture of the city and its politics, leading to the shrinking of budgets for health, policing, housing and education. The alpha city is surely one of the richest cities in the world that apparently doesn't have enough to provide essential public services to those most in need. Yet the sense that the wealthy are vital to the fortunes of the city retains a purchase on policy thinking and populist narratives that is hard to shake. The current mayor, Sadiq Khan, has trodden an uneasy line, appearing to be concerned about empty, second and investment homes while claiming that the rich have made a 'massive contribution' to the city over many years.[4]

The rich are often emulated within a society that is increasingly materialistic. Until recently there was a shop on Sloane Street called Billionaire, in which a small army of immaculately tailored and coiffed staff would assist wannabe rich kids. Whether anyone who was a billionaire actually shopped there is another question, but it illustrates a broader aspect of life in the city today. Watching and appearing to copy the rich has become part of the cultural life of the society we live in. Many appear to want to be part of what is in reality a curse, rather like the repeated refrain that permeates John Lanchester's novel *Capital* – 'we want what you've got'. The paradox is that we can read this both as a chant of envy by the masses or alternatively as a statement of the possessive desires of the rich themselves – we want what you have got and we are going to take everything we can wrest from you.

The wider point that flows from this ideological triumph of wealth and the notion of the inherent goodness of markets is that public goods have become stigmatised as inefficient, low quality or inept. Both the financial crisis and the straitening measures of austerity have entrenched the idea that market systems must be defended as the only game that can save us. The result is a continued competition for footloose capital with city competitors globally, notably New York and second tier 'beta' city contenders like Frankfurt, Paris and Dublin.

How did we arrive at a city whose only dedicated newspaper, all of its major football clubs and many of its iconic buildings are owned by partially resident billionaires, sovereign wealth funds and foreign investors (many using offshore shell companies to hide their ownership)? Alongside this sense of condensing and growing money power exists a city where a hundred public housing estates, numerous care homes, swathes of public land and other social assets have been passed over to capital with almost no public deliberation and ultimately little resistance.

The alpha city is one in which Lords are accused of taking bribes from billionaires while public institutions are compelled to accept tainted philanthropic funding and where public spaces are provided in the sky rather than being accessible to all on the street. Its wealth management system is unrivalled globally while being attached to one of the largest, if not the largest, ecosystem of tax evasion. A low sales tax and an annual service charge on property have allowed wealthy buyers to keep properties empty, with no meaningful penalty for doing so. While Ken Griffin's apartment in New York attracts an annual property tax of $280,000, his two London properties worth around £100m each have a combined annual council tax bill of just £2,842.[5] New York has gone still further, introducing in 2019 the kind of annual 'mansion tax' that appeared to hole Labour's ambitions in the 2014 general election, suggesting that it is possible to win the argument for public investment. Planning in London has allowed thousands of developments without provision of on-site affordable, let alone public, housing (the developers of such properties, a hedge fund manager and corporate titan were among those who helped bankroll the Conservative party leadership campaign of the city's former mayor Boris Johnson). This is a city in which 10 per cent of its planners and less than 1 per cent of its architects now work in the public sector, the remainder working in local authorities stripped of the bulk of their funding over the past decade, compelled to sell buildings and land, much of it at below-market prices to private developers.

An historically patrician elite has been increasingly substituted by a richer and more grasping class who measure success by their ability to escape the collapse of the public realm, a collapse that they themselves have brought about. A concern with the social fortunes and long-term vitality of a great city had something going for it. The attitude of the traditionally wealthy and the middle class to the city was one of engagement and responsibility, born of the sense that it was hard to escape an urban condition that brought a vital social patchwork so closely together. So we get to the crunch point, the core of this city as it stands today, a city in which the answer to any question we might wish to ask is money. Money is why political interests turn a blind eye to offshore and criminal purchases of real estate, no matter how shady the source. Money is the reason why public housing is being demolished in the name of 'affordable' housing. Money is why gentrification is seen as a good thing and poor residents are deemed to be better placed elsewhere, out of sight. Money lies at the heart of keeping taxes low and regulations slack. If we want to understand the zombie market of more than 500 new towers on the Thames, money will help to explain that too.

The city shaped by this dominating logic is like a negative doughnut, with wealth and high-rise housing at its core, falling away to suburbs increasingly marked by slow physical decay and a growing cohort of the city's poor. The city has become a sorting machine for opportunity and fortune – the rich in one door, the poor literally out of others made just for them. A million such portals sort, organise and categorise citizens by the size of their bank balances, while citizenship, residence and social contribution are ignored.

At the heart of this book is the suggestion that the relatively small numbers of the super-rich are the tip of a large iceberg whose deeper, submerged influence operates via a self-interested and successful class of enablers. These key agents working on behalf of both capital and capitalists can be found in the

finance, real estate, political and economic sectors. Critically
this is a highly urban and, more specifically, London-centric
group. This emerging constellation of complex interests, actors
and incentives is somewhat distinct from traditional ideas of
an establishment or ruling class made on the playing fields of
public schools. The cadres operating and running the city in
favour of capital are bred from old and money, but any shared
identity stems from their alignment with markets and economic
principles emerging from business schools, boardrooms and
a shifting, speculative form of capitalism that has brought in
many new players.

Stealth homes, blacked-out cars, high gates, walls and service
staff create a distributed enclave of privilege that is difficult to
peer into. Opaque offshore systems and untraceable property
owners facilitate systems of value extraction that feed the rich
and expropriate the city's core social resources. Yet this privacy
and enclosure appears increasingly vulnerable. Insights into the
workings of the alpha city are more evident today – we live
in a world of new academic research on the rich, Wikileaks,
social media coverage, entertainment rooted in documentary
journalism (such as *McMafia*) and the frequent reports of the
Tax Justice Network and Transparency International, among
others.

Insights from the front line of lives lived in poverty have the
potential to inform society and to restore a sense of conscience,
reports on life at the top may yet have the power to divide and
destabilise it.

The poverty of an affluent city

Various names have been used to suggest London's takeover
by the wealthy, whether Singapore on Thames (sometimes
Hong Kong or Moscow), Hedge City, Londongrad or the
Nincompoopolis of the Johnson mayoral regime.[6] Yet in many

ways the city is its own place, a more or less unique confluence of histories, economic flows, cultures, people and politics.
More than fifty years ago, the émigré social commentator
George Mikes commented that London was a kind of 'chaos
incorporated', and in many ways this casual observation has a
ring of truth to it today. The city is a highly organised machine
built from the disorder, uncertainties and wavering flows of
political and economic life in this and other parts of the globe.
It is a place primed for accumulation and the extraction of
value from a global economy and indeed from itself.

Despite moments of evident crisis – from the 2008 financial collapse (whose costs are still being tallied) to Brexit and
now to the reckoning to be tallied from the pandemic – the
city machine functions efficiently, riding the waves of global
and regional chaos to take advantage of cash-rich buyers and
investors. Indeed, the recurrent crises only create new momentum – even now a wave of concern about house price drops at
the top of the market has made way for a new round of purchases by cash-rich buyers from the US, China and elsewhere.

Underlying these conditions a mostly working poor remain
excluded from the ebbs or are damaged by the flows. This
restates a point made in Chapter 5, that the homes and
avenues of the alpha city generate a moral atmosphere that
acts rather like a social opiate – creating places of forgetting
in which it becomes permissible for the rich and for city elites
to forget about the losers and the excluded. The fabric of the
city becomes a screen onto which a faux reality is projected
in order to assuage the consciences of the wealthy and their
factotums. Such an environment feeds the sense that there is
little need to feel obligated to help those who are invisible
when life exists entirely behind plate glass, locked doors and
tall gates.

The alpha city shapes a distinctive psychology among the
alpha elite. To many it may seem simply outrageous to identify
the rich as value takers, rather than the creators of prosperity.

But the argument for extraction holds more water when we consider the way international chains of investment are designed precisely to take returns offshore, or empty homes are maintained by footloose owners for capital returns or to hide illicit cash. In 2019, amidst the feverish endgame of Brexit, the UK was being asked by the EU not to turn a blind eye to money laundering as a means of shoring up a post-Brexit future. This outcome seems almost assured as proposals for tax cuts, financial deregulation and the use of tax-free zones for artworks and treasures proposed for the north of England find renewed favour in the post-pandemic city. Meanwhile favourable currency rates and continued global wealth accretion by the rich had begun to boost house sales in London again.

The effect of alpha status is the creation of a multitude of slow-burning front lines that consume the working city. One of the more pernicious effects of this is a kind of creeping and deadening influence that touches the city's poorer groups and districts. In years gone by some analysts made the argument that inequality generated common problems. The sense, and indeed reality, that problems were in some way shared helped to incentivise reform – if one didn't want to be exposed to a lousy public realm, the risk of public violence or declining essential services, then the rationale for public investment was clear.

Now these relationships and responsibilities have become blurred, the incentive to act is diminished. This is because staggering wealth, combined with technology-driven mobilities and secure nodal points of residence, work and leisure, allow the wealthy to circumvent a degraded public realm, while their private resources create a world that competes with and exceeds anything provided by the state. In extremis, the microsecessionary spaces of the Shard, The Lancasters, The Mansion or The Chilterns and many other bunker spaces are produced according to the principles of a private security club, enabling sections of the city's rich to remain unseen.

The capital offers numerous schemes by which this escapology can be practised and honed. All of this adds up to the winner-exit strategy: once you have enough money the social world can effectively be jettisoned.

Should the city again melt down, the flames and sirens will not be seen or heard by the rich in their towers or behind their gates. A city built for the elites helps to deactivate some prospect of political action or intervention. Despite the sense of rage at the extent of unequal reward, there is little sense that a serious political challenge lies in wait. Even as reports by the UN suggesting that the political class have acted with real callousness towards those in want are batted away by that same group.

We need to return to the idea that place is important, enchanting almost, in bringing together a complex set of forces and factors. The concentration of the rich in the city's alphahoods is not simply a co-presence – it creates the potential for the development of networks and, thereby, a shared culture and interests. Wealth has an ideological form, with the capacity to bring many into the logic of its accumulation. Its combined holders share an interest in capital expansion and a commitment to enabling its reproduction while muting voices of opposition as party poopers or envious onlookers. In an environment so tied to the needs of capital even moderate arguments for public housing or progressive taxation are almost hysterically shouted down as illogical or masochistic.

Perhaps the real problem is that in activating the dominance of capital and its emissaries a city is created that fails to integrate its social subjects into some common understanding of sharing that space and benefiting from it. Here there is little identification with common values, few controls on individual desires, and the sense that no moral compass directs corporate or political life. This is simply another negative feature of the poverty of life that emerges in this, and indeed other, profoundly wealthy cities. Space becomes important because

Sunset or sunrise?

alpha environments operate to switch off empathy and connection via gated communities and fortress apartment blocks that create the sense of an embattled position of the affluent rather than their co-presence among other citizens.

The ultimate effect of the capture of the city by capital is akin to a repeatedly turning ratchet, where every turn only takes us further towards the privatisation of citizens, contracts, services and amenities, never back. How can the grip of this logic be uncoupled from the public city that is slowly being strangled by it? The more the various resources of the city – health services, schools, swimming pools, libraries, housing, education, even policing – become matters of private provision, the more their use relies on the ability to pay. In a society of massive inequalities this situation is simply a disaster for those struggling on lower incomes, but it is also a catastrophe for the social city itself, a denial of the basic elements that comprise urban life. How can a socially vivacious, encompassing and human place be sustained amid these disparities and in the face of a disinterested and emboldened political elite? Where do the homeless and the low-paid fit in to a future built of chrome and marble and propelled by jets and unending streams of cash? Money will kill the city.

Even in the city's long-standing affluent heartlands there is a palpable sense of anger. This comes in various forms and diffuses through the city and beyond. Among its objects are inequality, the lack of decent housing, the appalling conditions in rented accommodation, the rise of food banks, and the lack of culpability for the financial crisis that precipitated a multitude of acts against the poor. There is a general sense of a deepening social injustice compounded by gender and class pay gaps, unequal health and education outcomes, rising street violence, revelations of banker bonuses, tax evasion and political corruption, and planning decisions that favour the wealthy. There is rising anger directed at the excess, the lack of accountability, the double standards, the closed doors, the empty homes and the property brokering. Even many of those who are for capitalism are against what is happening to London because they recognise the regressive effects of cronyism, backhanders, blind eyes being turned to sharp practice, and of the unfair benefits accruing to agglomerations of capital.

To ask who the city is for and how it is run is simultaneously to ask about the place of its mere mortals – its middle classes and low-income citizens who feel outmoded, undone, displaced and ill at ease at the rapidity and scale of changes. They have been pushed to the margins of the new institutional, geographical and financial centres of the city. An emerging possible future for the city is one in which a pound sign hangs over every building, asset, public resource and facility in existence. This could be called the dead-city model, because within it there is ultimately no place for, or recognition of, the public city, the needs of citizens and of communities, or of that which cannot be assigned a money value. The only index of its vivacity is the speed with which cash is accumulated.

It is possible that London may not be the alpha city of tomorrow, that it may not be home to the most UHNWIs or property millionaires or CEOs who earn more than £1 million. Whether this would be a loss to the city is an open question. Perhaps the more challenging question is whether the super-rich are a sustainable gift to the city. Even so, London will likely maintain its position as a mainstay of the international global capitalist system, a system that will continue to generate enormously uneven rewards if left unchallenged. New winners will continue to be created, and many will seek refuge for themselves and their capital in this city of security, grand terraces, leafy suburbs and dynamic social circuits. Yet as those who live with fortunes well know, sustained pre-eminence is never a sure thing – in another phase of the global capitalist economy perhaps another metropolis will become the alpha city.

Afterword

Cacopolis Now

What does the pandemic mean for the alpha city? London contains some nine million souls. It's an area of concentrated wealth but also a city in which many institutions and elite actors have worked hard to further secure those gains while neglecting the needs of many others. Even in an emergency year, requiring support for the poor and the excluded, the alpha city's operations could still be observed.

The same year saw agents of the Vatican buying luxury homes in Chelsea amidst allegations of laundering. A media baron bought access to a minister's ear and as a consequence, the complaints of a London borough were swept to one side so that a multi-million-pound luxury development could be allowed to go ahead (albeit later deemed illegal). While work stopped for hundreds of thousands with little or no protection, cash-rich buyers snapped up 'cheap' homes in the city as investments, or became part of the booming market in stately homes. Street homelessness doubled. Covid infections led to half of all taxi driver deaths and to those of 42 London bus drivers. Everything seemed to change for so many, yet very little did for the city's elites, whether wealthy in their own right or those operating at the pinnacle of the corporate, legal and property sectors. Have no doubt, the alpha city is here to stay.

Even at this early point you may wish to take me by the arm and say: *But everything is different now. Landlords are suffering, rents are dramatically down, homes and apartments*

sit unsold and house prices are also down in the city's centre.
Meanwhile, the City is in crisis with 10,000 workers already
gone to Europe and fears remain of losing more like earlier
estimates of 75,000 of the 300,000 working in London's
financial services. Many other companies face near-existential
threats via the new tariffs or bars on their activity in mainland
Europe following Brexit. And here is the really big news: while
you talk down a slender few lucky winners and wealth genera-
tors, haven't you noticed that nearly a tenth of the entire city's
population (700,000 people) have deserted it? All in all, we
fear that your analysis is wanting – there isn't so much as a ray
of sunshine through an estate agent's window here right now.

Certainly the brunt of the prevailing storm has hit the city
hard. But its full force has been felt most by citizens on low
wages, precarious contracts, those without savings, tenants,
minority ethnic workers and struggling households, the disabled and those receiving support for their income from
governments. Conditions among these groups were grievous
and almost unending in their cruelty – and that was *before*
Covid had even hit the city. Now everything looks, if it could
be, even worse.

The result is a city that looks more like a cacotopia – a
state in which everything is as bad as it possibly could be.
Commentators dwelt on the deaths, hospital admissions and
lockdowns as many suggested that the pandemic revealed the
extent of poverty and inequality in the city. The almost daily
discussion focused on the extent of disparities between secure
work and precarious work, owners and renters, outcomes
for majority and minority ethnic groups, and, of course, rich
and poor.

For the majority of citizens who had lived in overcrowded
or vulnerable conditions for years, the observation that Covid
showed the extent of inequalities was offensive. Which bubble
had you been living in before the virus hit not to know how
hundreds of thousands were already pushed to the limit by

merciless welfare changes, or how Black citizens faced mea-surably poorer life-chances? Did scales really fall from the eyes of those suddenly seeing how genuinely bad contract working was, how widespread the loss of youth employment opportuni-ties or how unjust the takeovers of land by capital that pushed thousands from their homes? This had been the familiar busi-ness of national and city politics and everyday life for many, for more than a decade before the current crisis.

Despite all this, the city is neither dead nor dying but dormant. In this sense, *Alpha City's* central messages were in many ways emphasised, even amidst a global calamity that appeared, like an electromagnetic bomb, to knock out the city's engines while leaving its architecture standing. Elite institutions, actors and agents and the rich themselves continued their business more or less unimpeded. A city that appeared to have crashed was slowly rebooting in 'safe mode' to rebuild, protect and restore investments, lifestyles and leisure. Wealthy residents were shuttled to airports to escape – at Farnborough airport alone 900 private jet movements were recorded even during the peak lockdown months of April and May. Cash-rich buyers were given virtual tours of super-prime homes with more being spent, according to Knight Frank, in the first six months than the same period the previous year (£1.13bn vs £977m).

In sections of the central city, the construction of dozens of luxury apartment blocks has continued, while digital money flows rebuilt losses on the screens of hedge fund operators and financiers. What had long been true of the city – that it operated primarily for capital, capitalists and those working to support them – remained so. While many on the left looked at the current social disaster as a possible spur to a more equi-table and compassionate city politics, it became increasingly clear that little had or would change. The hunger of the pow-erful to return to pre-existing profit margins and for the wider population to go back to normal life pointed the way to such a future. So, where next for a cacopolis such as this, a place in which *anything* might seem a better situation to be in?

Power bloc(k)

The current crisis makes it clear that the alpha political and economic system is a durable vessel, a boat capable of moving even while in the doldrums. Its drive to rapidly reconstruct markets, rebuild growth and snap back into place its economic models is understandable. But this has also had the effect of returning a nakedly sectional politics. This politics is not simply one of right and left, but rather one formed of splits within governing elites between neoliberal and libertarian wings of national government, egged-on by lobbyists on Tufton Street.

It has become easier to spot how ideas of sovereign individuality, personal freedom and winner-takes-all mentalities pervade the lifestyles and interests of many of the world's billionaires as well as politicians in government as well. The move is from a politics barely still connected to city and community to one in which such quaint associations and possibilities only exist to the extent they form resources to be plundered by the winners of meritocratic and technocratic races.

Today Brexit, high-tech, freeports, open markets and closed borders are key elements of the emerging economic order, brought into focus by key players in government, allies in the City and analysts in the lobbying firms and paid employees of the super-rich, wealthy corporations and their allies. A dark future indeed for the many who will form the grist of such a mill. Such plans include ten freeports, effectively onshore tax havens in which art, wine and precious metals will be stored without paying duties. Since other examples of freeports around the world tend to consist more or less of large warehouses periodically subject to criminal investigation, with a few hundred staff at most, this looks more like a further victory for tax injustice than a boon to trade or employment prospects. A decade of investigations and declarations of the UK as one of the pre-eminent dark money hideouts appears not to trouble the government's further moves in this direction.

Perhaps the biggest question facing city and nation is who should pay to help us to recover. Debate about the scale of inequality and excessive wealth and its influence has intensified, accompanied this time even by pro-market wings of the press and other analysts who see that the unfairness of austerity needs to be replaced by hits on the enormously deep pockets of wealthier members of our community. For a right of centre government the question of financing recovery is thorny. Traditionally taboo areas, like wealth taxes, offshore tax havens and corporate tax, have been forced further to centre-stage by economists of all stripes, looking for ways to fund the cost of bailouts, vaccines and state supports. In this respect, the tide may have turned. Leader writers in the *Financial Times* have talked of reforming capitalism, the LSE has produced a report on the viability of wealth taxes and a series of other initiatives have driven debate about shareholder capitalism and more empathic re-makings of the city.

Such apparent progress is undermined by the government's very clear connections to big money, offshore capitalists and lobbying firms. The Conservative Party's own links have also come under close scrutiny in two reports to Parliamentary select committees, discussing links to Russian agents and to oligarchs living in the UK. Similarly, the business as usual of British banks and agents over the past year, enabling money laundering and fraud, has been revealed in several reports and at least one BBC documentary.

Such revelations set the scene for a contest between civic society and the excess, corruption and inaction of various elites connected by networks lined with cash. But this is not the only battle line and, if we look more deeply, we can see emerging contests within the capitalist elites themselves. In an interesting intervention in the *Le Monde Diplomatique* monthly, it has been suggested that the conflict is particularly intense between the different sections of the finance sector – particularly between banks and mainstream financial operators, on the one hand, and on the other the hot and fast money of hedge funds, the wealthy and private equity (who funded much of the Brexit campaign and, of course, the former Mayor of London's bid to be Prime Minister). Ideas of elites as being connected to class, or to nation and community here breakdown. Instead, we can see how different wealth elites, alongside political support wings and corporate actors, form a complex web of interests that are rarely simply aligned with something we might call national interest, a power bloc or establishment. In reality, something much more complex is at work rather like an animated Venn diagram of interests.

The current emergency will deepen the problems of those living on low, medium and indeed higher incomes in this super-rich city. Being a world centre of five-star hotels, opulent homes, luxury goods vendors and super-charged financial services means little to those affected by the new crisis. The majority of citizens would have been as well served had the city been a major centre of cake making. To make things worse, the current political powerhouse is generally not one schooled in hard knocks, set-backs or the experience of personal hardship. Many at its political centre are millionaires, hold significant property portfolios or have worked in private finance.

This disconnection has yielded a high-minded and often tone-deaf response to the pandemic and its social consequences. It often feels that the official game plan had been plotted over the expansive kitchens of Oxfordshire farmhouses or in the gardens of Somerset. This was, and all too likely will be, how much we are in this together in a post-Covid world. It is a sign of these times that even the traditionally staid cricket club at Lords had started to allow queue jumping for memberships. With 12,000 people on its list, waiting up to 29 years, it now offered the chance to pay £45,000 to join straightaway, to help cover a £30m shortfall due to Covid cancellation of matches. The story connected to other emerging disparities, with many reports circulating about Harley Street doctors selling Covid vaccines to super-rich clients and others among them buying additional passports in EU countries to keep their options open in a Brexit world (Cyprus being a notable vendor).

In 2020 the world's rich continued to get (much) richer, many doubling their fortunes even during the darkest days of the pandemic. For Evgeny Lebedev, co-owner of the *London Evening Standard*, the year ended with his being made a lord. The close friend of Boris Johnson chose the eye-catching title of Baron Lebedev, of Hampton in the London Borough of Richmond upon Thames and of Siberia in the Russian Federation. The chancellor of the Exchequer, whose wife holds billions in various investments, was found not to have declared significant wealth, raising questions about conflict of interest due to the blind trust that he was later found to own. Perhaps it was therefore symbolic that in November an entire West End street had to be evacuated as two houses being excavated for an extensive basement collapsed. Fortunately, no one was hurt. But homes were not the only places in which mega basements were being built. Even with the crisis in full flow 2021 brought the grand reveal of Claridges' new hotel basement, where the builders dug down 100ft using massive cylinders of concrete to stop the hotel collapsing in on itself, and a new penthouse with a rack rate of £50,000 per night (though still not the most expensive in the city).

The sense of disconnection between sections of the political class and the imperatives to act on questions of inequality, corporate fraud, offshore evasion and laundering has made the administration seem out of touch as well as callous. This appeared to be highlighted by the claim by Conservative MP Jacob Rees-Mogg (himself a hedge fund manager) that UN assistance to provide emergency food for the poor and malnourished in a first-world nation was a 'political stunt'. During this same year the entire street homeless population were helped into hotels to save them from the risk of infection, only to be turfed out again some months later. The pandemic acted like a kind of rotavator – turning over the social soil of the city to reveal numerous additional injustices and problems (its record 60,000 plus in temporary accommodation, for example), many of which had been sowed during years of inaction or policies that had only undermined the position of many. So how to shape the future of the city in a more positive direction?

Towards a beta or better city?

How best to advocate for and seek greater claim to the city for its long-suffering working residents? Might it be possible to offer clear answers on how to make the city a fairer and better place for all? Can we help to assemble a city engine that runs on a cleaner fuel when the existing model is proclaimed the best and most efficient that can be found? Today the neoliberal tenets, of uncaring but efficient markets in the name of a greater social good, seem to offer a kind of political immaturity, a childlike denial of the lessons of growing up.

Social life, even in lockdown, persists and highlights our interconnected nature, as well as revealing the ambitions of the wealthy few to escape. Without recognition of our social bonds the idea of triumphing as an individual unfettered by community, state or even family persists as mythology of the monied. Despite this we know that even billionaire *uber*men and women went to school, received (often abundant) familial support, drive on public roads, are protected by the police and laws, and have many others working for them in their own businesses or others they invest in. Life on an island is ultimately an illusion of social severance.

The lack of social cohesion in the current depression,

significantly driven by inequalities in property wealth or its absence, highlights how a politics of the self has generated divided and, in turn, less resilient communities. In all of this the rich are of course notable symbols, standing for what many wish to exemplify as all that is unsustainable and wrong with the excess of reward and the way that political and economic resources are now plundered and hoarded.

Yet we also need to see how western affluence more broadly is implicated in questions of inequality and the lack of sustainability. The rapidity and ferocity of the climate crisis, fuelled by the affluence of the global north and the richest within it, seem likely to compel some form of political action as growth models, carbon-hungry lifestyles and excessive consumption appear ever more unsustainable. We must mature to painfully recognise that separating from civic society is impossible, that both markets and states run through, and are connected to, community life.

Civic society is now bursting with viable and exciting proposals that seek to disabuse the wealthy (whether corporations or individuals) of their sense of themselves as uniquely placed winners. There is intense interest in new and tested ideas that focus on fairer ways of living, working, being housed and educated. Yet the many bodies and institutions looking to create even modest proposals around tax, work, land reform, housing, social care and other 'costs' to the public purse are feverishly shouted down by pro-market, pro-individual and pro-wealth lobbies.

Work has not yet begun to balance a Covid recovery with urban vitality and, in the mix, also achieve a much greater sense of fairness and social justice. Too much had already been lost for working Londoners even before the pandemic arrived; now the question is how to recover this social ground. The fulcrum of this debate for many in mainstream politics is likely to be, how do you do 'X' without destroying our finance economy, scaring away investment and reducing jobs in these sectors?

But to ask this question is itself a betrayal of the imagination of many who see that the current system is already destructive, unfair and unsustainable. The real question is less how can we do this than what will happen if we don't?

London's ostensible aim to grow to a city of 10m always looked like an unattractive goal. But while the current situation may appear to be one of trying to fill, rather than to build, housing we need to remember prevailing levels of housing need (households on the waitlist for local authority and housing association homes) and overcrowding that will not be alleviated by population loss. In this sense markets will continue to fail as the primary method to provide. London's dramatic recent population loss is already leading to steeply declining rents, lowering the returns to many individual landlords. Yet few tears will likely be shed at the prospect of rentiers selling up, and it seems possible that a glut of resulting sales would help to reduce prices.

At the time of writing no real innovations are being proposed by government, whether in the form of an economic plan to build affordably, a green new deal, or effective spatial policies to tackle regional and social divides. Emerging proposals would do better to eschew talk of levelling up and replace this with more effective designs to level down and help redistribute property and land wealth – too many people with more than one home and too many others with no home or no personal wealth to keep them going in times of need. The fault lines here are not only regional but intergenerational, tenurial, ethnic, educational – how can these be addressed in ways that might lead to a better city for all? Here are some reflections on where things might be going.

On taxing wealth

Tax goes to the heart of the question of inequality and what fair contribution might mean. Tax is now a key site of debate and new ideas. Support is growing for some model of wealth tax that finds methods of fairly helping the asset-rich to contribute to the collective good. While the bogeyman of annual added taxes on million-pound homes has killed debate about reform in the past, this year brought a major new report from the London School of Economics and University of Warwick which proposed that a one-off tax at a 1 per cent rate applied to wealth over £2m paid over 5 years would raise £80bn (the same rate applied to all household wealth over £500,000 would raise £260bn). While the chancellor has said there is never a good time to discuss a wealth tax, the public appears to feel that an opportune moment has indeed arrived with 75 per cent believing that this is a valuable strategy when compared to taxes on work income.

On the issue of asset and wealth tax another key proposal is to level the playing field so that these are taxed at the same rates as income. Abolishing 'non-dom' tax status in favour of taxing the wealth of self-proclaimed citizens should come as part of the package. As an interim measure, publish the extent of wider wealth known to HMRC to assist in public discussion of future measures. Another key tax issue being widely examined is the need to close offshore tax havens (British overseas territories or crown dependencies are among 4 of the top 10 in the Tax Justice Networks index of Corporate Tax Havens, including top place to the British Virgin Islands) and to find methods of common accounting between nations that would eliminate the advantages of these loopholes. In this, the UK is a notably bad actor, as are sections of the EU (including Luxembourg) and the US. Public anger and movement to act is growing; all of us should join that movement, particularly those fighting for fairer cities (because that is where the money lands) and a revised model of capitalism that delivers for the social good at its core.

Right now, it is worth reminding ourselves of the estimate that addressing corporate and personal wealth in the havens, even say a very low target of 10 per cent on all dark money (estimated at $35 trillion globally), would generate enough to pay for the entire Covid crisis. All of this is difficult but possible with an effectively funded tax department working transparently to address these issues. In the meantime, it is interesting to look at other alpha cities, like San Francisco with its silicon billionaires, and New York, where tax proposals on the wealthy have been hotly debated and seem likely to see implementation. As always, the question arises as to whether the rich will leave. But existing research highlights that the super wealthy in particular are among the least likely to move from higher tax jurisdictions where they clearly enjoy rich leisure, lifestyle and social benefits.

On laundering and crime

Crime is a major part of the wealth-finance economy, whether this be in terms of fraudulent and sharp practices, or in terms of the laundering of illicit cash. As *Alpha City* shows, the property sector has been a major beneficiary of criminal cash, helping to bankroll developments pitched at the cash-rich, and to further bolster profits by attracting buyers who are almost immune to real-world price signals. Global Witness has called for a register of beneficial owners of all UK property to prevent laundering, enabling the owners of all land and property to be trackable. Remarkably this is still not possible in many cases, made more difficult also by offshore ownership. Despite the UK's lamentable progress on these issues the authorities in charge of such matters, the Financial Conduct Authority (FCA), remain under-funded and under-staffed, lampooned in *Private Eye* magazine as the Fundamentally Complicit Authority (now run by the chancellor appointed former head of the London Stock Exchange) – by January 2020 it had still not prosecuted anyone under its new anti-money laundering powers. It is in this area that pressure is particularly needed because it is

becoming clear that easing regulation and policing allow cash to continue flowing in a climate where such injections are hard to find.

Housing and planning for all

A city captured by the rich and its allies in the property lobby needs to see a revitalisation of the planning system, dramatically privatised and defunded over the past decade. Two key issues stand out. First, the way that viability tests are used to avoid contributions of affordable housing by developers. Second, the need to promote on-site social housing contributions as a standard, non-negotiable aspect of all new provision. Communities in social rented housing should be presented with options only for investment and refits, never for demolition or any loss of homes, paid for through the first measure. Rehab should also take place using green new deal principles of sustainable design and involving local labour and training systems.

As Owen Hatherley argues in *Red Metropolis*, a major argument of the Mayor's office has been that any new supply is desirable because it helps the middle classes and others to move out of stock which can then cascade down. The problem begins when the new housing is bought by people not part of the locality. The answer here is to follow the money and to seek greater contribution from wealthy international buyers who add pressure to the market by inflating prices, under-using, in many cases, these homes and contributing less to the local economy.

Other reforms have been widely discussed. One possibility is that continuing sales of social housing be abandoned, as could all plans for housing demolition. Rent controls should be put in place alongside other measures to reduce the attractiveness of being a private landlord (now a quarter of London's housing stock). The general push in policy terms should be to move in the direction of a 50/50 tenure structure – with much closer to half owning, and half renting in social housing that is of good condition, affordable and secure, and which is spatially mixed with private housing. The current mayor has made efforts to increase affordable housing (which is often very expensive in reality) but has often been timid in his approach – international buyers have not been challenged and are unlikely to be in the coming years.

What is needed is a revitalisation of strategic thinking with an understanding of how public housing can indeed offer the single most cost-effective pathway to providing secure, good quality and spacious homes. Such possibilities will, we are told, rankle with 'tax payers' and others with interests in the kind of property economy that the UK has become. Yet some of the most popular, sustainable and even beautiful homes in the city were built by municipal institutions - the London County Council, the 32 boroughs and the Greater London Council over a hundred years. Many of the best of these, due to the commodification of public housing through the right to buy, saw homes among them resold for many hundreds of thousands of pounds in the best developments. In Rowan Moore's *Slow Burn City*, all of the best neighbourhoods he cites are notable for being public housing developments. We won't see a 50-50 city any time soon, but decisions that move us in that direction by de-financialising public housing and building more and better public homes could be a key way of engaging a green new deal and helping medium-sized builders to recovery, instead of bunging billions through redundant schemes like Help to Buy.

Choose a more social city

Individuals can and should support any initiative that challenges the narrowly economistic vision of what and who the city should be for. This includes several of the above proposals but also more sustainable transport systems, provision of green and play space, moves to better value the contribution of BAME citizens, women and the disabled, to see greater investment in schooling and health through central government funding allocations and the ending of austerity-driven welfare measures. All of this to be paid for by publicly deliberated discussions about fair wealth taxes and equitable contribution to public life by all who claim the citizenship of the city of London.

On philanthropy

Good money for key public services and cultural infrastructure, such as for hospitals, universities, museums and other institutions should come through strategic allocation by publicly accountable bodies. All should contribute to these provisions through general forms of taxation. Large personal gifts to elite bodies, based on whim, interest or personal favour, should be denied in favour of the tax measures described above. This would prevent much of the reputation washing that goes on, the most recent example being the £100m from Ineos billionaire Jim Ratcliffe to Oxford University.

In all of this a rediscovery of civic life and the deep virtues of municipalism is long overdue. These keywords are not the preserve of the left or a metropolitan intelligentsia elite; rather they should be used to define the joint project of making places better for all people. And this is their danger. Because to embrace the idea of common provision, effective planning and fair contribution is a direct threat to models of private and excessive profit and wealth.

Arm yourself with knowledge

It is worth knowing that in a survey commissioned by Action on Empty Homes it was found that two-thirds (68 per cent) of Londoners think the London property market is now focused on building for investors, and almost nine in 10 (86 per cent) Londoners think expensive housing is a significant problem in London (figures from Pretty Vacant, Action on Empty Homes, 2020).

The next argument we may face from those representing capital, the wealthy, finance and the development sectors is that the city is again in crisis so we need the money of the rich, property and international investment to keep the machine going. Many will claim that the treasury is dependent on receipts of housing sales and on the contribution of the City of London (around 7 per cent of the UK economy). All of this true, but the preferable alternative for a future city is one that delivers for a much greater number of its citizens and is built on a more balanced and much greener economy, for social investment, greater social protections, a revised urban equilibrium in which property prices sustainably deflate, where affordable housing is guaranteed in all new development.

Conclusion

The alpha city is like an octopus with its tentacles integrated into its streets, suites and fine neighbourhoods. Yet despite London's status as one of the single largest metropoles for the world's wealthy it is also a complex mosaic of 'red' boroughs and civic organisations. Many of these organisations and their supporters are involved in efforts at preventing big money destroying community life. London's citizens have long fought against national government directives that see the city as the de facto property of capital and those in charge of it. This made the city both playground and battleground of ideas and policies that ultimately enlarged the powers of the City and embedded ideas that see markets and inequalities as legitimate or necessary features of a modern urban-national economy. In strategic terms the city's mayor has relatively few resources to manage the city in ways that might run counter to national political directives. Meanwhile its many citizens, irritated by labour councils following pro-market, pro-property plans to do land deals and alienated from a Brexit they did not vote for, are similarly estranged by the city economy's tendency to over-determine social life in the city.

A new reality is coming into focus, with falling numbers of migrants and a less certain future for the finance and real estate sectors as well as wavering public health risks. In all of this any such risks are unlikely to impact the wealth or lifestyles of the rich, nor will they affect the desirability of the city as a socially or economically strategic place in which to live as a post-Covid world begins to emerge. As the *Financial Times* tells us daily, London today faces a fight for its future. Yet of course its implied object is the city of high finance, while for so many others the London fighting for its future is the one still gasping for air after being knocked down first by a decade of austerity and then by the effects of the pandemic.

The decade to come is unlikely to be the new 'roaring 20s' heralded by one elite property agency moments before the pandemic hit the city. Few will believe that the super-rich have firmly switched to ESG (environment, social, governance) goals above their strategies to preserve inheritances or rebuild their reserves. Outside elite networks all talk is now about fairness, economic recovery, the nature and rewards of work, and climate change. Citizen and NGO engagement with questions of tax justice, political reform, the role of big money and big corporate interests, the paid-for lobbying by Tufton Street advisers and so on all offer some hope to provide that such a fairer future may become a reality.

Bibliography

The following is a selection of readings that underpin the analyses offered in each chapter, including articles from journals that are free to access for the general reader.

Chapter 1: Capital's City

Dorling, D., *Inequality and the 1%*, Verso, 2019.

Forrest, R., Koh, S. and Wissink, B. (eds.), *Cities and the Super-Rich*, Palgrave Macmillan, 2017.

Hall, S., *Global Finance*, Sage, 2018.

Hay, I. and Beaverstock, J. (eds.), *Handbook on Wealth and the Super-Rich*, Edward Elgar, 2016.

Lanchester, J., *Capital*, Faber and Faber, 2012.

Luyendijk, J., *Swimming With Sharks: Inside the World of the Bankers*, Faber and Faber, 2015.

Wright Mills, C., *The Power Elite*, Oxford University Press, 1956.

Chapter 2: The Archipelago of Power

Di Muzio, T., *The 1% and the Rest of Us: A Political Economy of Dominant Ownership*, Zed Books, 2015.

Hay, I. and Muller, S., '"That Tiny, Stratospheric Apex That Owns Most of the World": Exploring Geographies of the Super-Rich', *Geographical Research* 1, 2012, pp. 75–88.

Norfield, T., *The City: London and the Global Power of Finance*, Verso, 2016.

Piketty, T., *Capital and Ideology*, Harvard, 2020.

Sampson, A., *Who Runs This Place? The Anatomy of Britain in the 21st century*, John Murray, 2004.

Savage, M. and Williams, K. (eds.), *Remembering Elites*, Blackwell, 2008.

Scott, J., *The Upper Classes: Property and Privilege in Britain*, Macmillan, 1982.

Scott, J., *Who Rules Britain?* Cambridge: Polity, 1991.

Thorold, P., *The London Rich: The Creation of a Great City*, St. Martin's Press, 1999.

Westergaard, J. and Resler, H., *Class in a Capitalist Society*, Penguin, 1975.

Chapter 3: Accommodating Wealth

Atkinson, R., Parker, S. and Burrows, R., 'Elite Formation, Power and Space in Contemporary London', *Theory, Culture & Society* 5–6, 2017, pp. 179–200.

Burrows, R. and Knowles, C., 'The "HAVES" and the "HAVE YACHTS": Socio-Spatial Struggles in London Between the "Merely Wealthy" and the "Super-Rich"', *Public Culture* 1, 2019, pp. 72–87.

Burrows, R., Webber, R. and Atkinson, R., 'Welcome to "Pikettyville"? Mapping London's Alpha Territories', *The Sociological Review* 2, 2017, pp. 184–201.

Mordaunt Crook, J., *The Rise of the Nouveaux Riches*, John Murray, 1999.

Webber, R. and Burrows, R., 'Life in an Alpha Territory: Discontinuity and Conflict in an Elite London "Village"', *Urban Studies* 15, 2016, pp. 3139–54.

White, J., *London in the Twentieth Century*, Vintage, 2001.

Chapter 4: Crime, Capital

Bullough, O., *Moneyland: Why Thieves and Crooks Now Rule the World and How to Take It Back*, Profile Books, 2018.

Harrington, B., *Capital Without Borders: Wealth Managers and the One Percent*, Harvard University Press, 2016.

McKenzie, R. and Atkinson, R., 'Anchoring Capital in Place: The Grounded Impact of International Wealth Chains on Housing Markets in London', *Urban Studies*, 2019.

Platt, S., *Criminal Capital: How the Finance Industry Facilitates Crime*, Palgrave, 2015.

Shaxson, N., *Treasure Islands: Tax Havens and the Men Who Stole the World*, Bodley Head, 2011.

Chapter 5: Cars, Jets and Luxury Yachts

Atkinson, R., 'Limited Exposure: Social Concealment, Mobility and Engagement with Public Space by the Super-Rich in London', *Environment and Planning A* 7, 2016, pp. 1302–17.

Birtchnell, T. and Caletrío, J. (eds.), *Elite Mobilities,* Routledge, 2013.

Knowles, C., 'Walking Plutocratic London: Exploring Erotic, Phantasmagoric Mayfair', *Social Semiotics* 3, 2017, pp. 299–309.

Chapter 6: My Own Private Stronghold

Atkinson, R. and Blandy, S., *Domestic Fortress: Fear and the New Home Front*, Manchester University Press, 2017.

Harding, L., *A Very Expensive Poison: The Definitive Story of the Murder of Litvinenko and Russia's War with the West*, Guardian Faber, 2016.

Hollingsworth, M. and Lansley, S., *Londongrad: From Russia with Cash – The Inside Story of the Oligarchs*, HarperCollins, 2010.

Schimpfossl, E., *Rich Russians: From Oligarchs to Bourgeoisie*, Oxford University Press, 2018.

Shrubsole, G., *Who Owns England? How We Lost Our Green and Pleasant Land, and How To Take It Back*, HarperCollins, 2019.

Chapter 7: Life Below

Lees, L. and Ferreri, M., 'Resisting Gentrification on its Final Frontiers: Learning From the Heygate Estate in London (1974–2013)', *Cities* 57, 2016, pp. 14–24.

Minton, A., *Big Capital: Who is London For?* Penguin, 2017.

Watt, P., *Estate Regeneration and its Discontents: Public Housing, Place and Inequality in London*, Policy Press, 2020.

Chapter 8: Too Much

Atkinson, R., Burrows, R., Glucksberg, L., Ho, H. K., Knowles, C. and Rhodes, D., 'Minimum City? The Deeper Impacts of the "Super-Rich" on Urban Life', in R. Forrest, S. Koh and B. Wissink (eds.), *Cities and the Super-Rich*, Palgrave Macmillan, 2017.

Davis, A., *Reckless Opportunists: Elites at the End of the Establishment*, Manchester University Press, 2018.

Freeland, C., *Plutocrats: The Rise of the New Global Super-Rich*, Penguin, 2013.

Murphy, D., *Nincompoopolis: The Follies of Boris Johnson*, Repeater Books, 2017.

Sayer, A., *Why We Can't Afford the Rich*, Policy Press, 2015.

Shaxson, N., *The Finance Curse*, Bodley Head, 2018.

Streeck, W., *How Will Capitalism End?*, Verso, 2017.

Notes

1 Capital's City

1   Capgemini, *World Wealth Report 2017*.
2   In 2013 it was estimated that the entire London and South East housing market was worth £2trn. J. Pickford and E. Hammond, *Financial Times*, 1 February 2013.
3   J. O'Neill, 'London Unites the World But Splits the UK', *Financial Times*, 8 February 2013.
4   D. Dorling, *Peak Inequality*, Policy Press, 2018.
5   N. Shaxson, *The Finance Curse*, Bodley Head, 2018.
6   Semi-detached £581,000, Terraced £495,000, Flat £421,000 (UK House Price Index for May 2018, HM Land Registry data).
7   Capgemini, *World Wealth Report 2018*.
8   Ibid.
9   World Bank International Debt Statistics, 2017.
10 These are $666bn (OMB/US Treasury) and £52bn (UK Treasury).
11 In 2015 there were a reported 4,364 UHNWIs in London (Knight Frank, *The Wealth Report 2015*), compared to 3,008 in New York and 3,575 in Tokyo. Such estimates do vary: in the Wealth-X *World Ultra Wealth Report 2017* the figure is put at 3,630 UHNWIs for London.
12 New York has 393,000, but measured in terms of population size London's population is proportionally higher. New World Wealth, London, *Global Wealth Migration Review 2018*.
13 CapGemini, New World Wealth Report 2018.
14 *The Guardian*, 15 August 2018.
15 Credit Suisse, *Global Wealth Report 2017*.
16 Wealth-X, *Global Billionaire Census 2018*.

17 THE World University Rankings, 2019.
18 Skyscraper Centre, 2019 data.
19 J. Westergaard and H. Resler, *Class in a Capitalist Society*, Penguin, 1975, p. 42.
20 W. Buiter, *Lessons from the Global Financial Crisis*, Discussion Paper 635, London School of Economics, 2009.
21 A. Davis, *Reckless Opportunists: Elites at the End of the Establishment*, Manchester University Press, 2018.

2 The Archipelago of Power

1 P. Atkins, 'The Spatial Configuration of Class Solidarity in London's West End 1792–1939', *Urban History* 17, 1990, pp. 36–65.
2 N. Shaxson, 'A Tale of Two Londons', *Vanity Fair*, April 2013.

3 Accommodating Wealth

1 S. Baldwin, E. Holroyd and R. Burrows, *Mapping the Subterranean Geographies of Plutocratic London*, Working Paper, Newcastle University, 2018.
2 F. Sá, *The Effect of Foreign Investors on Local Housing Markets*, London School of Economics, 2016.

4 Crime, Capital

1 M. De Simone, *Corruption on Your Doorstep: How Corrupt Capital is Used to Buy Property in the UK*, Transparency International, 2015.
2 Global Witness, Secret Property Database 2015.
3 O. Bullough, *Moneyland: Why Thieves and Crooks Now Rule the World and How to Take It Back*, Profile Books, 2018.
4 B. Cowdock, *Kept in the Dark: Analysis of New Home Purchases at 375 Kensington High Street*, Transparency International, 2017.
5 Transparency International, *Faulty Towers: Understanding the*

Impact of Overseas Corruption on the London Property Market, 2017.

6 'The secret of a great fortune made without apparent cause is soon forgotten, if the crime is committed in a respectable way.'

7 *Guardian*, 30 October 2018.

8 Transparency International, Faulty Towers; 'Foreign Investors Snapping up London Homes Held in Off-Shore Tax Havens', *Guardian*, 13 June 2017.

9 Analysis of census and MOSAIC socio-demographic data, Dave Rhodes, University of York.

10 R. Neate, 'Anger Over Glut of "Posh Ghost Towers" Planned for London', *Guardian*, 4 February 2018.

11 P. R. Keefe, 'The Kleptocrat in Apartment B', *The New Yorker*, 21 January 2016.

12 Office of National Statistics, Analysing Low Electricity Consumption Using DECC Data, 2015.

13 Live Tables on Dwelling Stock (including vacants), gov.uk.

14 A. Wallace, D. Rhodes and R. Webber, *Overseas Investors in London's New Build Housing Market*, University of York, 2017.

15 K. Scanlon et al., *The Role of Overseas Investors in the London New-Build Residential Market*, London School of Economics, 2017.

16 Foreign Affairs Committee, *Oral Evidence: Russian Corruption and the UK*, HC 932, 28 March 2018.

5 Cars, Jets and Luxury Yachts

1 Data sourced from Civil Aviation Authority annual reports.

6 My Own Private Stronghold

1 P. Atkins, 'How the West End Was Won: The Struggle to Remove Street Barriers in Victorian London', *Journal of Historical Geography* 19, 1993, pp. 265–77.

2 D. Sudjic, *The Edifice Complex: How the Rich and Powerful, and Their Architects, Shape the World*, Penguin, 2006.

7 Life Below

1 Greater London Authority, *Poverty in London*, 2019.
2 J. Allen and J. Pickard, 'London Councils Urged to Demolish and Redevelop Council Estates', *Financial Times*, 22 March 2015.
3 T. Copley, *Right to Buy: Wrong for London*, London Assembly Labour, 2019.
4 Greater London Authority data, reported by BBC News, 19 June 2019.
5 A. Adonis and B. Davies (eds), *City Villages: More Homes, Better Communities*, IPPR, 2015.
6 L. Lees, P. Hubbard, N. Tate and A. Elliot-Cooper, *Estate Renewal and Displacement*, ESRC Grant ES/N015053/1, 2020.
7 G. Audickas, P. Loft and A. Bellis, *Knife Crime in England and Wales*, House of Commons Briefing Paper, 2019.
8 A. Baker, G. Epstein and J. Montecino, *The UK's Finance Curse? Costs and Processes*, University of Sheffield, 2018.

8 Too Much

1 A. Davis, *Reckless Opportunists: Elites at the End of the Establishment*, Manchester University Press, 2018.
2 B. Harrington, *Capital Without Borders: Wealth Managers and the One Percent*, Harvard University Press, 2016.
3 New London Architecture, *London Tall Buildings Survey*, 2019.
4 *The Times*, 11 May 2019.
5 S. Jenkins, 'Why is the Tax on a London Mansion a Tiny Fraction of that in New York?', *Guardian*, 8 February 2019.
6 D. Murphy, *Nincompoopolis: The Follies of Boris Johnson*, Repeater Books, 2017.

Index

Abramovich, Roman, 49, 51, 54, 120
Abu Dhabi Investment Authority, 130
Abu Dhabi, 43, 130
Admiralty Arch, 59
AirBnb, 190
Al-Fayed, Fayed, 132
Albert Memorial, 60
Albertopolis, 60
Alderley Edge, 80, 121
Alfa, 51
Amsterdam, 214
Anglia Ruskin University, 55
Antibes, 127, 128
Apple, 78, 121
Arsenal, 51
Ashcroft, Lord, 54, 55
Aspen, 216
Aspinall, John, 52
Aston Martin, 123, 125
Athenaeum, 38
Athlone House, 51
Audi, 124

Auriens, 192
Aykon, 74
Azerbaijan, 84

Balfron Tower, 165
Ballard, J. G., 77, 98
Balzac, Honoré de, 94
Bamford, Anthony, 55
Banham, 140
Bank of England, 21, 49, 94
Bannatyne, Duncan, 50
Barclay, Jack, 122
Barts Hospital, 192
Barts Square, 192
Battersea Power Station, 77, 98, 217
BBC Panorama, 86
Beadles, 134
Beckwith, John, 50
Bedford Estate, 146
Beechwood House, 51
Belgravia, 18, 58, 62, 133, 145, 173, 174
Bentley, 110, 122, 123, 125

Berezovsky, Boris, 160, 161
Berkeley Square, 36, 64, 122
Berkeley, Lord, 36
Berlin, 188, 214
Bermuda, 48
Biggin Hill, 118, 121
The Bishops Avenue, 64, 97, 146
Blavatnik, Leonard, 51, 55
Bloomberg, Michael, 50
Bloomsbury, 36, 42
Blow-up (Antonioni), 70
Boeing, 120
Boodles, 135, 149
Bordeaux, 16
Botton, Alain de, 215
Brexit, 53, 102, 160, 202, 222, 223
British Grand Prix, 123
British Museum, 55
British Virgin Islands, 51, 84
Brompton Road, 67, 123
Buckingham Palace, 21, 38, 43, 51, 73, 86, 129, 130
Bugatti, 127
Bulgari, 23, 129
Burlington Arcade, 134
Burwood Park, 156

Caan, James, 49
Cadogan Square, 86
Cameron, David, 50, 94, 176, 187

Canary Wharf, 59, 217
Candy Brothers, 22, 53, 69, 161
Candy, Christian, 50, 54
Candy, Nick, 61
Cannes, 127, 128
Capgemini, 17
Capri, 128
Carlton, Jumeirah, 23, 129, 149
Carney, Mark, 49
Carvalho-Heineken, Charlene de, 50
Casablanca, 101
Cavendish Square, 36, 37
Center Point, 21, 22
Charles I, 21, 22
Chelsea Barracks, 59, 135
Chelsea Bridge, 76
Chelsea Tractor Company, 124
Chester Square, 64
Cheyne Walk, 64
Circus West, 98
Civil Aviation Authority, 121
Clarges Mayfair, 9, 72
Clermont Club, 52
Compton Avenue, 99
Connaught, 129, 130
Conservative Party, 55, 105, 202, 217, 219
Cool Britannia, 2
Corbyn, Jeremy, 105, 106
Corinthia Hotel, 126
Courtauld Gallery, 55

Courtney Avenue, 156
Covent Garden, 36
Coward, Noel, 84
Crosfield, Arthur, 73
Crown Jewel, 154
Cundy Street Quarter, 174
Cundy Street, 173, 174
Curtis, Stephen, 160

Daily Mail, 49
Daily Telegraph, 130
Dark Matter (report), 95
Davos, 216
Deripaska, Oleg, 54
Desmond, Richard, 50
Deutsche Bank, 95
Diggers, 80
Dorchester Hotel, 121
Dorchester House, 132
Downing Street, 21
Drones Club, 196
Dubai, 19, 52, 57, 79, 117,
    129, 133
Dublin, 117, 218
Duke of Westminster, 42, 43,
    173
Dyson, James, 54

Earl of Dorchester, 132
Earl of Oxford, 36
Earl of Scarborough, 36
Earls of Bedford, 36
East End, 125, 193
East India Company, 37
Eaton Square, 64, 68, 81

Ebury Estate, 177
Ecclestone, Bernie, 50
Ecclestone, Tamara, 51
Edifice Complex, 159
Edwardian Era, 63, 132,
    167, 192
Edwardian London, 192
Eisenhower, Dwight, 131
Elephant Park, 175
Elite Crown Jewel, 154
Elmbridge, 15
Embassy Gardens, 9, 76, 77,
    148
Epstein, Jacob, 22
EU, 217, 223
Evening Standard, 50
Exchequer, 94
Exhibition Road, 55

Farnborough, 118–121
Fenchurch St, 22
Financial Times, 55, 89, 210
Fitzgerald, F. Scott, 118
Forbes, 121
Foreign Affairs Committee,
    102, 160
Four Seasons Hotel, 133
Foxtons, 51
Frank, Knight, 215
Frankfurt, 218
Fridman, Mikhail, 51
From Russia With Cash, 94

Gallagher, Liam, 73
Garden Bridge, 29

Garrick, 38

Gatwick, 118

Geneva, 52, 57, 117

George IV, 60

Gerrards Cross, 79, 145

Getty, John Paul, 131

Glasgow, 15

Goldfinger, Ernö, 165

Goldin, Nan, 216

Goldsmith, James, 52

Graff, Anne-Marie, 50

Great Ormond Street Hospital, 55

Green, Philip, 54

Grenfell Tower, 174, 209

Griffin, Ken, 50, 61, 219

Grosvenor Crescent, 62

Grosvenor Family, 36, 42

Grosvenor Square, 36, 64, 125, 133, 160, 217

Guardian, 97, 174, 179

Guriev, Andrei, 51, 76

Hajiyeva, Zamira, 84, 87, 89

Hamilton, Lewis, 49

Hampstead Gardens, 192

Hanover Square, 36, 37

Harrodsburg, 117

Heathrow, 118, 119, 150, 217

Hedge City, 93, 221

Helmsley, Leona, 96

Heygate Estate, 174, 175

Highgate Hill, 59

Hinduja, Ashok, 50

HMRC, 48, 96

HNWI (High Net Worth Individuals), 17, 18

Holland Park, 70

Hong Kong, 50, 53, 57, 65, 214, 221

House of Lords, 42

Houses of Parliament, 21, 59, 198

Hunt, Jeremy, 18

Hunt, John, 51

Hyde Park Corner, 121

Imperial War Museum, 55

Jacobs, Jane, 145

Johnson, Boris, 20, 29, 47, 78, 196, 219

Kensington High Street, 91, 140

Kensington Palace Gardens, 51, 55, 64, 147

Kensington Road, 9

Kensington Row, 174

Kew Gardens, 55

KGB, 160

Khan, Sadiq, 218

Klass, Myleene, 16

Labour Party, 170, 176, 219

The Lancasters, 148, 223

Lanchester, John, 218

Lanesborough, 129, 130

Lansdowne Crescent, 71

Law, Jude, 73
Lebanon, 52, 54
Lebedev, Evgeny, 50
Leicester Square, 36
Lewis, Bernard, 50
Lewis, Wyndham, 71
LIBOR, 89
Lisbon, 214
Litvinenko, Alexander, 160, 161
London Building Act of 1894, 146
London Business School, 55
London Streets (Removal of Gates) Acts of 1890, 146
Louvre, 131
Lunajets, 120

Macintosh, Sir Cameron, 50
Manchester, 121
Mandarin Oriental, 69, 132
Mandelson, Peter, 29
The Mansion, 223
Marylebone Town Hall, 55
Maybourne Group, 130
McLaren, Richard Mille, 124
Melbourne, 214
Metro London, 121
Metropolis (Lang), 167
Mexico City, 121
Michael, George, 73
Mikes, George, 222
Millbank Tower, 20
Millennium Hotel, 160

Mills, C. Wright, 205, 210
Mittal, Lakshmi, 49, 51, 55
Montagu Square, 160
Moscow, 57, 221
Moss, Kate, 73
Mount Street, 67, 122

Nash, John, 51
National Crime Agency (NCA), 87, 90, 95
National Gallery, 55
National Health Service (NHS), 197
NatWest Tower, 20
NetJets, 120
Newport Street, 19
Nichols, Harvey, 22, 23, 50, 54, 113, 126
Nine Elms, 66, 78, 98, 121, 176
Noble, Ross, 209
North London, 97, 99
Northumberland, 25
Notting Hill, 70, 178

Odey, Crispin, 50
Ofer, Idan, 55
One Kensington Gardens, 59
One Tower Bridge, 98
Orient Express, 131
Overfinch, 123, 124

Palace Street, 59
Panama Papers, 96

Paradise Papers, 106
Paris, 57, 120, 129, 131, 178, 188, 194, 214, 218
Park Avenue, 100
Park Lane, 23, 64, 121
The Passenger (Antonioni), 70–1
Piccadilly Circus, 127
Piccadilly, 38, 122, 127, 131
Pimlico, 20, 177
Platt, Michael, 50
Politically Exposed Persons, 96
Poon, Dickson, 50
Portland Street, 70
The Power Elite (Mills), 205
Prince of Brunei, 51
Princes Gate, 133

Qatar, 22, 51, 54, 59, 69, 124, 135, 136
Queen Mary Hospital, 192

Ratcliffe, Jim, 54
Rausing, Sigrid, 49
Regent Street, 12, 60, 127
Rogers, Richard, 22
Roland, Tiny, 52
Rolex, 134, 135
Rothchild Family, 42
Rothermere, Viscount, 49
Rue de Rivoli, 131
The Rush of Green (Epstein), 22

Ruskin, John, 215
Russia, 23, 41, 43, 65, 76, 88, 90, 94, 95, 102, 105, 119, 120, 160–163, 202

Sackler Bridge, 55
Sackler Family, 55
Sackler Hall, 55
Sackler Studio, 55
Safran Holdings, 51
Sainsbury Family, 55
Saint Laurent, Yves, 149
San Francisco, 211, 214
Sebag-Montefiore Family, 42
Serpentine Gallery, 55
Shard, 22, 109, 209, 216, 217, 223
Shinjuku, 96
Silicon Valley, 78
Singapore, 57, 94, 203, 214, 221
Skripal, Sergei, 89, 105, 160
Slater, Jim, 52
Sloane Square, 149
Sloane Street, 67, 135, 218
Sotheby's, 16
Soviet Union, 17
St George Wharf Tower, 76, 99
St George Wharf, 75, 76, 99, 148
St Georges Hill, 159
St James, 38, 61, 122
St Paul, 20

Stansted, 118
Stirling, David, 52
Streatham Common, 158
Sudjic, Deyan, 159
Sultan of Brunei, 51, 132
Sultan of Oman, 51
Sunday Times, 18
Surrey, 51, 113, 119, 154, 158, 160
Suspicious Activity Reports, 87, 95
Sutton Place, 51
Sydney, 214

Taipei, 214
Taiwan, 54
Taj Mittal, 51
Tata Motors India, 123
Tate, 55, 158
Tax Justice Network, 221
Thomas, Mark, 106
Tiffany, 149
The Time Machine (Wells), 167
Titz, 131
Tokyo, 11, 15, 25, 57, 96, 214
Toon, Donald, 90
Tory Party, 38
Trafalgar Square, 21
Transparency International, 88, 92, 221
Trellick Tower, 165

Trussell Trust, 182
Turf Club, 38

Ultra High Net Worth Individuals (UHNWI), 17, 18, 29, 118, 124, 226
Unexplained Wealth Order (UWO), 87
University of Oxford, 55
Usmanov, Alisher, 51, 54

Vancouver, 214
Vauxhall, 66, 74, 99
Venice, 128
Versace, 74
Victoria and Albert Museum, 55, 60, 216
Victoria Cross, 55
Victoria, Queen, 38
Victorian Era, 132, 167, 192

Walden House, 173
Wall Street, 29
Wallace, Dougie, 117
Wang Jianlin, 51
Wells, H. G., 167
Westminster, 21, 42, 43, 85, 86, 100, 173, 217
Whitehall, 21
Wikileaks, 88, 221
Wodehouse, P. G., 196

Young, Scot, 160